FAUX PAS?

FAUX PAS?
A No-Nonsense Guide to
Words and Phrases
from Other Languages

PHILIP GOODEN

Walker & Company
New York

First published in the United Kingdom in 2005 by
A & C Black Publishers Limited
First published in the United States of America in 2006 by
Walker Publishing Company, Inc.
Distributed to the trade by Holtzbrinck Publishers

For information about permission to reproduce selections
from this book, write to
Permissions, Walker & Company,
104 Fifth Avenue, New York, New York 10011.

All papers used by Walker & Company are natural, recyclable products made from wood grown in well-managed forests. The manufacturing processes conform to the environmental regulations of the country of origin.

Visit Walker & Company's Web site at www.walkerbooks.com

Library of Congress Cataloging-in-Publication Data has been applied for.

ISBN-10 0–8027–1473–0
ISBN-13 978–0–8027–1473–2

1 3 5 7 9 10 8 6 4 2

Typeset by RefineCatch Limited, Bungay, Suffolk
Printed in the United States of America by Quebecor World Fairfield

INTRODUCTION

Language gives a snub to borders in a way that is denied to any other human invention. There are no controls or checks to prevent words crossing boundaries, there are no duties to be paid when phrases migrate from one culture to another. In the basic and simplest sense of the phrase, language is a free market.

Among world languages, English has some claim to provide the freest market of them all, not only because it is compounded from a variety of sources but also because it has made itself open to linguistic influences from around the globe. This is a matter of history – the original settlement in Britain by the Angles and Saxons and other northern European peoples, followed by the Norman invasion, laid one stratum of language on top of another. The extensive centuries of exploration and colonisation which followed brought back verbal riches as well as physical wealth. Geographically, the position of the British Isles at the western end of Europe has also helped to ensure that the language remains wide open to the linguistic ebb and flow across the oceans.

Every period has brought in new terms from other cultures. To take a few examples: long connections with India in the eighteenth and nineteenth centuries gave us 'bungalow' and 'chutney' and 'verandah', as well as 'thug' and 'loot'. Our age-old and sometimes uneasy relationship with France and the French has provided hundreds of terms in the past, ranging from 'champagne' to 'routine', 'canteen' to 'manoeuvre'.

Language does not stand still and so the process of importing words from other countries goes on. There must be a moment, very hard to pinpoint, when a new expression – new to us, that is – is feeling its way. Eventually, if it's useful, it will be permitted to stay. If it doesn't serve some purpose, however, it will become nothing more than a curiosity known only to a few. The German term *Schadenfreude* ('pleasure in the misfortunes of others') is a good example of the former. I don't remember seeing or hearing much of this word, say, twenty years ago. But a search of a couple of newspaper web-sites throws up over 600 uses of it in the recent past. The expression is being used two or three times a week in one newspaper alone – not bad for an obscure, 'foreign' word. *Tsunami* is another and more recent example of a term which was (unaccountably) in vogue even before the natural disaster of December 2004. These words obviously have the potential for a long life in English. Others, such as 'ad lib' or 'chic' or 'status quo', have been around in English for so long that they are hardly perceived as coming from other languages at all.

Is there something lacking in our home-grown English? Why do we want to use foreign expressions? The simplest answer is that we need them. To go back to our newish friend, *Schadenfreude*. There are English ways of expressing the ideas contained within the German word, but none of them are as compact or as expressive or, simply, as right-seeming. At the opposite end of the scale, is there any word among recent imports that fits the bill so well as the Italian-by-origin *bimbo*? It sounds right, it looks right. We'll take it! And we'll add to it and refine it so that we get spin-offs like *bimbette* and *himbo*, a process that is a sure sign of the vitality of the original expression and a demonstration of our real need for it.

There are, of course, less practical reasons for employing foreign terms. One might almost say less creditable ones. We use words to impress as well as to communicate, and choosing an appropriate and exotic term may be a short cut to impressing others. If you've chosen the right word and the right audience, that is. You also run the risk of being misunderstood or thought pretentious.

It is interesting to see how the different languages are deployed in differ-ent fields. French is traditionally the language of diplomacy, of *détente* and *démarche*, but it is just as traditionally the language of sex and romance (*billet doux, cinque à sept*). Latin, functional and precise, provides us with many of the abbreviations we still use (*e.g., i.e., etc.*) as well as a number of legal terms, some of which are discussed in *Faux Pas?* From Spanish come a handful of 'masculine' terms like *macho* and *cojones*. At times it is difficult to avoid the feeling that an entire culture may be contained within an expression that remains tantalisingly elusive even when translated. One thinks of the sombre northern European quality of the German *Weltschmerz* or the way an entire (Mediterranean) quality of life seems to be embodied in the Italian *dolce far niente*. Whatever their meanings, they are contained and discussed within the pages of *Faux Pas?*, the familiar and the unfamiliar, the useful and the pretentious.

Each entry in this book has been given a phonetic indication of pronunciation. This should be taken as a rough guide only. In many cases there may be more than one way to say the word. Where the pronunciation is obvious I have put 'pronounced as spelled'.

Each entry has also been given a rating on the so-called – or *soi-disant* – Pretentiousness Index. For many entries it does not apply at all, either because they are 'technical' terms (like *in camera* or *ultra vires*) or because they are so well-established in English that using them is about as natural as breathing. Other terms, however, are graded by a system of exclamation marks: ! for mild pretension, !! for moderate, !!! for the extreme. Using a Pretentiousness Index might seem rather pretentious in itself, but I hope that readers of *Faux Pas?* will find it useful and amusing – if only as something with which to disagree.

Every entry has been illustrated with an example of actual use, sometimes very recent use. The sources are generally what used to be called the broadsheets (*The Times, Guardian, Daily Telegraph* and *Independent* in particular), even if two of the newspapers no longer fit the 'broadsheet' description. Quite a few examples have been drawn from fiction as well as sources such as the *Spectator* magazine. The entries reproduce the way the 'foreign' expressions appeared at source. For instance, if they were originally italicised – one of the signs that a word is still being treated as not quite English – then that is reproduced in the typography of this book (i.e. by putting them in Roman type to contrast with the italic of the rest of the example). Similarly with accents, which have been included in the definitions and commentary whenever they occur in the original language but only in the examples if they were actually in place. Again, the use of accents is quite a good guide to how domesticated these foreign expressions have become. On the whole, the fewer the accents, the more at home the words are over here.

Not included in *Faux Pas?* are foreign terms relating to currency or, with a couple of exceptions, to food. That would require a whole book to itself.

Philip Gooden

A

AB INITIO *ab in-ishio* (Latin)

'from the beginning':

But he might care to remind himself – or understand ab initio, as the case may be – of the factors regarding the infantry order of battle. (Spectator)

PRETENTIOUSNESS INDEX **!**

This is a rarely used and rather formal – or stuffy – phrase which does not accomplish much more than English near-equivalents such as 'in the first place'. There's a rather magisterial quality to it. Appropriately, the article from which the *Spectator* example is taken was written by General Sir Mike Jackson, Chief of the General Staff.

A CAPPELLA *ah kappella* (Italian)

literally 'in the church style'; 'without instrumental accompaniment':

Medulla, an almost entirely a cappella album [...] was recognised by critics and Björk herself as a return to full-lunged, warm-blooded power.
(Daily Telegraph)

PRETENTIOUSNESS INDEX **Nil**

A cappella is a slightly specialist term to describe a style of singing which is, itself, something of a specialist taste.

ACCIDIE *aksidi* (French)

'apathy', 'despair':

And while Welles concluded his career advertising sherry on television, Tynan's life drifted into inconsequence, silliness, cruelty and accidie.
(Daily Telegraph)

PRETENTIOUSNESS INDEX **!**

The English language is not fertile ground for terms connoting a kind of spiritual boredom, and we need to go to Europe for expressions such as *ennui, malaise* and *weltschmerz* (see entries). *Accidie* (in fact from Old French via Latin) is perhaps more extreme than these others but, like them, it gives dignity and (self?) importance to a condition which is more serious than anything produced by a wet Sunday afternoon.

ACTUALITÉ *ack-tew-ali-tay* (French)

'actuality', 'objective reality':

The tunnel, Kaletsky reckoned, had 'made cross-Channel ferries technologically obsolete' [...] Seven and a half years on, the actualité is a slightly different story. (Guardian)

PRETENTIOUSNESS INDEX *!!*

The primary meaning of the word in French (where it is used in the plural, *actualités*) is 'current affairs' or 'news' but it occurs on this side of the Channel only in the sense of 'truth', often when the writer or speaker wants to make a distinction between what someone has said and the real state of affairs. The relative popularity of *actualité* can probably be traced back to a 1992 court case involving illegal armsdealing. While he was giving evidence, Alan Clark – the one-time Defence Minister and all-round maverick Tory MP and diarist – talked about being 'economic with the *actualité*', a euphemistic reference to lying. The phrase has stuck.

À DEUX *ah de* (French)

'of two', 'involving two people only':

We're even more romantic, because every penny we spend on sexy dinners à deux *is probably shaved off the mortgage.* (Independent)

PRETENTIOUSNESS INDEX *!*

This phrase quite frequently occurs in the context provided by the example, implying some link (romantic, sexual) between the two people concerned. At the least, any meeting or activity which is *à deux* is likely to have some exclusive or confidential aspect to it.

AD HOC *pronounced as spelled* (Latin)

'organised for a particular purpose rather than being permanent':

No longer would massed-start races, on open roads from town to village and back again, be organised in that ad hoc way, without permanent facilities or even the vaguest notion of safety precautions. (Daily Telegraph)

PRETENTIOUSNESS INDEX **Nil**

Ad hoc is a versatile expression, applicable to almost anything for which one-off arrangements are required. There is generally the implication of 'makeshift' to the term.

AD HOMINEM   *pronounced as spelled*   (Latin)

literally 'to the man'; 'appealing to the known views of the listener or reader', 'personal':

> *This kind of below-the-belt, ad hominem criticism is nothing new, but it seems suddenly to have become acceptable, even fashionable.*   (Observer)

PRETENTIOUSNESS INDEX **!**

An *ad hominem* argument is one which seeks to work on the other side's known prejudices and feelings, rather than being based on reason. An *ad hominem* attack or criticism, not so unusual in the arts (as in the example), is aimed not at what someone has produced but at the producer. It may therefore be seen as unfair and 'personal' (which could usually be substituted for *ad hominem* in this context).

AD INFINITUM   *ad in-fi-nigh-tum*   (Latin)

'to infinity'; 'endlessly':

> *Twelve hours later he [Michael Schumacher] revealed his intention to race on ad infinitum. There was, he said, no end in sight to a career that has already spanned 14 years.*   (Daily Telegraph)

PRETENTIOUSNESS INDEX **Nil**

Rarely applied to anything which genuinely goes on for ever (perhaps because very little does), *ad infinitum* tends to mean no more than 'lasting a long time' or 'as far as the eye can see'. The Latin expression is sometimes useful as an alternative to equivalents such as 'endless' or 'interminable', since it sidesteps the faintly critical or threatening overtones of those English words.

AD LIB   *pronounced as spelled*   (Latin; abbreviated from *ad libitem* – 'at will')

'spontaneous', an 'unrehearsed remark':

> *Just before the end [of the speech], there was another interruption, the huge noise of his helicopter arriving to pick him up. Instinctively, the audience looked skyward, and in a beautiful ad lib Lord Hanson quipped: 'Don't worry, it's one of mine!'*   (The Times)

PRETENTIOUSNESS INDEX **Nil**

The term *ad lib* generally applies to an off-the-cuff remark rather than any other kind of response. It implies quickness of thought or wit (Lord Hanson's remark quoted above hardly seems to qualify on either ground). It's a widely used term, as shown by the formations *ad-libber* and *ad-libbing*.

AD LITEM   *ad lie-tem*   (Latin)

'for the case in law':

> *All parental submissions to the court had to be in before those of social services or the guardian ad litem (the voice of the child), so the professionals were always able to respond to Emma and Martin's defence.*   (Daily Telegraph)

A technical and legal term, *ad litem* generally appears linked to 'guardian', as in the example, where it describes the person appointed by a court to speak or act for the interests of a child.

AD NAUSEAM   *pronounced as spelled*   (Latin)

'to the point of disgust or sickness':

> *You know a comedy cult is born when its catchphrases are quoted* ad nauseam *by unfunny people trying to be funny.*   (The Times)

PRETENTIOUSNESS INDEX **Nil**

Ad nauseam sounds worse in translation. Rarely if ever used about anything that would provoke genuine sickness, *ad nauseam* – a less polite version of *ad infinitum* (see entry) – conveys no more than the yawn-inducing tedium produced by something which is insistent and repetitive.

AFICIONADO   *affisheon-ah-doh*   (Spanish)

person who is an 'enthusiastic and knowledgeable follower of some activity':

> *Then creative kingpin Brian Wilson, through a combination of drugs and depression, was felled by a nervous breakdown, and the uncompleted album became the stuff of legend among aficionados.*   (Independent)

PRETENTIOUSNESS INDEX **Nil**

Originally used to describe devotees of bullfighting, *aficionado* is well accepted in English and occupies a useful middle ground between fandom and expertise. Perhaps the essential component is that the *aficionado* is an amateur. (*Aficionado* is related to the Latin word *affectio* – which in turn gives us *affection* – but note that the usual spelling in Spanish is with a single 'f.')

A FORTIORI   *ah for-tee-or-eye*   (Latin)

'with a more compelling reason', 'even more strongly':

Every reason they have given for making war on Iraq applied a fortiori to Soviet Russia.   (Guardian)

PRETENTIOUSNESS INDEX *!*

A fortiori is a logical link, part of a chain of argument in which the truth of one assertion is based on the acceptance of another assertion that is less important or pressing. It's one of those weighty terms which adds *gravitas* (see entry) to whatever claim is being made but which can generally be substituted by an English equivalent like the ones given in the definition.

AGENT PROVOCATEUR   *ah-jon prov-ock-aterr*   (French)

literally 'provocative agent'; 'someone employed by authority to tempt others into committing crimes':

'It matters too, because television is becoming an agent provocateur. I'm intrigued to know how the producers who give money to people to take their clothes off outside Sainsbury's would explain to their kids why flashers are a bad thing.'   (quoted in the Guardian)

PRETENTIOUSNESS INDEX **Nil**

Originating in the nineteenth century, an *agent provocateur* was a police agent who infiltrated suspect groups, usually ones with a political orientation, and encouraged them to commit crimes for which they could then be punished. More broadly, it now applies to anyone who knowingly provokes others to some activity which is illegal or outrageous.

AGITPROP   *ajit-prop*   (Russian)

'system of spreading political propaganda':

He also grabbed attention in the theatre with Close the Coalhouse Door *(1969), a musical slice of agitprop about Durham miners.*   (The Times)

Agitprop is a shortened form of '*Agitpropbyuro*', a Soviet-era bureaucracy using agitation and propaganda to promote the Communist cause. Always used in a disparaging sense, the term can be applied to any overt piece of political propaganda – especially when in the form of a film or play – although, given its Soviet source, it tends to be reserved for material which is perceived as being 'left-wing'.

AIDE MÉMOIRE   *aid memoir*   (French)

'aid to memory', 'reminder':

> *In fact, once you were in the right frame of mind, the billboard adverts depicting the build-up of fatty deposits in a smoker's artery were immensely effective at offering constant, graphic* aides-mémoires...   (Independent)

PRETENTIOUSNESS INDEX **Nil**

Aide mémoire usually refers to something actual or concrete which is carried to jog the memory, often written material like a memorandum. But it can also be pictorial, as in the *Independent* quote above. More specific than the straightforward 'reminder', *aide mémoire* has no exact equivalent in English and so is a useful term.

À LA   *alla*   (French)

'in the manner of':

> *[Condoleeza] Rice's deputy is to be Bob Zoellick, a veteran of Bush's father's administration – and an old-style Republican internationalist à la James Baker.*   (Guardian)

PRETENTIOUSNESS INDEX **Nil**

A la frequently precedes a French word (see some examples below), but it can happily be placed before an English one, quite often someone's name. A versatile three letters, *à la* stands for 'in the style of' – not quite the same as a simple 'like' and so carrying a useful shade-of-meaning difference.

À LA CARTE   *alla cart*   (French)

literally 'according to the menu'; describing 'a menu where each dish is individually priced'; by extension, 'giving freedom to choose':

> *But a retreat from collective responsibility in favour of reactionary à la carte platforms and 'boutique' politics would be a step backwards.*   (The Times)

PRETENTIOUSNESS INDEX ARGUABLY **!** WHEN FOUND ANYWHERE APART FROM ITS PROPER PLACE ON A MENU.

A la carte is the counterpart of *table d'hôte*, a menu at a fixed price in which there is little or no choice. The *à la carte* idea of giving the customer freedom to choose between a wider range of options can be extended to other areas like politics, at the risk of making them sound frivolous (if such a thing is possible).

À LA MODE *alla mod* (French)

literally 'according to the fashion'; 'fashionable':

You need only the faintest brush with fashion pages to know that dressing like a granny is highly à la mode. (Guardian)

PRETENTIOUSNESS INDEX **!**

A la mode doesn't just apply to clothes but to anything which is 'of the moment'. I've done no kind of survey on this but I would bet that most uses of the phrase in English have a touch of mockery to them, just a *soupçon*.

AL DENTE *al dentay* (Italian)

applied to food which is cooked so as to be slightly 'firm when bitten into':

It is paddy-rat season again in southern Cambodia, and gourmands from all over the country [...] are polishing their chopsticks at the thought of stir-fried rat, boiled rat al dente *and Vietnamese-style barbecued rat.*

(Independent on Sunday)

PRETENTIOUSNESS INDEX **Nil**

Al dente (originally used to describe the neither-hard-nor-soft texture which pasta ought to have when cooked) can be applied to other kinds of food, as above. This is an expression that has made itself at home in English.

ALFRESCO *pronounced as spelled* (Italian)

'open air'; 'in the fresh air':

Pa and I would carry the dining-room table out onto the lawn [...] and there recreate what my father was convinced he had once seen in a Cognac commercial, a large family eating and drinking and chatting alfresco.

(Daily Telegraph)

Alfresco has firmly anchored itself in mainstream English, mostly when applied to eating and drinking outside. It wasn't always so – the *Telegraph* quotation above, describing an *alfresco* Sunday lunch some 50 years ago, makes it sound like a very unusual activity. But *alfresco* is a word associated with leisure. Those who have to work outside for a living, for example on a building site, would probably not welcome a lyrical description of their *alfresco* lives.

ALIBI *ali-by* (Latin)

literally 'elsewhere'; 'excuse', 'defence (often produced in court) that a person could not have committed some offence because he/she was elsewhere at the time':

> *Aimed primarily at cheating spouses who need an excuse to get away from home for a day or two, or explain away a lost night after an unplanned indiscretion, Dmitry Petrov sells copper-bottomed alibis for as little as £120.* (Daily Telegraph)

Pretentiousness Index **Nil**

Alibi is a term so thoroughly fixed in English that it's unlikely to register as 'foreign' at all. Although frequently used in the sense of 'excuse', an *alibi* is more solid, something usually requiring proof (witnesses, photos, etc.) and which, if shown to be true, must be accepted.

ALMA MATER *al-ma marter* (Latin)

literally 'generous mother'; 'something which provides care and sustenance':

> *If you go back far enough everything lived in the sea: watery alma mater of all life.* (Guardian)

Pretentiousness Index **Nil**

Alma mater is very frequently used to describe a person's school or college, although it can apply to any institution which has had a benign and formative influence in the earlier stages of life. And, as the *Guardian* example shows, this can extend even to sea-water.

ALTER EGO *al-ter ego* (Latin)

'another self', 'intimate friend':

> *The transvestite potter Perry, 44, has become a popular figure about*

town in the dress of his alter ego Claire since his [Turner Prize] win.
(Independent)

PRETENTIOUSNESS INDEX **Nil**

Alter ego is sometimes used in the sense of 'alternative identity' or 'pseudonym', particularly in the field of the arts. In addition, it can describe a particularly close friend, someone who is a 'reflection' of oneself. An *alter ego* lacks the sinister overtones of a *doppelganger*, who is more likely to be an unwelcome shadow (see entry).

ALUMNUS   *pronounced as spelled*   (Latin)

'former student of school or college':

Nonetheless there are quite a few basket cases in the acting profession [...] The Method school produced armies of them, with the late Marlon Brando being one of its foremost alumni.   (The Times)

PRETENTIOUSNESS INDEX **Nil**

Alumnus – with a feminine form *alumna* – is probably more often found in the US than in Britain (whose schools may have Old Boys and Girls and whose colleges can boast of Old Members instead). Rather like *alma mater* (see entry above), *alumnus* does not make any discrimination between levels of education and, as the quote about Marlon Brando shows, the 'school' can be anywhere which gives some sort of instruction.

AMANUENSIS   *ah-man-ewe-ensis*   (Latin)

'literary assistant', 'someone who writes what another person dictates':

Is he not aware that almost every Communist dictator was [...] followed by an eager amanuensis capturing for posterity his on-the-spot guidance to farmers about how best to harvest potatoes, and to car mechanics about how best to change the spark plugs?   (Daily Telegraph)

PRETENTIOUSNESS INDEX **Nil**

A slightly specialist term, *amanuensis* might seem to be a secretary of a rather basic sort, one whose life is confined to writing down what he or she is told to write. However, the word is not as disparaging as the definition suggests. John Milton's epic poem *Paradise Lost* was dictated to a series of *amanuenses* on account of the poet's blindness. Similarly the composer Frederick Delius, blind and paralysed at the end of his life, dictated his final works to his *amanuensis*, Eric Fenby.

AMICUS CURIAE   *amicus cue-ree-eye*   (Latin)

literally 'friend of the court'; 'legal adviser who does not represent a party in a case but whose knowledge is required in court on points of law or other matters of public interest':

During the preliminary hearing Sir Stephen Brown, president of the Family Division, is likely to ask for an amicus curiae to be appointed, an expert lawyer to advise the court on a grey area of the law in which Parliament has been reluctant to tread.   (Daily Telegraph)

PRETENTIOUSNESS INDEX **Nil**

Amicus curiae is a specialist term in law. The key point is that he or she does not have an interest or bias in the case going forward, but is called on simply for expertise about some aspect of the proceedings.

AMOUR FOU   *amoor foo*   (French)

literally 'mad love'; 'obsessive love', 'passion':

The plots of such films are classic silliness: in some exotic locale, world-weary Marlene [Dietrich] would, against her best instincts, fall for a legionnaire or spy or soldier and sacrifice herself for him. These were exercises in amour fou, in which even the most experienced woman on the globe [...] could become a selfless martyr to romance.   (Guardian)

PRETENTIOUSNESS INDEX *!*

There are English equivalents for *amour fou*, but this is a not uncommon expression. As often, we turn to the French when it comes to love and sex.

AMOUR-PROPRE   *amoor prop'r*   (French)

'self-love', 'self-esteem':

The blow to an entire nation's amour-propre comes as evidence emerges from Brussels that if the outside world is no longer quite so enamoured of one prized Gallic icon, another has fallen from favour as well: the French language.   (Guardian)

PRETENTIOUSNESS INDEX *!*

This is a term that sounds better in French than in translation. We don't talk much about 'self-love', while 'self-esteem' seems to be a loaded expression only used about the many who are said to be running low on it. There may be a touchy, comic side to *amour-propre*, but the term is not entirely negative or egotistic.

AMUSE-BOUCHE *amooze-boosh*   (French)

literally, 'something to please the mouth', 'starter':

After an amuse-bouche *of codfish foam with sea-urchin mousse, we propose a starter of snail porridge followed by yeast soup...*   (Independent)

PRETENTIOUSNESS INDEX *!*

The term *amuse-bouche* is less often used than *amuse gueule* (see below). Not so elaborate as a *hors d'oeuvre* (see entry), it's the little thing – usually involving a fragment of pastry for some reason – brought to your table before you've had time for a proper look at the menu.

AMUSE-GUEULE *amooze-gerl*   (French)

literally, 'something to please the mouth', 'taster':

[He] then proceeds to regale me with a selection of delicious but irrelevant gossipy amuses gueules *about his grandmother and various maiden aunts.*
(The Times)

PRETENTIOUSNESS INDEX *!*

Amuse-gueule describes any pre-meal titbit but can be used metaphorically, as above. It is the term used by the French for an appetiser, even though *gueule* is on the edge of slang ('Ferme ta gueule!' is 'Shut your gob!').

ANCIEN REGIME *an-sienn regime*   (French)

literally 'old regime'; historically the 'government of pre-Revolutionary France' and, by extension, any 'old and discredited system of rule':

Faced with tyranny, Europe's anciens regimes *preferred appeasement to confrontation.*   (The Times)

PRETENTIOUSNESS INDEX **Nil**

Always a pejorative expression, ancien regime characterises a system of authority which is redundant – or deserves to be redundant.

ANGST *pronounced as spelled*   (German)

'anxiety', 'fear':

And it is a relief not to be overwhelmed by the angst about secondary education that grips the London middle classes.   (Independent)

PRETENTIOUSNESS INDEX *!*

Angst has philosophical overtones suggesting troubled soul-searching rather than run-of-the-mill nail-biting. It is anxiety with attitude, and a term or concept with which English users are not entirely comfortable. Most uses of the word have a slightly ironic tinge to them.

ANNUS HORRIBILIS *ann-us horree-bilis* (Latin)

'horrible year':

Thankfully, her annus horribilis – which included checking into the Meadows Institute in Arizona as a result of exhaustion – is now a closed chapter. (Daily Telegraph)

PRETENTIOUSNESS INDEX **!**

The Queen is responsible for the popularity of this phrase, which doesn't date from Roman times but was created recently as a counterpart to *annus mirabilis* (see below). In a speech made towards the end of 1992 she looked back on that year, marked by the collapse of two of her children's marriages as well as a major fire at Windsor Castle, and called it a personal *annus horribilis*. In one of the *Sun* newspaper's inspired headlines, the Queen's speech was referred to as 'One's Bum Year'. *Annus horribilis* has enjoyed quite a wide circulation ever since to describe a disastrous period in someone's life, usually a celebrity's.

ANNUS MIRABILIS *ann-us mirrah-bilis* (Latin)

'remarkable year':

Dominic Masters, The Others' singer-songwriter, is much too young to have seen Bowles in action, though the lyric does include reference to 'QPR 1974', the club's annus mirabilis. (Daily Telegraph)

PRETENTIOUSNESS INDEX **!**

Although originally signifying a year which was historic (remarkable for things which could be very good or bad), *annus mirabilis* is now used only in the sense of 'wonderful year', and is the opposite to *annus horribilis* (see above).

ANOMIE *anomee* (French)

'lawlessness'; 'sense of despair (produced by breakdown in traditional standards)':

Instead, the modern vampire incarnates many things – sexual fantasies, fears of urban anomie, especially for teenagers. (Guardian)

Anomie was originally a term used in sociology. A relatively unusual expression, it tends to appear as part of a catalogue of contemporary emotional and spiritual ills whose other members may include *angst* (see entry), alienation and anger. Vague but impressive-sounding, *anomie* may sometimes be included for its alliterative value or for its echo of 'anonymity' (another popular 'urban' problem).

ANTEBELLUM *anti-bellum* (Latin)

'before the war':

> *[Dave] Allen became an underground star in Poland, Romania (where there was a thriving black market in his tapes) and antebellum Yugoslavia, to which he was once invited by Tito.* (The Times)

PRETENTIOUSNESS INDEX **Nil**

Principally a US term, *antebellum* is used to describe the period before the American Civil War – in other contexts, 'pre-war' would be the usual expression. Possibly some association with civil wars prompted its application to Yugoslavia in the *Times* quote above.

APARTHEID *apar-tite* (Afrikaans)

'separateness'; applied to the 'policy which, in pre-majority-rule South Africa, kept the black and white races segregated from each other'; more generally, any 'scheme or policy which aims to separate people into different groups or categories':

> *The physical layout of the shop reflects a sort of hi-fi apartheid. On the raised floor at the back, rows of CDs rise to ceiling height [...] Downstairs, it is a different world. Nicotine-stained fingers flick impatiently through racks of LPs.* (Daily Telegraph)

PRETENTIOUSNESS INDEX ARGUABLY *!* WHEN USED OUTSIDE ITS ORIGINAL SOUTH AFRICAN CONTEXT.

The term *apartheid* – once the stuff of banners and headlines – has lost much of its political sting, as shown by its application in the *Telegraph* quote to the way CDs and records are sorted. On a more serious level, the term is quite frequently used to describe different systems of schooling or some gap between the sexes in a particular field. Like the policy it once enshrined, *apartheid* is still a loaded and ugly word, one to be used with care.

APERÇU   *a-per-sue*   (French)

'survey', 'glimpse', 'insight':

Until [Alan Clark], diaries by public figures had mostly been stodgy memoirs shedding little light on anything but the author's self-regard; more rarely they followed the trend started by Samuel Pepys – aperçus and anecdotes that exposed the values and foibles of society.   (Observer)

PRETENTIOUSNESS INDEX **Nil**

A genuinely useful term imported from French, *aperçu* occupies the ground somewhere between glimpse and insight. An *aperçu* is more valuable and informative than a simple glimpse – which may be accidental or unrevealing – but it lacks the heavyweight undertones of insight. In other words, the perfect home for an *aperçu* is in a diary.

APOLOGIA   *apo-low-gee-ah*   (Latin)

'formal statement in defence or vindication of a particular position':

In his passionate foreign policy apologia in Sedgefield last week, [Tony Blair] declared Britain to be 'in mortal danger'.   (Spectator)

PRETENTIOUSNESS INDEX **Nil**

Despite the echo of 'apology', there's no suggestion of regret in an *apologia* – rather the reverse since the word implies a thought-out and often robust justification of oneself or someone or something else. The person who makes such a statement is an *apologist*.

APPARATCHIK   *pronounced as spelled*   (Russian)

'member of the (Soviet) bureaucracy'; now extended to any 'inflexible organisation man, particularly in a political party':

As he said, having to make people redundant gave him insights into human frailty that are denied to MPs who are full-time apparatchiks.   (The Times)

PRETENTIOUSNESS INDEX ARGUABLY **!** IF USED OUTSIDE A SOVIET/HISTORICAL CONTEXT.

Like other terms deriving from the USSR such as *nomenklatura*, *apparatchik* is always used pejoratively. It suggests a bureaucrat who willingly follows and implements the 'party' line, either in a spirit of blind obedience or one of cynical ambition. As an insult for a person sitting in an office, it's stronger and more exotic than 'suit' or 'jobsworth'.

APPELLATION CONTROLÉE   *appel-assion con-trow-lay*   (French)

literally 'controlled appellation'; when appearing on French wines (and some other products) a 'guarantee' that the product satisfies certain standards to do with its source, quality, and so on:

> *The industry is worth £400 million a year and produces shellfish so renowned that they have a distinctive appellation controlée style stamp of origin.*   (Daily Telegraph)

PRETENTIOUSNESS INDEX **Nil**

Now that the pre-eminent position of French wine has been toppled by vintages from all round the word, the long-standing and slightly snobbish significance of the *appellation controlée* label (sometimes abbreviated to AC) has faded. But it still has a little authority, and can be extended to other foodstuffs, as in the example.

A PRIORI   *a pry-ory*   (Latin)

literally 'from what is before'; of a conclusion 'believed to be so but not (yet) supported by evidence', 'to the best of one's knowledge':

> *And their children are not, a priori, any more likely to be bad eggs than yours.*   (Daily Telegraph)

PRETENTIOUSNESS INDEX **Nil**

A priori has a particular meaning in philosophy (to describe reasoning from causes rather than from effects), but in general use it carries the sense of 'as far as one knows'. A formal and not very widely used phrase, *a priori* nevertheless describes a pretty usual way of assessing things.

APROPOS   *ah pr'poe*   (French)

'on the subject of', 'to the purpose', 'timely', 'relevant':

> *...but occasionally he strikes an excessively literary note, as when a gangster observes, apropos the word abstemious, 'You know what else I learned about that word? It's one of just two words in the English language that uses all five vowels and in order.'*   (Daily Telegraph)

PRETENTIOUSNESS INDEX **Nil**

Apropos is an oddly versatile expression, encompassing several related meanings. So, a person's arrival on the scene may be *apropos* (opportune or timely) while their words could be *apropos* in two more senses

(directed towards a particular subject but also relevant to the occasion). This is one foreign term that does a lot of work.
See also *malapropos*.

ARCANUM *ar-kay-num* (Latin; generally found in the plural **arcana**)

'secrets', 'mysteries':

Rather, he explains the arcana of genetics in as clear and concise a manner as he can to the person to whom the double helix is a matter of general knowledge but who knows nothing else. (Daily Telegraph)

PRETENTIOUSNESS INDEX **Nil**

Arcana are not bog-standard secrets but ones which are comprehensible only to experts or the initiated. One of the original associations of the term was with the alchemists, who searched for the elixir of life, among other things. So *arcana* retain a slight aura of magic.

ARRIÈRE-PENSÉE *arry-air ponsay* (French)

literally 'behind-thought'; 'unspoken reservation', 'hidden intention':

Note how every statement has its unspoken agenda, its background silence, its awareness of what cannot be said, the arriere-pensees no politician will utter. (Guardian)

PRETENTIOUSNESS INDEX **!**

Arrière-pensée is not a much used expression and may stick out when it occurs. Perhaps it should be more widely used since we don't have a straightforward English equivalent – something like 'back thought'? – for what is a very ordinary part of everyone's mental processes, politicians or not.

ARRIVISTE *aree-vist* (French)

'go-getter', 'upstart':

Holland is sensitive enough to bring out the essential insecurity of this arriviste [the Roman writer Cicero] who had no fancy ancestors or inherited supporters. (Guardian)

PRETENTIOUSNESS INDEX **Nil**

Arriviste derives from the French *arrivisme* ('pushy ambition') and describes someone who has 'arrived' from obscure origins and is determined to make his mark. Definitely a term of disapproval, if not quite as pejorative as its English equivalents.

ARTISTE   *arteest*   (French)

'person who performs in public, usually singing or dancing':

I learnt, several months in advance [from a fortune-teller], of the success of my present Broadway show, thus sparing myself the torments of self-doubt and first-night jitters other artistes experience as they wait up till dawn to read the reviews.   (Spectator)

PRETENTIOUSNESS INDEX **Nil**

On the face of it, *artiste* might sound like a rather twee and affected term but using it seems to me an example of inverted pretension. In fact, *artiste* may be actively avoided by those in the performing trade either because it's a bit dated or because it doesn't sound grand or serious enough. Those performers (singers, actors, comics, etc.) who might once have been quite happy to describe themselves as *artistes*, now prefer to be 'artists'. It sounds more classy.

ASHRAM   *pronounced as spelled*   (Sanskrit)

'place of religious retreat':

Later, the Beatles spent time in the Maharishi's ashram on the banks of the River Ganges studying transcendental meditation.   (Guardian)

PRETENTIOUSNESS INDEX NIL AS FAR AS THE WORD AND THE PLACE ITSELF ARE CONCERNED. BUT THE PEOPLE WHO VISIT AN *ASHRAM* MAY BE A DIFFERENT MATTER...

Ashram, which can describe both the place of retreat and the community that gathers there, was brought back from the East in the hippy backpack in the 1960s, like *guru* and *karma* (see entries). Unlike those terms it doesn't seem to have gathered any negative or comic connotations, and its use remains fairly specific to Hindu culture.

ATELIER   *ah-tell-ee-a*   (French)

'workshop', 'artist's studio':

A romantic back-story, which (in Dolce and Gabbana's case at least) probably involves shambolic ateliers off Italian back streets and years surviving on pasta, love and a shared dream...   (Observer)

PRETENTIOUSNESS INDEX *!!*

An *atelier* is a workshop of a fairly specific sort, associated with artists and fashion designers, and by definition a place for mental creativity rather than hard sweat. Even so, the word can sound a little precious in an English context when we have the more versatile 'studio'.

AU CONTRAIRE   *oh con-trair*   (French)

'on the contrary':

> *...the columnist opined that Janet [Street-Porter] was doing womankind no favours by showing her cellulite. Au contraire. Janet speaks for every woman who'd rather grow old disgracefully than save up for the plastic surgeon.*   (Independent)

PRETENTIOUSNESS INDEX *!!!*

On the face of it there seems no reason to prefer *au contraire* to 'on the contrary'. The meaning is obvious whether it's expressed in French or English. True, the French version is two words rather than three but the saving is minimal and beside the point. The value of *au contraire*, therefore, lies with the slightly camp context in which it's usually found. An earnest argument demands 'on the contrary'. But an opposing point of view, not meant too seriously and delivered with a flap of the wrist or a raised eyebrow, justifies *au contraire*.

AU COURANT   *oh cooron*   (French)

'well-informed', 'in the know':

> *When I tell someone I'm hooked on CSI, I get pitying or baffled looks by the same determinedly au courant people who've seen the latest play or art film.*   (Guardian)

PRETENTIOUSNESS INDEX *!*

As the example above suggests, *au courant* can carry the sense of being 'aware of what's fashionable'. This is probably its shade-of-meaning difference from *au fait* (see below). Any pretension may lie more with the people who are claimed to be *au courant* rather than the expression itself.

AU FAIT   *oh fay*   (French)

'knowledgeable', 'well acquainted with':

> *Not completely au fait with the workings of the programme [...] Bez was also unaware he was in the final.*   (Guardian)

PRETENTIOUSNESS INDEX *!*

Au fait is a more widely used expression than *au courant*. One is usually *au fait* with something specific, a situation, a set of facts. Both expressions lack the pseudo-urgency of the English 'up to speed with'.

AU FOND   *oh fon*   (French)

'at bottom', 'basically':

Above all, the Tories believe that au fond *most voters' values are still conservative*   (Independent)

PRETENTIOUSNESS INDEX *!!*

There are a couple of perfectly good English equivalents for *au fond*, so the most likely reasons for using the French term are to avoid the slight snigger-value of 'at bottom' or the over-emphatic 'basically'. A third possibility is 'fundamentally'.

AU NATUREL   *oh nat-you-rel*   (French)

'in the natural state', 'without extras or adornments':

The 57-year-old property mogul's barnet is not quite as ridiculous as that of ex-wife Ivana, but that has not prevented rumours that his 'flip-flop' style [...] wasn't quite au naturel.   (Guardian)

PRETENTIOUSNESS INDEX *!*

The context for *au naturel* is frequently humorous or sly, as in the example above or when it is used as a knowing alternative to 'nude'. When applied to food, *au naturel* describes anything which is prepared without fuss and served without dressing, etc.

AUTEUR   *aw-ter*   (French)

'author'; 'film director':

Nine Songs is a self-proclaimed attempt by Michael Winterbottom, the British auteur highly regarded by many, to push the boundaries of how we see explicit sexuality in film at a time when we are becoming more prudish.   (Guardian)

PRETENTIOUSNESS INDEX *!!*

Although *auteur* in the French language can have a variety of applications, covering those producing books or music or films, in English it only describes a film director. And furthermore a particular type of film director, one who puts an individual stamp on his or her films rather than churning out formula movies. This 'high art' term originated in the early 1950s with the influential Parisian magazine *Cahiers du*

Cinema, where director-in-waiting François Truffaut and others laid out the foundation of an *auteur* theory that elevated the director to the position of a creative artist. The pendulum has swung back, recently, however, and current thinking tends to see film-making once more as a collaborative process rather than the expression of the artistic vision of a single individual.

AUTO-DA-FÉ *auto-da-fay* (Portuguese)

literally 'act of faith'; applied to the sentence passed by the Inquisition against heretics and the public burning which followed; any 'public burning':

The curator proudly led me past hideously realistic scenes of torture, whippings, executions, auto-da-fé's, and other ghastly depictions of the barbarities practised by the Church and State. (Daily Telegraph)

PRETENTIOUSNESS INDEX **Nil**

Auto-da-fé has a very specific historical meaning but it is sometimes used to describe a public burning in the present day, for example of books, particularly if they are being destroyed for religious reasons.

AUTRES TEMPS, AUTRES MOEURS *oh-tr tom, oh-tr merr* (French)

literally 'other times, other customs':

The White House, eve of millennium, historians summoned to pronounce on how other millennia have been greeted (autres temps, autres moeurs)
(Guardian)

PRETENTIOUSNESS INDEX **!**

This French saying means essentially 'they did things differently then' (the *Guardian* reference is to a White House reception hosted by Bill and Hillary Clinton), and is an acknowledgement that manners and customs change with shifts of power and fashion as well as with the passing of the years.

AVANT LA LETTRE *ah-von la lett're* (French)

literally 'before the letter' and so 'before the word existed':

In many respects he [Labour Minister, Jack Straw] was consistently ahead of the game. An Islington councillor before they became a cliché, soft left before the term existed, and even a Blairite avant la lettre, he has a track record of being in the right place ahead of the right time. (Guardian)

Avant la lettre may not be very often used but it is a practical phrase since it fits a particular requirement to describe the history of something or someone in terms that relate only to the present or to another, later time. In short, the expression describes a deliberate anachronism in choice of words. (In the *Guardian* quote above, Jack Straw apparently showed the symptoms of being New Labour and Blairite before those concepts had been created.) There are ways of expressing the same idea in English but they are not so straightforward as *avant la lettre*.

AYATOLLAH *eye-ah-tolla* (Persian/Arabic)

literally 'sign of God'; a 'leader of the Shia Muslim sect' and, by extension, a 'powerful figure representing some party or dogma':

The big question is, will Tokyo's tax ayatollahs kill off Japan's economic recovery? (The Times)

Pretentiousness Index *!* if used outside its original Muslim context.

Ayatollah was transformed from a relatively obscure term in the late 1970s after the fall of the Shah of Iran and the coming to power of Ayatollah Khomeini. The rule of the ayatollahs in Iran and their influence elsewhere across the Middle East has made the word a convenient shorthand to describe a figure who is perceived as being rigid or doctrinaire in the way he exercises authority. Whenever the word is used in a non-religious context, as in the *Times* quote above, there is likely to be an undertone of scepticism or hostility.

B

BADINAGE *baddy-narj* (French)

'light-hearted talk', 'banter':

> *Questions for Campbell were mostly either cues for celebrity badinage – does he dye his hair? – or respectful explorations of his political views.* (Guardian)

PRETENTIOUSNESS INDEX *!!*

Badinage is an alternative to 'banter', and there's not much more to be said about it apart from the fact that the first syllable echo of 'badminton' reflects the back-and-forth sense of the word.

BAKSHEESH *pronounced as spelled* (Persian)

'gift of money', 'tip':

> *Power systems were privatised from Brazil to Pakistan and the baksheesh flowed. Or so say Pakistan's anti-corruption prosecutors although the World Bank dismissed the allegations.* (Observer)

PRETENTIOUSNESS INDEX **Nil**

Although a standard term for 'tip' in parts of the world, *baksheesh* may also carry overtones of 'bribe', as in the example. There's generally something slightly disdainful about the use of the term in English.

BAGATELLE *bag-atell* (French)

'something very insignificant':

> *In the great scheme of things, another point dropped was a mere bagatelle.*
> (Daily Telegraph)

PRETENTIOUSNESS INDEX *!*

A term with several meanings, *bagatelle* also describes a game and a brief, unserious piece of music. Its application to something trivial is an earlier definition. Not a very common term in this sense, perhaps, but quite an effective way of dismissing a topic which other people might be fussing about, and usually preceded by 'mere'.

BARRIO   *pronounced as spelled*   (Spanish)

'district in Spanish town or Spanish-speaking community elsewhere':

Much is made, correctly, of the President's appeal to white Christian voters. But he has also tried, explicitly, to reach out to other constituencies – 'the barrios of LA', for example.   (Daily Telegraph)

PRETENTIOUSNESS INDEX **Nil**

The *barrio* tends to define the poorer areas of a city, particularly when applied to the US or to countries in South America, and is sometimes synonymous with 'slum'. Not yet a term in general circu-lation but as the Spanish-speaking population of some American states rises, we'll hear more of the *barrio* and its impact on politics and culture.

BATHOS   *bay-thos*   (Greek)

'unintentional drop from a high level to the absurd or banal', 'anti-climax':

But I ended up finding Meet the Fockers distasteful (for its title among other things) and suggest that the comedy of embarrassment can at times be more embarrassing than comic. I also disliked the happy ending, a descent into sentimental interfaith bathos.   (Observer)

PRETENTIOUSNESS INDEX **Nil**

Examples of *bathos* don't have to occur at the end of a book or speech or film, although this is where they find their natural place, as it were. Rather, *bathos* characterises any jarring clumsiness in organising material so that the overall result is comic or banal when the intention is serious. A very useful term (which shouldn't to be confused with *pathos*).

BEAU MONDE   *bow mond*   (French)

'fashionable, socially superior world':

A young woman from the London beau monde is en route to a Scottish isle to marry Sir somebody or other, a wealthy et cetera.   (Guardian)

PRETENTIOUSNESS INDEX *!*

It's hard to imagine anyone using *beau monde* about a group or class now, except tongue-in-cheek, and the expression looks and sounds as dated as 'high society'. But, like that English phrase, it may be the right one in an appropriate historical context.

BELLA FIGURA *bella fig-you-ra* (Italian)

'fine figure', 'good impression':

When you deal with the Mediterraneans, remember, again and again: bella figura. You must cut a dash. You must use colour and style. That was what Diana was able to do on behalf of this country. (Guardian)

PRETENTIOUSNESS INDEX **!** IF USED BY OR ABOUT ANYONE OTHER THAN AN ITALIAN.

Bella figura is a concept that hasn't found much of a home in Britain – 'cutting a dash' is probably the closest we can come to it. Partly a matter of how you look and what you wear, *bella figura* also concerns itself with style, flair, attitude and other intangibles.

BELLES LETTRES *bell lett're* (French)

literally 'fine letters' and so 'pure literature':

'While one cannot expect a butler to be a master of belles lettres,*' said Andrew Roberts, who deigned to review A Royal Duty in the Sunday Telegraph, 'one might have imagined that Penguin could have employed a ghost-writer for these toe-curling outpourings.'* (Guardian)

PRETENTIOUSNESS INDEX SOME WOULD SAY THAT *BELLES-LETTRES* ARE INTRINSICALLY PRETENTIOUS.

The world of *belles lettres* has been essentially dead since the early years of the 20th century. The expression conjures up a network of little magazines, leisured esssayists and men (rarely women) who devoted their life to the study of Literature. As such, it describes a historical period. If used about contemporary writing, it is likely to be ironic.

BÊTE NOIRE *bet nwah* (French)

literally 'black beast'; 'pet hate':

[TV programme Club Reps] A ratings winner but bete noir of Daily Mail for encouraging British louts on Rhodes. (Guardian)

PRETENTIOUSNESS INDEX **Nil**

This widely used expression must be in the top 50 linguistic imports, and is useful for describing a strong dislike without resorting to words like 'hate' or 'aversion'. In any case, the term doesn't really convey loathing. Don't people – and newspapers – frequently enjoy sounding off about their *bêtes noires*, in the same way that we enjoy scratching an itch?

BÊTISE   *bet-eez*   (French)

'stupid remark or action', 'folly':

Still, the Republicans have only themselves to blame for the bêtise of indicting Mr Clinton on Monica Lewinsky charges.   (Daily Telegraph)

PRETENTIOUSNESS INDEX *!*

This isn't a very usual term in English, and doesn't do much that 'folly' wouldn't accomplish – arguably, it lacks the force of that word or equivalents such as 'stupidity'. However, what *bêtise* does convey, I think, is a kind of weary impatience with someone else's idiocy.

BIBELOT   *bib-ello*   (French)

'small ornamental object', 'trinket':

[This] bronze figure of a ballerina is the sort of bibelot you might find for sale at Harrods. This isn't art, it's kitsch of a sort that would appeal to Hyacinth Bucket.   (Daily Telegraph)

PRETENTIOUSNESS INDEX *!*

Bibelot is an up-market and relatively unusual way of referring to a knick-knack. It is a dismissive term, as the example indicates.

BIEN PENSANT   *be-an ponson*   (French)

literally 'well thinking' and so 'right thinking'. But *bien pensant* is almost always used in a derogatory sense to describe people (usually of liberal or left-leaning views) who are 'conventional and unquestioning' in their outlook and assumptions:

In the world of bien pensant educationalists, 'celebrating diversity' is an article of faith.   (Daily Telegraph)

PRETENTIOUSNESS INDEX *!*

Like the expression 'Politically Correct', *bien pensant* has become a standard term of abuse in the hands of right-of-centre commentators. Those who are *bien pensants* are woolly-minded liberals who believe unquestioningly in high taxes, state intervention, etc. The right-of-centre commentators are, of course, never guilty of thinking in stereotypes.

BIJOU *bee-joo* (French)

'small and elegant':

> …*he faces a venue so tiny that, were it a living room, an estate agent would describe it as 'bijou'.* (Guardian)

PRETENTIOUSNESS INDEX *!!*

As a noun *bijou* means 'jewel' or 'trinket' (see below), but it usually crops up in English as an adjective, and a somewhat thread-bare one at that. At some stage estate agents must have begun to employ it as a euphemistic alternative to 'small and poky', and *bijou* has never made a complete recovery since. The word carries overtones of elegance, or prettiness, but it is doubtful whether it can be used as a straightforward compliment now. No great loss.

BIJOUTERIE *bee-joo'terri* (French)

'jewellery', 'trinkets':

> *Jewels are the fashion accessory du jour, and from Bond Street to the high street, there are stacks of bijouterie, priced to suit every budget.* (Daily Telegraph)

PRETENTIOUSNESS INDEX *!!*

Bijouterie is on the trinket end of the jewellery spectrum. The word doesn't even sound serious, and any usage is likely to be slightly tongue-in-cheek or camp.

BILDUNGSROMAN *bil-dungz-romahn* (German)

literally 'education novel'; a 'novel telling the story of a person's moral or emotional growth and change':

> *Updike has written a Bildungsroman in which family, work, friends and history are all ruthlessly subjugated to Owen's sexual consciousness – from his first encounters with obscene graffiti to his heyday as a fully-fledged Man of Pleasure.* (Daily Telegraph)

PRETENTIOUSNESS INDEX **Nil**

Something of a specialist term, the *Bildungsroman* had its heyday in the nineteenth century when that kind of novel was in vogue.

BILLET DOUX *billay doo* (French)

literally a 'sweet note'; 'love letter':

In the old days [before texting], it was a lot simpler: billets doux could be retrieved and thrown in the fireplace, making proof elusive for the accuser.
(Independent)

<small>PRETENTIOUSNESS INDEX</small> *!*

Billets doux may no longer be written with pen, ink and paper but they still exist in other forms like texting. The closest English equivalent, 'love letter', suggests something a bit more formal, even lengthy. But a *billet doux* need be only a couple of lines. As often, French is more expressive when it comes to love and sex.

BIMBO   *pronounced as spelled!*   (Italian)

literally 'an affectionate way to refer to a small boy' (bimba is a small girl) but in English usage generally meaning 'young, sexy but dim woman':

And the hilarious dumb-blonde secretary isn't the brainless, sexually available bimbo she seems.   (Daily Telegraph)

<small>PRETENTIOUSNESS INDEX</small> **Nil**

There are some foreign imports that hit the spot so precisely that we wonder how we could ever have done without them. *Bimbo* – the word means 'little child' in Italian – is one such. Its success can be seen by other words it has spawned: *bimbette* (for a particularly young or dim *bimbo*) and *bimboy* or *himbo* (for the male of the species).

BLASÉ   *blah-zay*   (French)

'familiar with [something] to the point of boredom':

I'm fairly blasé about European decadence these days – I barely raised an eyebrow at the news that an unemployed waitress in Berlin faces the loss of her welfare benefits because she's refused to take a job as a prostitute in a legalised brothel.   (Daily Telegraph)

<small>PRETENTIOUSNESS INDEX</small> **Nil**

Blasé is a very common expression in English, suggesting boredom rather than disapproval. The implication is that one might have once been shocked or surprised at whatever it is that makes one *blasé*, but that familiarity and cynicism have dulled those reactions.

BLITZKRIEG   *blitzkreeg*   (German)

literally 'lightning war'; 'military campaign marked by great speed and force', 'burst of activity':

German politicians, meanwhile, launched their own rhetorical blitzkrieg, arguing that his choice of fancy dress demonstrated the need for a continent-wide ban on Nazi insignia. (Daily Telegraph)

PRETENTIOUSNESS INDEX **Nil**

Blitzkrieg has a specific historical sense when applied to the strategy of the German army in World War Two, and in the shortened form of *blitz* describes in particular the Luftwaffe air raids on Britain. But even the most ferocious words can be tamed. *Blitzkrieg* may still be used in its military sense but its prime application now is figurative (see example above). More common still is the sense of the word to mean no more than a 'strenuous bout of activity', as in 'Let's have a blitz on that paperwork.'

BONA FIDES   *bow-na fy-deez*   (Latin)

'good faith', 'sincerity':

This time around, his [Arnold Schwarzenegger's] carefully plotted indecision appears to have been designed to reassure California voters of his moderate bona fides while at the same time doing his duty to his party. (Independent)

PRETENTIOUSNESS INDEX **Nil**

As a noun, *bona fides* is both an abstract idea and something concrete, in that it can describe documents or any other type of proof which establishes that a person is trustworthy or genuine. As an adjective *bona fide* (without the 's') means 'genuine', 'authentic'. This is a well-established term, and one which hardly registers with most users as non-English.

BONHOMIE   *bon-ommee*   (French)

'good nature', 'geniality':

The worst aspect of New Year's Eve is the false bonhomie on which the whole affair is built. (Daily Mail)

PRETENTIOUSNESS INDEX **Nil**

Quite a widely used term, *bonhomie* is very much the public face of a person's good nature, shading into other descriptions like 'sociable' or 'extrovert'. There occasionally seems to be a grudging or sceptical undertone to the use of the word, or even outright dislike as in the quotation above. (There is also the adjectival form, *bonhomous*.)

BON MOT   *bon moh*   (French)

literally 'good word' and so a 'clever or witty remark':

The police broke [the demonstration] up with a baton charge, and [philosopher Sidney] Morgenbesser got hit over the head. The experience lead to one of his most quoted but least revealing bon mots. He was asked whether the police had treated him unjustly or unfairly. 'Unfairly yes, unjustly no,' he said. 'It was unfair to be hit over the head but not unjust since they hit everyone else over the head too.'   (The Times)

PRETENTIOUSNESS INDEX **Nil**

Bon mot is quite widely used in English, probably because two three-letter French words express an idea which it takes us several more syllables to say. The economy of the expression, and its near rhyming quality, also point to the polish and precision of the true *bon mot*.

BONSAI   *bon-sigh*   (Japanese)

'miniature tree, specially cultivated'; by extension, something which is 'very small but complete':

Most of the richest places in the world are bonsai states: Singapore, Brunei, Monaco, the Channel Islands.   (Spectator)

PRETENTIOUSNESS INDEX **Nil**

Bonsai is not a term much found outside its proper horticultural context, although it may be used to characterise something which is small but perfectly formed. So the word is a rather apt, if slightly patronising, description of the small states listed in the example.

BON VIVANT   *bon vee-von*   (French)

literally someone 'good living'; describing a 'person with a discriminating taste in food and drink':

...as any bon vivant will tell you, you rarely expect anything [in a station buffet] other than a smeared glass of gassy lager and an indigestible sausage roll when close to rolling stock.   (Daily Telegraph)

PRETENTIOUSNESS INDEX *!*

Bon vivant appears less frequently than *bon viveur* (see below), which is sometimes mistakenly used for this first expression. Although there's an overlap of appetites between the two phrases and a shared taste for – in that creaky old phrase – the good things of life, the *bon vivant* should be confined to the dining table.

BON VIVEUR   *bon vee-ver*   (French)

'pleasure-lover', 'man-about-town':

An 'emotional' court hearing in London revealed the tangled love life of the screen-writer and notorious bon viveur, who married three times and embarked on a love affair with Miss Minutolo in his 70s.   (The Times)

PRETENTIOUSNESS INDEX **!**

Bon viveur, an expression which isn't used by the French, is often confused with *bon vivant* and mistakenly applied to someone who has well-developed tastes in food and drink. In fact, it has more of the 'playboy' sense, as in the newspaper example above. Perhaps because of its fake-Frenchness, *bon viveur* has a rather dated naughtiness about it. Think of winks, nudges and twirled moustaches.

BORDELLO   *bor-dello*   (Italian)

'brothel':

Just because he comes from a working-class family in Liverpool – and was caught frequenting the local bordellos – it doesn't follow that we can expect an autobiography describing a life of booze, birds and regrets.   (Daily Telegraph)

PRETENTIOUSNESS INDEX **!**

One of a number of linguistic imports which mean 'brothel', *bordello* has a slightly euphemistic tinge to it. It simply sounds better or more fancy – or at least less unrespectable – than 'brothel', as can be seen if the plainer English term is substituted in the example above.

BOUDOIR   *boo-dwah*   (French)

'a woman's private room':

For a start, the interior of Roddick's place is decorated like a Victorian boudoir with sumptuous wall coverings.   (Guardian)

PRETENTIOUSNESS INDEX **!!**

Like *lingerie*, this is one of those French terms that come equipped with a nudge and a wink. Deriving from a verb meaning to 'sulk', a *boudoir* describes the place where a woman can be alone or where she can receive a chosen few. The word *boudoir* is often attended by a handful of equally select adjectives such as 'sumptuous', 'intimate', 'Victorian', 'cosy'. This is an expression that the English really don't know what to do with, but can't leave alone.

BOULEVERSEMENT *bool-er-verss-mon* (French)

'violent upset', 'reversal of fortune':

> *One writer suggested that France's 'prospects of winning are little more than negligible' and a former British Lion was moved to predict 'a crushing defeat'. I quote these forecasts, not out of any sense of superiority [...] but to illustrate just how astonishing a bouleversement this semi-final was.*

(Daily Telegraph)

PRETENTIOUSNESS INDEX **!**

This isn't a frequently used expression but sports writing, with its search for drama, is a popular venue for *bouleversements* and the term is an elegant if slightly formal alternative to its English equivalents.

BOURGEOIS *bor-jwa* (French)

'middle class'; 'respectable', 'conventional':

> *...our first hours in Marseille bring out the bourgeoise in me: the litter; the graffiti; the bibulous bums in the squares and gardens of the Vieux Port.*

(Daily Telegraph)

PRETENTIOUSNESS INDEX **Nil**

Bourgeois is a loaded term, almost always used in a disparaging way (as in the example) to mean not merely 'conventional' but often 'narrow-minded' as well. In fact, you can throw in 'petty', 'easily outraged' and 'materialistic' while you're about it. *Bourgeois* (feminine: *bourgeoise*) can mean almost whatever the user requires it to mean, as long as it's negative. Interestingly, but characteristically, the most critical users of the term are members of the *bourgeoisie* themselves. There is a less frequently found expression, *haute bourgeoisie*, to describe the 'upper middle class'. See also *épater les bourgeois* and *petit-bourgeois*.

BRAGGADOCIO *bragga-doe-chee-o* (fake-Italian)

'loud boasting':

> *Classic American conservative realists [...] understand this, and even if Bush holds on to the White House may yet persuade him to employ less braggadocio and more real understanding of power.* (Spectator)

PRETENTIOUSNESS INDEX **!**

Braggadocio may sound like an Italian word but it does not exist in that language. Rather, it was taken from the name of a character in a late sixteenth-century epic poem, *Faerie Queene* by Edmund Spenser. Any use of the relatively unfamiliar *braggadocio* might, I suppose, be taken as an example of the word itself – a case of linguistic boasting. On the other hand, it could be claimed that English alternatives such as 'boasting' and 'bragging' lack the swagger of the sham-Italian word.

BRAVURA *brav-you'ra* (Italian)

'daring and skilful' (particularly of artistic performances):

> *Amis was a master of sentences, but a novelist who papered over the cracks in his narratives with the bravura exercise of style.*   (Observer)

PRETENTIOUSNESS INDEX **Nil**

Bravura is most frequently found in commentary on musical performances but it can be applied to the other arts. It suggests supreme confidence, style, dash – all in seven letters.

BRIO *bree-o* (Italian)

'liveliness', 'energy':

> *His vulnerabilities, his desire to cut a dash with women, his tenderest and most private emotions are worn with Byronic brio for the reader's entertainment.*   (Daily Telegraph)

PRETENTIOUSNESS INDEX **Nil**

A term in music-playing, *brio* can also be applied to a person's manner, the performance of a team in a match, etc. One of those terms which can be translated by half a dozen equivalents – from 'vim' to 'vigour' – and yet one which hardly needs translation.

C

CABALLERO *cab- ayer-o* (Spanish)

'gentleman':

Paul forgets himself and nearly behaves like something less than a perfect caballero with a willing Victoria... (Daily Telegraph)

PRETENTIOUSNESS INDEX *!*

Spanish gives us a fair number of terms to do with men and masculine behaviour (see also entries for *cojones, macho, mano a mano*). I don't know whether it's English sniggering or envy at the supposedly hot-blooded Mediterranean male, but it seems almost impossible to employ them without at least a hint of the tongue-in-cheek. *Caballero* is obviously no exception.

CAMARADERIE *cammerah-deree* (French)

'comradeship', 'fellowship':

Her father, refusing to see that this is their chance to bond, is short-tempered and opaque – as he is, to be honest, most of the time. Her plans for intellectual camaraderie are, like the food, best abandoned.
(Charlotte Mendelson, *Daughters of Jerusalem*)

PRETENTIOUSNESS INDEX **Nil**

This is a genuinely useful term since the English equivalents can sound rather heavy-going to English ears. For this reason it may be preferable to characterise a long-term relationship of trust and companionship between people by the French *camaraderie* – if only to avoid the masculine, Lord-of-the-Rings overtones of terms such as 'fellowship'.

CAMERA OBSCURA *pronounced as spelled* (Latin)

literally 'dark chamber'; a box or room which allows light through a narrow aperture and inside which is projected a picture of the outside world:

...this is positively the only comedy I have seen in which the leading lady sees her true love kissing his dentist in a camera obscura.   (Guardian)

PRETENTIOUSNESS INDEX **Nil**

Both *camera obscura* and 'dark chamber' are evocative phrases in different ways. But the device was popularised by a 16th-century scientist from Naples so it is perhaps appropriate that the Italian phrase is the one which is still in use.

CANAILLE   *can-eye*   (French)

'rabble', 'mob':

We find it shocking that in Spain [at international football matches] the canaille make monkey chants. (The Times)

PRETENTIOUSNESS INDEX *!!*

Although the word is French, *canaille* derives from the Latin *canis* or dog. So the word suggests a baying pack of animals. There are several English equivalents for it but *canaille* comes with a kind of in-built, aristocratic sneer. Handy also in that none of the *canaille* will know what you're talking about.

CANARD   *can-arr*   (French)

literally 'duck'; used only in the sense of 'hoax', 'ridiculous story':

Like so many British institutions, it [BBC TV's Panorama] is often said to 'not be what it used to be'. This canard is backed up by much tut-tutting about its late Sunday evening slot.   (The Times)

PRETENTIOUSNESS INDEX *!*

This odd usage comes from one of several old French sayings connected with pretending to give away or sell a duck, and then withdrawing the offer. However feeble the trick or joke may have been, the 'hoax' associations of *canard* have stuck, and the term is quite often used in English to apply to a false story or belief which is in general circulation. A French satirical magazine called *Le Canard Enchainé* has been in existence for nearly a century.

CAPO   *pronounced as spelled*   (Italian)

'head of a Mafia branch', 'leader of a band of individuals':

As happy as a corpulent Mafia capo working the old family Parma ham slicing machine, I turned out eighth of an inch slice after slice.   (Daily Telegraph)

I have seen *capo* used to describe the head of a political group – specifically, the United Kingdom Independence Party (UKIP) – but the term is generally reserved for the head of a Mafia grouping. As with *consiglieri* (see entry), when used outside the context of US crime, *capo* carries a faint whiff of sulphur.

CARAVANSERAI   *caravan-ser-igh*   (Persian)

'inn in the East where parties of travellers can shelter for the night':

We crossed the plain where the Silk Route once passed and explored an echoing brick caravanserai [...] where light poured down in dusty shafts from ventilation holes in the roof.   (Daily Telegraph)

PRETENTIOUSNESS INDEX **Nil**

The *caravanserai* was particularly associated with desert travel. The word is very often used to describe a strung-out line of individuals or even a queue of vehicles, but in fact refers only to the place where travellers shelter for the night.

CARPE DIEM   *carpay dee-em*   (Latin)

literally 'seize the day' and so advice to 'live for the present moment':

A sense of history happening, even. Call it pompous tosh, but this is what we had come for: the moment. Carpe diem, and all that.   (The Times)

PRETENTIOUSNESS INDEX **!**

Carpe diem is a piece of advice from the Roman poet Horace. There is no exact equivalent in English, or at least nothing so economical, and the phrase is more resonant than rather vapid exhortations like 'go for it'.

CARTE BLANCHE   *cart blonsh*   (French)

literally 'white paper'; the 'giving of the right to act as one wants'; 'free hand':

When, why and how is it right to disobey the law? If it is never right to disobey, then tyrants have carte blanche.   (The Times)

PRETENTIOUSNESS INDEX **Nil**

The paper reference in *carte blanche* is to a signed but otherwise blank sheet on which the person receiving it can state his or her own conditions. The phrase is quite often used in contexts where a person has simply taken *carte blanche* rather than being granted it, as in the reference to dictators in the *Times* example above. This is a convenient alternative to English expressions such as 'free hand' or 'blank cheque'.

CASUS BELLI *carsus bellee* (Latin)

'cause of war', 'something which would justify a war':

> *The decision to overlook Thierry Henry and instead give Zinedine Zidane the world player of the year award should be a casus belli for more than just the North Bank regulars.* (Guardian)

PRETENTIOUSNESS INDEX *!*

Casus belli can be used about a literal war, but it is quite frequently applied to disputes between individuals or teams, the outbreak of hostile feelings, etc. Useful when the actual term 'war' may be a little too strong for the context.

CAUSE CÉLÈBRE *corze celeb're* (French)

literally 'famous case' and so a 'very newsworthy trial' or, more usually, any 'famous controversy':

> *Tracey Emin is upset because far from being a cause célèbre for angry female teenagers, her debut feature film Top Spot is being described as 'boring' even by her friends and allies.* (Independent)

PRETENTIOUSNESS INDEX **Nil**

Cause célèbre can describe a controversy or a scandal. If the latter, it nicely straddles the boundary between fame and notoriety. The English language forces a choice between one and the other, good or bad – even if, these days, being notorious isn't what it was. But the *cause célèbre* expression does not pass judgement on the trial or event to which it refers.

CAVEAT EMPTOR *cavvy-at emp-tor* (Latin)

'let the buyer beware':

> *…some of the oldest adages hold good; spread your risk, caveat emptor, remember that the past is no guide to the future and if it looks too good to be true it probably is.* (Guardian)

PRETENTIOUSNESS INDEX **Nil**

Caveat emptor is an old and familiar warning stressing the responsibility of the buyer to check the quality, etc. of goods purchased rather than taking the seller on trust. It's still valid even in the days of guarantees and consumer rights, and, despite the Latin, probably easier to understand than many pages of rights legislation.

CF (Latin) abbreviation of *confer* (from *conferre*) meaning

'compare':

> *We might think of the pairings that happen at parties as comically lustful (cf the office party)* (Guardian)

<small>PRETENTIOUSNESS INDEX</small> **Nil**

This widely used abbreviation generally appears inside brackets and introduces an item related to the main topic of the sentence. Less specific than *e.g.* (see entry), *cf* is more of a request to the reader to 'look at...'

CHACUN À SON GOÛT *shack'un ah sonn goo* (French)

'each to his own taste':

> *My own attendance at numerous European Councils did not trigger in me a deep urge to transfer more sovereignty to Brussels but, I suppose, chacun à son goût.* (Daily Telegraph)

<small>PRETENTIOUSNESS INDEX</small> *!*

Chacun à son goût is one of those French phrases – like *plus ça change* – which come equipped with an in-built shrug of the shoulders. It's a plea for tolerance but also an expression of amusement at the odd tastes of other human beings. So *Gallic*.

CHAGRIN *shag'ran* (French)

'great annoyance', 'vexation':

> *Much to her chagrin, as Argento got older, she inherited the 'dark lady' mantle from her mother.* (Daily Telegraph)

<small>PRETENTIOUSNESS INDEX</small> **Nil**

Chagrin can also suggest the idea of 'sadness', one of its older meanings. It does not characterise door-slamming irritation but is connected to disappointment or frustration.

CHARIVARI *sharri-varee* (French)

'discordant mixture of sounds':

> *The publication of a new book by Peter Ackroyd is an occasion for the kind*

of falderal and charivari that the author so vividly describes in his histories of London. Up and down the high streets, tills ring out like Bow bells…

(Observer)

P<small>RETENTIOUSNESS</small> I<small>NDEX</small> **!**

A *charivari* was originally a mocking serenade, played on kitchen implements, in 'honour' of a newly married couple. The practice of tying pots and pans to honeymooners' bumpers may still go on, but the word that would describe it has pretty well disappeared. Perhaps it should be revived.

CHATELAINE   *sha-tell-ane*   (French)

'female keeper of a large house':

Cherie Blair is making history again. She is the first chatelaine of Downing Street to appear in a television commercial.   (The Times)

P<small>RETENTIOUSNESS</small> I<small>NDEX</small> **!**

There is a masculine equivalent of the word (*chatelain*), but this term is generally found in the feminine form. A *chatelaine* is the mistress of a place but the word may suggest occupancy rather than ownership.

CHEF-D'OEUVRE   *shef d'erv're*   (French)

'masterpiece':

'This should put things into perspective,' said Gerry, handing me a leather-bound copy of his chef d'oeuvre, The Definitive Rotherham United.

(Daily Telegraph)

P<small>RETENTIOUSNESS</small> I<small>NDEX</small> **!**

Chef-d'oeuvre is not a widely used expression now, if it ever was. Although applicable to 'proper' masterpieces, the term is sometimes used with a touch of humour, as in the example, to describe someone's personal achievement, especially if it has a quirky or eccentric quality.

CHIAROSCURO   *kyah'ro scuro*   (Italian)

literally 'light and dark'; 'arrangement of light and shadow in a picture', 'contrast':

It [cigarette-smoking] simultaneously blurred and illuminated the mise-en-scène with its blue chiaroscuro, drawing attention to the shadows and ambiguities of life and softening the boundaries.   (Independent)

Chiaroscuro has expanded from being a term in paintings or photos to a more general, non-literal application to any subtle contrast of darkness and light in, say, a novel. The implication of the original Italian term is that each half, darkness or light, is dependent on the other for a full appreciation of itself.

CHIC *sheek* (French)

'smart', 'fashionable':

Andrei Piontkovsky, a well-known political scientist, says KGB chic and glorification of the armed forces is going down well among the Russians.

(Independent)

Pretentiousness Index **Nil**

A truly indispensable four-letter word, *chic* is both noun and adjective. You can be it, you can have it, you can wear it. Nor is *chic* careful about the company it keeps, since the term can even be associated with the secret police of the former USSR (see example).

CHUTZPAH *khoots-pah* (Yiddish; also **hutzpah**)

'cheek', 'effrontery':

You have got to hand it to Kay Burley for sheer chutzpah. In the interview with the woman at the centre of the Beckham affair tomorrow night, the queen of Sky News asks Rebecca Loos. 'Are there any identifying marks on his body?' (Guardian)

Pretentiousness Index *!*

Chutzpah is an increasingly popular term, pushing confidently into mainstream use. Like a number of Yiddish words, *chutzpah* has come into British English via the US, and brings with it a whiff of the big city.

CINÉASTE *sinn ay-ast* (French)

'maker of films':

The French word for a film buff is cinéphile. The word cinéaste, repeatedly misused in the British media, means 'filmmaker'. Please don't make the mistake again. (Guardian)

Pretentiousness Index *!!*

As the writer (Gilbert Adair) of the example above complains, *cinéaste* is misused in English. Not frequently perhaps, given that it's a some-what specialist piece of vocabulary. Anyway, just make sure you don't do it.

CINQ À SEPT   *sank ah set*   (French)

literally 'five o'clock to seven'. The phrase covers the stretch of time in the late afternoon when French lovers enjoy an illicit get-together or when a man makes a visit to a brothel, reputedly:

  'I'm staying the night for once. Mercedes, cinq à sept doesn't quite cover it.'
  (Martin Amis, *Money*)

PRETENTIOUSNESS INDEX *!!*

This is a phrase which is not so much useful, perhaps, as interesting. For many British people, the time between five and seven is occupied by the homeward slog from work. Any stop-over is likely to be invol-untary (traffic jam, broken-down train) or, at best, the pub or the station buffet. But it's different for the French.

CLAQUE   *clack*   (French)

Originally a 'group hired to applaud a theatre performance' and so any 'group of flatterers' in the arts, politics, etc:

  Naturally this was because of the claque, instructed by the whips to whistle and cheer him and jeer at everyone else.   (Guardian)

PRETENTIOUSNESS INDEX *!*

Claque is a fairly rare word – although one much favoured by Simon Hoggart, the parliamentary sketch-writer in the *Guardian*, probably because it fits neatly into the theatrical world of politics. It may some-times be taken as a misprint for 'clique', and the two words have some-thing in common, both denoting tight-knit, rather self-congratulatory groups. Of the two terms, *claque* is slightly more pejorative.

COGNOMEN   *cog-no-men*   (Latin)

'title', 'nickname':

  [Philadelphia] the City of Blubberly Love, the unlovely cognomen given it by Men's Fitness magazine, which pronounced it the country's fattest city.
  (Guardian)

PRETENTIOUSNESS INDEX *!*

Used originally in Latin for the final word in someone's name, *cognomen* now implies a different or alternative title to the one normally found – a kind of *sobriquet* (see entry) or nickname, but more dignified-sounding than the second term.

COGNOSCENTE   *con-yosh-entee*   (Italian; plural **cognoscenti**)

'someone with a claim to knowledge', an 'expert':

The lucrative Premiership is thereby peerless as the delight of couch potatoes all across the planet, but in the process its reputation with the self-appointed cognoscenti is damaged.   (Guardian)

PRETENTIOUSNESS INDEX *!*

Cognoscente is not quite as respectful as *connoisseur* (see entry), since the second term implies critical judgement as well as sheer knowledge. In fact, *cognoscente* is sometimes used with the underlying sense of 'someone who (thinks he) knows', and there may be a touch of mockery to the word.

COJONES   *ko-ho-naze*   (Spanish)

'testicles', 'courage':

And, yes, credit where it's due, it takes cojones to sing in front of a crowd who are there only because of your regal bloodline. But it takes cojones of brass to use the family name when you have so little to offer.
(Guardian)

PRETENTIOUSNESS INDEX *!!*

Of course, the most accurate translation of *cojones* is 'balls' since the English term is both literal and metaphorical, just like the Spanish one. *Cojones* haven't really caught on in Britain. They are big in the United States at every level, partly because of the influence of Spanish on the language. (Speaking to Alistair Campbell, George W. Bush reportedly said of Tony Blair: 'Your man has got cojones.') However, as long as we retain the perfectly serviceable 'balls', any reference to *cojones* is generally going to be tinged with irony.

COMME IL FAUT   *com eel foh*   (French)

literally 'as it is necessary'; 'as it should be', 'correct and proper':

Even in my profoundly hazy grasp of the beautiful game [...] there has for some time lurked the knowledge that Milwall are not quite comme il faut.
(The Times)

Comme il faut defines the territory between what is correct and what is fashionable, and so does a job which no single English expression is quite equipped to do. For all that, there is something a little pretentious about the expression.

COMMUNAUTAIRE *commoon-oh-tair* (French; also **communitaire**)

'community-minded'; used almost exclusively in relation to the European Union, and indicating a person, group or country which places a high value on the EU:

> *Abroad, [President Chirac] plans to [...] show Europe that France remains true to its communautaire history with a 'yes' vote in the referendum on the new EU constitution.* (The Times)

Pretentiousness Index !

This is an expression that comes with a lot of baggage, since it describes an attitude of mind, a willingness to think of pan-European interests rather than narrowly nationalistic ones. To be *communautaire* might therefore be regarded as a good thing. But for those who do not believe in the European Union, or think that Britain should have no part in it, being *communautaire* is the equivalent of wearing the mark of the beast. Not only is it a French word, it is a French concept. Enough said.

COMPOS MENTIS *composs mentiss* (Latin)

'in one's right mind' and so 'sane', 'rational':

> *He gets more lucid as the night goes on, but throughout MacGowan clicks in and out, a mumbled verse followed by a fairly compos mentis chorus, or vice versa.* (Observer)

Pretentiousness Index **Nil**

This little term is surprisingly popular, given that there are several perfectly good English equivalents. I suspect that *compos mentis* is used because, for all its Latin weight, it somehow sounds less serious than the English alternatives would in the same context. To describe someone's words or actions as 'sane', etc. might be a bit clinical. However, the opposite of *compos mentis* – that is, *non compos mentis* – tends to be found precisely in such cold, clinical contexts.

CONFER see cf

CONFRÈRE *con-frair* (French)

'fellow member of group or profession':

The creator of the Alex Cross novels has been besting the sales of his confrères in crime-writing for many a moon, and his finely-honed, utilitarian prose really gets the job done. (Independent)

PRETENTIOUSNESS INDEX *!*

Confrère, implying something more than a 'colleague', suggests membership of a brotherhood or fraternity, linked by shared aims and practices rather than by place and business. That said, the word is sometimes used in an ironic or less than serious context.

CONNOISSEUR *con-ess-er* (French)

'person of knowledge and taste, particularly in the arts or food and drink':

Yes, if you're going to be a connoisseur about [smoking cigarettes], you should hold the flame a couple of centimetres under the end without touching, so that you avoid the rush of carbon. (The Times)

PRETENTIOUSNESS INDEX **Nil**

In the arts field *connoisseur* has generally been replaced by 'art expert' perhaps because of the air of amateurism hanging about the French term. There is also a slightly old-fashioned feel to its use about someone who has a knowledgeable appreciation of food and drink – or even cigarettes. Nevertheless, the *connoisseur* is a cut or two above the *cognoscente* (see entry).

CONSIGLIERI *con-sil-yairee* (Italian)

'adviser'; the *consigliere* is the older (or at least wiser) counsellor to the *capo* or head of a Mafia 'family':

Though that's not his [Tony Blair's] image in the States, where Bush supporters see him as the intellectual backing for Bush, the consiglieri if you like, and Democrats are just deeply disappointed. (Guardian)

PRETENTIOUSNESS INDEX *!!* IF USED IN A NON-MAFIA CONTEXT.

This faintly sinister term won't convey much to British ears unless the reader or listener picks up on the Mafia overtones, something that is more likely to happen after exposure to *The Godfather* or *The Sopranos*.

CONTRETEMPS   *contra-tom*   (French)

'embarrassing hitch', 'argument', 'confrontation':

> *Sensibly, the Football Association are overlooking the brief pre-match contretemps between Vieira and Keane, yet continuing tensions are wearisome.*
> (Daily Telegraph)

PRETENTIOUSNESS INDEX **Nil**

Contretemps has a range of meanings but is most usually applied to a face-to-face dispute between two people. There may be a slightly euphemistic quality to the term in this sense.

CORDON BLEU   *cor-don bler*   (French)

literally 'blue ribbon'; applied to an 'excellent cook' or to food which is 'of the highest standard':

> *Pure pursuit of happiness in the NHS might risk offering cordon bleu meals and a smiling doctor, but lethal results.*   (Guardian)

PRETENTIOUSNESS INDEX **!**

Cordon bleu derives from the highest French order of chivalry, and so signifies general excellence. Its almost invariable application is to cooks and cookery. The term is quite widely used even though it seems to have a slightly dated feel to it now, perhaps because France is no longer seen as the culinary king of the world.

CORDON SANITAIRE   *cor-don sanee-tair*   (French)

literally a 'sanitary line' [of soldiers]; 'demarcation line between an infected area and a non-infected one, put in place to stop the spread of disease'; any 'area cleared to prevent contamination':

> *You will have noticed that a frigid Mr Blair shook hands at full stretch, creating a cordon sanitaire between himself and his host, the better to lessen the peril that the Libyan dictator would press his lips on the prime ministerial cheek.*   (Observer)

PRETENTIOUSNESS INDEX **Nil**

Cordon sanitaire is used more often figuratively than literally, although it can still describe the physical restrictions placed round an area where there is an epidemic or other disaster. There is no exact

English equivalent – hence the 'nil' rating for pretension – and the literal translation of the phrase, 'sanitary cordon', sounds like a chemist's item.

COSA NOSTRA *co-sah nostra* (Italian)

literally 'our thing'; the 'American arm of the Mafia':

...the sounds of Italy's untamed south have been sniffing around world music's mainstream with the urgency of the Cosa Nostra around a Vegas casino. (Daily Telegraph)

PRETENTIOUSNESS INDEX **Nil**

The term *Cosa Nostra* was supposedly coined by a 'boss of bosses' in New York in the early 1930s to describe the US branch of the Mafia. It has been popularised through books and films ever since.

COUP DE FOUDRE *coo de food're* (French)

literally 'lighting stroke' and so an 'extraordinary event'; most often used to describe 'love at first sight':

A friend who met Howard shortly after he had met Sandra (then married to her third husband) in the mid-Seventies recalls: 'He was glowing. It was a complete coup de foudre. *He adores her.'* (The Times)

PRETENTIOUSNESS INDEX **Nil**

Coup de foudre is a bit literary and dated perhaps but it still crops up (or darts down) from time to time, the 'lightning' of the phrase being a more aggressive form of Cupid's arrow. There seems to be no English equivalent.

COUP DE GRÂCE *coo de grass* (French)

literally 'stroke of grace'; the 'death-blow that puts an end to suffering'; any 'stroke which finishes the matter once and for all':

The Sun's editor, Larry Lamb, adds the coup de grâce *by repeating Terry's pejorative précis in a huge front page headline 'CRISIS, WHAT CRISIS?'*
(Francis Wheen, *How Mumbo-Jumbo Conquered the World*)

PRETENTIOUSNESS INDEX **Nil**

A very familiar expression in English, *coup de grâce* once referred to the pistol shot delivered at close range by a firing-squad officer to finish off the fatally injured victim. Current applications of *coup de grâce* tend to be more innocuous, referring to anything from a killer headline to the goal scored in the closing seconds of a game.

COUP DE THÉÂTRE   *coo de tay-art're*   (French)

'sensational effect in the theatre', 'unexpected and startling turn of events':

> *In his first coup de theatre as Labour leader, Tony Blair sprung upon an unsuspecting party conference his plan to change its constitution.*
>
> (Observer)

PRETENTIOUSNESS INDEX **!**

A *coup de théâtre* was originally associated with the theatre but it is more often used figuratively now to describe any kind of showy and calculated surprise. Politics provides a natural context for the term.

CRÈME DE LA CRÈME   *crem de la crem*   (French)

literally 'cream of the cream'; 'the best in any field':

> *This is not an aristocratic* crème de la crème *hermetically sealed in country seats or a clutch of high-flying politicians with No 10 in their sights.*
>
> (Observer)

PRETENTIOUSNESS INDEX **!**

If rendered literally into English 'cream of the cream' sounds silly. Alternatives such as the 'best' lack colour. The nearest equivalent for *crème de la crème* is probably another French term, the *élite*.

CRESCENDO   *cresh-endo*   (Italian)

'increasing loudness':

> *One of the marvellous things about Augusta is that you know when anyone big is coming because you hear this murmur, which grows in a crescendo of cheers…*   (quoted in the Daily Telegraph)

PRETENTIOUSNESS INDEX **Nil**

Crescendo is very useful, whether the term is employed 'correctly' or not (it is often used – and used wrongly – to mean 'climax' or 'high-point'). Of all the musical terms which have come from Italian, *crescendo* is probably the one most often found in mainstream English. Strictly speaking, the word should be applied to anything which is growing in volume (or in seriousness, excitement, etc.) but hasn't yet reached a climax.

The plural of *crescendo* is *crescendos* and the opposite of it is *decrescendo*, although the more usual musical term is *diminuendo*.

CRI DE COEUR   *cree de curr*   (French)

'cry from the heart', 'passionate plea':

Her cri de coeur was: 'I've run out of Branston.' It is simply a matter of personal priorities.   (Guardian)

PRETENTIOUSNESS INDEX **Nil**

A *cri de coeur* can be a protest or a plea for help. It may describe an action as much as a statement. However, the phrase tends to appear in less serious contexts (see example); an SOS from a sinking ship would not count as a *cri de coeur*.

CRIME PASSIONNEL   *creem passy-on-ell*   (French)

'crime (usually murder) motivated by passion (usually sexual jealousy)':

He was released on appeal after convincing the court that his was a crime passionnel, triggered by uncontrollable grief and misinformation peddled by the media.   (Daily Telegraph)

PRETENTIOUSNESS INDEX **Nil**

Crime passionnel is essentially a phrase that belongs to a particular culture. To be driven to murder by passionate jealousy is not merely a mitigating factor but, in France at least, appears to be a get-out-of-jail card. If one was falling back on national stereotypes, one would say that it was typical of the French both to recognise jealousy as a unique motive and to make special allowance for it.

CRITIQUE   *cri-teek*   (French)

'thought-out estimate of a work of art or an institution, idea, etc.':

The advance publicity from NBC projected the tapes as a caustic critique of the British monarchy.   (The Times)

PRETENTIOUSNESS INDEX **Nil**

Critique, both a noun and a verb, is quite a formal term, implying a measured assessment of something. You can't *critique* a person. The term may sometimes be confused with 'criticism', but even if a *critique* is negative, it should at least make the pretence of being balanced.

CUI BONO? *cue-ee bone-oh* (Latin)

'to whose good?', 'for whose advantage?'

Cui bono? Who benefits from Mr Brown's tax and spending?

(Daily Telegraph)

PRETENTIOUSNESS INDEX *!*

This is a slightly shortened form – in full it is *Cui bono est?* – of a question once used by the Roman orator Cicero, and likely to be just as valid today. *Cui bono?* is, in effect, a cut-to-the-chase method of saying 'Who is getting something (financially, politically, etc.) out of this initiative or action?', the implication being that the gainer will be behind whatever has happened.

CUM *pronounced as spelled* (Latin)

'with':

…her French publicist, who has accompanied her to London as chaperone-cum-translator… (Daily Telegraph)

PRETENTIOUSNESS INDEX **Nil**

This is a valuable link word showing a double position or function: cook-cum-proprietor; cafe-cum-bar. *Cum* suggests a slightly closer connection than the straightforward 'and', and is generally hyphenated with the words on either side of it. There is no single English term which will do quite the same job and it's a valuable addition to English.

(Cum is quite frequently mispelled as come – as in the erroneous 'actor-come-director'. This is a mistake, and a fairly stupid one at that, since a moment's thought will indicate that 'come' makes no sense in this context. What or who is coming? Where are they going?)

CURRICULUM VITAE *cur-rick-u-lum vee-tigh* (Latin; usually abbreviated to CV)

literally 'course of life'; 'brief, organised list of qualifications, previous jobs, etc. used when applying for new employment'; more generally, a person's 'history of work and achievements':

With games such as as England 1 Australia 3 on his CV, Sven-Göran Eriksson has already proved himself the ultimate farceur… (The Times)

PRETENTIOUSNESS INDEX **Nil**

This near-universal term is an elastic one since a CV is like a stew into which people can throw whatever they want (obsessions, places lived, positions of responsibility held). The expression can also be used more loosely to apply to the ups-and-downs in someone's career or fortunes, as in the *Times* quote above. In other circumstances, the Latin term may give dignity to an otherwise random-seeming stroll from pillar to post.

D

DACHA *datcha* (Russian)

'house or cottage in country':

The Today programme has already cost a BBC chairman and a director general their jobs in 2004 so you imagined their replacements holding their breath at their holiday dachas.   (Guardian)

PRETENTIOUSNESS INDEX **!** IF USED IN A NON-RUSSIAN CONTEXT.

A *dacha*, which can be any size, is essentially a country retreat. Normally applied to a Russian city-dweller's bolt-hole, it can be used half-humorously to describe anybody's 'place in the country'.

DANSE MACABRE *donce mak-ahb're* (French)

literally 'macabre dance'; 'dance of death':

But Sars has also highlighted the danse macabre between liberty and mortality.   (Observer)

PRETENTIOUSNESS INDEX **Nil**

Danse macabre originally described the images, popular in the Middle Ages, in which a skeletal death was shown leading everybody – rich and poor, young and old – on a dance to the grave. Now the phrase can characterise any sinister interplay between death and some other element.

DÉBÂCLE *day-bah-kl* (French)

'total failure', 'collapse':

In the years that followed the dot-com debacle, the public's faith in financial markets and their participants was shaken to its foundations.   (The Times)

PRETENTIOUSNESS INDEX **Nil**

Frequently used, *débâcle* tends to describe the collapse of a project, etc. for which there were high hopes and ambitions. It also carries a suggestion of disgrace or humiliation. *Débâcles* are not acts of God and somebody will be blamed.

DÉCLASSÉ *day-cla-ssay* (French)

'(person who has) lost social status or position':

Ultimately, indeed, it had been sex appeal which had redeemed him [the Roman dictator-to-be Sulla] from the ranks of the déclassés, for one of Rome's best-paid courtesans had grown so obsessed with him that in her will she had left him everything she owned.

(Tom Holland, *Rubicon*)

PRETENTIOUSNESS INDEX *!*

This is a fairly rare term but one which economically sums up what it takes a whole English phrase to say. Class is such a minefield that the safest applications of *déclassé* are probably retrospective, if not positively historical.

DÉCOLLETAGE *daycoll-e-'taj* (French)

literally 'exposure of the neck'; applying to a 'low-cut neckline revealing the cleavage':

Her spectacular decolletage is also winning her armies of young male fans, not least her support act, the comical Italian crooner Patrizio Buanne, 'the Voice of Romance.' (Guardian)

PRETENTIOUSNESS INDEX *!*

Like *embonpoint* (see entry), this is a vaguely coy and titillating term, with the adjectival form *décolleté*. Dictionaries define a *décolleté* dress as one which shows off the neck and shoulders but it is really the breasts which are meant – and the term may serve as a teasing euphemism for just that (or them).

DECREE NISI *decree nigh-sigh* (Latin)

literally a 'decree unless'; 'provisional decree from a court in a divorce case which ends a marriage for the time being':

To get custody of their daughter she had to divorce Dennis and marry Ginger. The decree nisi on grounds of adultery was reported in the Evening Post. (Guardian)

The *nisi* part of the phrase indicates that the court order for divorce will become absolute 'unless' some reason is shown why this should not happen. The simple, four-letter Latin word is probably better understood and less cumbersome than English equivalents like 'provisional' or 'conditional'.

DE FACTO   *day facto*   (Latin)

'in fact', 'actually':

> *In the US, there is virtually no legal protection for a public figure, especially a political one, from defamation. Libel laws are de facto defunct.*

> (Guardian)

PRETENTIOUSNESS INDEX **Nil**

De facto applies to a situation that exists without regard to what is rightful or what the law says about it and the phrase is almost always used in actual or implied contrast with *de jure* (see entry).

DÉGAGÉ   *day-ga-jhay*   (French)

'detached', 'casual':

> *The poem is about Williams dressing himself up in a variety of clothes in an effort 'to look natural, dégagé'.*   (Daily Telegraph)

PRETENTIOUSNESS INDEX *!*

Dégagé applies not merely to appearance but to attitude. It suggests lack of involvement, indifference.

DÉGRINGOLADE   *day-gran-go-lard*   (French)

'rapid decline', 'fall into decadence':

> *During an earlier, much ventilated, sexual* dégringolade, *the leader column of this newspaper shook its head over the affair, while observing with wry wisdom that whatever organ governed male sexual desire, it was not the brain.*   (The Times)

PRETENTIOUSNESS INDEX *!!!*

The imported *dégringolade* is an oddity. Since it is rarely used in English – in fact, it seems to be the preserve more or less of a single newspaper columnist – its appearances are as likely to baffle as to enlighten. However, a general sense of scandal or failure is usually evident.

DE HAUT EN BAS *de ote on bah* (French)

literally 'from high to low' and so 'condescending', 'in a superior or patronising manner':

> *The* de haut en bas *manner adopted by both [Conrad] Black and [Martha] Stewart cloaked, in fact the insecurity of the outsider.* (Observer)

PRETENTIOUSNESS INDEX *!*

De haut en bas describes a tone of voice or an attitude. Implying superiority, especially of the social or cultural sort, it is the less appealing side of *noblesse oblige* (see entry). Possibly more subtle than the pejorative terms 'condescending' or 'patronising'.

DÉJÀ-VU *day-jah-voo* (French)

literally 'already seen' and so applied to an experience that is 'familiar through repetition':

> *Royal watchers could be forgiven for a sense of déjà-vu when examining this year's Christmas card from Prince Charles. The picture of the prince with William and Harry is similar to the one released earlier this year when Harry turned 20.* (Observer)

PRETENTIOUSNESS INDEX **Nil**

Déjà-vu is comfortably in the top fifty of 'foreign' expressions, as shown by invented variants such as *déjà-lu* ('already read'). Originally the term was used to describe the psychological illusion of living through the same moment twice, but it has been diluted so that it can apply to just about anything which seems repetitive (and probably a bit boring as well).

DE JURE *day you-ray* (Latin)

'by right', 'according to law':

> *For one thing, Hitler, Mussolini and Hirohito were all sovereign rulers, de jure as well as de facto.* (Daily Telegraph)

PRETENTIOUSNESS INDEX **Nil**

De jure almost always appears in company with *de facto* (see earlier entry). The two phrases draw a distinction, respectively, between what is permitted by law and what is actually the case (irrespective of what the law says). *De facto* sometimes appears by itself, but *de jure* depends on the contrast with the other expression for its full meaning to be drawn out.

DELIRIUM TREMENS *pronounced as spelled* (Latin)

literally 'trembling delirium'; 'hallucinatory, trembling state associated with extreme alcoholism':

When I finally stopped drinking, aged 24, there was a nightmarish period of delirium tremens, a time when it was quite normal for me to hallucinate flocks of beautiful blue birds flying through my bedroom.

(Guardian)

PRETENTIOUSNESS INDEX **Nil**

Usually shortened to DTs, *delirium tremens* was a term coined by a nineteenth-century doctor (although it was not at first associated with alcoholism).

DÉMARCHE *day-marsh* (French)

'diplomatic move', 'policy initiative':

You might have got the impression [...] that the bill was a radical post-Madrid demarche by our ever-vigilant home secretary in the fight against terror. (Guardian)

PRETENTIOUSNESS INDEX *!*

Démarche doesn't mean much more than a 'step' although it usually carries the sense of an opening action. Its application is almost always to politics and particularly to diplomatic business.

DEMI-MONDE *demee-mond* (French)

literally 'half world'; originally applying to a nineteenth-century world of mistresses and prostitutes which was half-in, half-out of respectable society, the term can now describe any 'shady section of society':

As he pleads to the kangaroo court set up by thieves of the unnamed city to try him (the demi-monde *having hunted the killer down themselves to draw off the police heat), inner demons compelled him to kill again and again...* (Independent)

PRETENTIOUSNESS INDEX **Nil**

Le demi-monde was the title of a play by Alexander Dumas, first appearing in 1855, and dealing with a woman who had a 'dubious' reputation. The term has a historical significance – suggesting a social area between straight society and the underworld – but arguably not a great deal of contemporary relevance.

DE NOS JOURS   *de no jorr*   (French)

'of our days', 'of our time':

Nigella has become the idealised home maker de nos jours, *the domestic cook we would all like to aspire to be, Mrs Beaton cum Constance Spry cum Jane Grigson cum Caroline Conran.*   (Observer)

PRETENTIOUSNESS INDEX *!!*

De nos jours has truly become one of the key foreign phrases *de nos jours*. I'm not quite sure why this is so. Perhaps an English equivalent like 'of our time' sounds a little too heavy and historical, while 'at present' is simply flat.

DÉNOUEMENT   *day-noo-mon*   (French)

'unravelling of a story', 'conclusion':

In fiction, theatre and film we have been taught to expect a denouement before the curtain comes down, but in politics there are few denouements.   (The Times)

PRETENTIOUSNESS INDEX **Nil**

Denouement – from a French term to do with the unpicking of knots and so domesticated in English that it generally appears without the acute accent over the first 'e' – describes not merely the ending of a story but the satisfactory resolution of that story. The term is therefore not often applicable to real life.

DEO VOLENTE   *day-oh vol-en-tee*   (Latin)

'God willing':

A man at 65 can expect another 21 years while the average woman of this age will live for another 24 years and six months deo volente.   (Daily Telegraph)

PRETENTIOUSNESS INDEX **Nil**

Deo volente was once in quite common use, especially when abbreviated to *d.v.* But I suspect that this expression – the half-religious equivalent of touching wood when looking into the future – already sounds a bit quaint.

DE RIGUEUR   *de rig-err*   (French)

literally 'from strictness'; 'obligatory as a matter of form or style':

'Placard-waving student militants have left the campus. Anti-heroes like David Brent are now de rigueur.'   (quoted in The Times)

De rigueur can be applied to what's fashionable, the equivalent of the English 'must-have' (accessory, etc). But it is slightly more than a matter of style alone and implies custom or tradition. So, while fashions in clothes may change constantly, it is pretty well *de rigueur* to wear something sombre at a funeral as a mark of respect.

DERNIER CRI *dernee'eh cree* (French)

literally 'the last cry'; 'the newest fashion':

> *Could twin sets and pearls, carpet slippers, and shabby tweed sports jackets with leather patches on the elbows and cuffs be about to become le dernier cri?* (The Times)

Pretentiousness Index *!!*

Dernier cri is one of those phrases which is more likely to be used tongue-in-cheek than straight, and is the camp or chic equivalent of 'all the rage'.

DERRIÈRE *derry-air* (French)

'buttocks', 'bottom':

> *…the satin hot pants they […] customise with their own diamante logos ('Cheeky' on one girl's derrière, 'Girls' on the other's).* (Daily Mail)

Pretentiousness Index *!!*

Derrière is a soft substitute for the plain English of 'behind' or 'buttocks' or colloquialisms like 'bum'. It falls somewhere between the titillating and the euphemistic, and it's hard to envisage the word being used in any serious context.

DÉSHABILLÉ *daze-a-bee-eh* (French)

'undressed or partially dressed':

> *Nobody wants to be thought buttoned-up and repressed, but that doesn't necessarily mean you should go all-out for the untucked, déshabillé chic of TV lad (patron saint: J. Oliver).* (Observer)

Pretentiousness Index *!!*

To describe someone as being 'in a state of *déshabillé*' can be an irritatingly coy way of referring to nakedness or near-nakedness, although the term can also be employed with a sharper touch, as in the *Observer* quote where it has more the sense of 'scruffy'.

DÉTENTE *day'tont* (French)

'relaxation', 'easing of (previously poor) relationship between countries':

> *Indians gave Gen Pervez Musharraf, Pakistan's president, a rousing reception at a New Delhi cricket match yesterday in a show of support for detente between the two nations.* (Daily Telegraph)

PRETENTIOUSNESS INDEX **Nil**

Détente really had its vogue in the 1970s as relations between the communist east and the capitalist west started to thaw slightly, although it still has relevance as the contemporary reference above to India and Pakistan indicates. The word is used almost exclusively in a diplomatic context.

DE TROP *de troh* (French)

literally 'too much'; 'unnecessary', 'not wanted':

> *There are, needless to say, no provocative chips on the Beauty in the Box menu. Nor anything as de trop as wheat, dairy or sugar.* (Observer)

PRETENTIOUSNESS INDEX **!!**

De trop is quite widely used although often, I suspect, with slight irony. That is, its appearance reproduces – and undermines – a fashionably weary dismissal of something as really not wanted. A person may also be *de trop* when their company is not required.

DEUS EX MACHINA *day-us ex makinah* (Latin)

literally a 'god from the machine'. The expression derives from the practice in Greek and Roman drama of having a god descend from the sky to sort out problems on earth when they became too much for mere humans to solve. The actor playing the god was lowered from above, using chairs, ropes, etc. Now the expression may be applied to any surprising or 'god-given' answer to a difficulty:

> *As Ehrenreich points out, the cleaning lady is a deus ex machina, a marriage saver. She enables women to go out to work.* (Observer)

PRETENTIOUSNESS INDEX **Nil**

A convenient expression, more colourful than equivalents like 'surprise solution'. Ironically the appearance of the *deus ex machina* is usually the result of human ingenuity rather than any 'spiritual' intervention.

DIASPORA *dye-ass-pera* (Greek)

originally describing, in the Greek version of the Old Testament, the 'dispersing of Jews outside their homeland'; now applied to those 'Jews who live across the world and outside Israel'; more generally, any 'group which has migrated or become scattered':

> *...like many people in the black diaspora, he [Bob Marley] embodied a tension between where he happened to be (Jamaica) and where he thought he should be (Africa)* (Guardian)

PRETENTIOUSNESS INDEX **Nil**

When spelled with a capital, *Diaspora* refers to the Jewish dispersion round the world; with lower case spelling, *diaspora* can apply to any scattering of a people.

DICTUM *dikt'm* (Latin)

'saying, 'pronouncement':

> *I subscribe to Auberon Waugh's dictum that if you want to increase the sum of human happiness in the world, then the best thing most of us can do is just be happy, rather than wringing our hands every time we open the Guardian.* (Observer)

PRETENTIOUSNESS INDEX *!*

A *dictum* can usually be laid at a particular person's door, as in the example above, while a maxim or proverb is rarely laid at anybody's. And while a *dictum* may be a (personal) point of view, the choice of this word suggests that it comes with a certain authority.

DIKTAT *pronounced as spelled* (German)

'order which can't be contradicted':

> *Religious Jews are familiar with rabbinical diktats that restrict their actions, especially on the Sabbath when many forms of work are forbidden.*
>
> (The Times)

PRETENTIOUSNESS INDEX **Nil**

A *diktat* comes from an authority (usually religious or governmental) which is considered beyond challenge. If the term is used to describe a ruling emanating from another source – a local authority, say – there may be an ironic element to its use.

DILETTANTE   *dillytantee*   (Italian)

**'person who has an extensive but amateur interest in the arts';
'dabbler'; 'superficial':**

*On the whole, British fascism was a rather dilettante expression of Italian
fascism.*   (Daily Telegraph)

PRETENTIOUSNESS INDEX **Nil**

Dilettante is both noun and adjective. It ought to describe something
quite admirable but in practice the word tends to be a sneer, since it
implies a lack of seriousness and a picky taste. Originally applied to
the arts, the term can be expanded to cover other fields like politics.
The *Telegraph* quote above somehow suggests that *dilettante* fascism
was inferior to the real thing.

DIRIGISME   *diri-jeesm*   (French)

'state control over the economy or social matters':

*To all this must be added the relentless concentration of power in
Whitehall, which has not only belittled local democracy and discouraged
the best from leading it, but has fostered a dirigisme which has resulted in
resentful dependence.*   (Observer)

PRETENTIOUSNESS INDEX **Nil**

Dirigisme is essentially a technical term to do with the way a government governs, although it spills over into more general use. The
context in which the word is found is generally disapproving, and use
of the French term may reinforce an underlying hostility to a concept
which some consider 'foreign' to British politics. (There is also a
noun/adjective form *dirigiste* to describe those who believe in state
direction or their policies and attitudes.)

DISTRAIT   *distray*   (French)

'distracted', 'absent-minded':

*Wayne Rooney is a distrait young man who risks making the wrong profes-
sional move because of the tornado sweeping through his personal life.*

(Daily Telegraph)

PRETENTIOUSNESS INDEX *!!*

Distrait may seem like a high-falutin' way of saying 'absent-minded',
and so it is. Useful only in so far as the user doesn't have to specify

what the source of the distraction or absent-mindedness is. One is simply *distrait*.

DIVA *deevah* (Italian)

'famous or distinguished female singer':

> …*it emerged yesterday that Sarah Jessica Parker [...] was to be replaced by Joss Stone, the teenage diva, as the face of Gap.* (Independent)

PRETENTIOUSNESS INDEX *!*

The term *diva* might once have been restricted to opera singers, particularly *prima donnas* (see entry), but the word has widespread application to just about any female singer now. Spreading the term even more thinly (and losing most of its original sense in the process), *diva* is sometimes used about a celebrity whose behaviour is particularly egocentric or demanding – hotel suites for pets, instructions not to look the star in the face, etc.

DIVERTISSEMENT *dee-verteess-mon* (French)

'entertaining interlude':

> *Patch provided a divertissement by jumping into the River Orne, and having to be dragged up a steep bank by the collar.* (Daily Telegraph)

PRETENTIOUSNESS INDEX *!*

Divertissement can have a specialist application in ballet or theatre to mean a brief dance sandwiched between longer pieces. Otherwise it describes any brief action which diverts attention (pleasurably) from the main business. It is a quite useful alternative to 'distraction', which might be good or bad.

DOLCE FAR NIENTE *dol-chay far nee-entee* (Italian)

literally 'sweet doing nothing' and so the 'pleasure of idleness':

> *Hodgkinson recognises, however, that* il dolce far niente *[...] doesn't come easily to those raised on the Protestant work ethic. 'Idling does take practice so that you don't feel guilty about it,' he says.* (The Times)

PRETENTIOUSNESS INDEX *!*

Like the *dolce vita* (see below), a life of *dolce far niente* seems quintessentially Italian, not merely in the words themselves but what they express. I can't think of anything like it in English – 'doing sweet FA' is always an insult directed at others – and the lack of any equivalent to *dolce far niente* may suggest that English speakers are not properly equipped for strenuous inactivity.

DOLCE VITA *dol-chay veetah* (Italian)

literally 'sweet life' and so a 'life of pleasure':

> *The nearest I got to the dolce vita was the appetising remains of a cake in a cafe where we were filming. But it was a prop and I wasn't even allowed to pick the icing off.* (Daily Telegraph)

PRETENTIOUSNESS INDEX **!**

Dolce vita has become shorthand for a hedonistic, self-indulgent way of life teetering on the edge of decadence. The expression became better known outside Italy after the release of the 1960 film *La Dolce Vita* (starring Marcello Mastroianni and Anita Ekberg, and directed by Federico Fellini). Any English application tends to be ironic or self-mocking, as in the passage (by Andrew Marr) above. It is as if northern Europeans are incapable of leading *la dolce vita*, even if they would like to.

DOPPELGÄNGER *pronounced as spelled* (German)

literally 'double goer'; 'ghostly double':

> *Another journalist has moved in down the road. I visit him. He has the same bubble bath [...], the same wall paint [...], and on and on. It is chilling. He's my aesthetic doppelganger.* (Guardian)

PRETENTIOUSNESS INDEX **!**

Dopplegänger is the sinister equivalent of a second self or an *alter ego* (see entry). Doubles are familiar in mysteries and folk tales, and they are rarely benevolent. However, the term is generally used in a more innocent context, as in the *Guardian* quote above.

DOUBLE ENTENDRE *doo-bl on-tond're* (French)

describing a remark 'with two meanings, one innocuous, the other (usually) sexual':

> *Having the hump is one of Lindi's favourite expressions. She uses it all the time, apparently unaware of the double entendre.* (Independent)

PRETENTIOUSNESS INDEX **Nil**

Double entendres are something of an English speciality (see any *Carry On* film or any 1970s' sitcom), although we require a French term to express an idea for which we have no exact equivalent.

DOUCEUR *doo-serr* (French)

'sweetener', 'bribe':

> *The Treasury has waived £13 million – mostly capital gains tax payable by the Duke on the sale, and a small douceur, a traditional sweetener paid to owners of art when they sell to a public institution.*   (Daily Telegraph)

PRETENTIOUSNESS INDEX *!*

Douceur has the specialist sense (used above) of a tax benefit given to someone who sells an artwork to a public collection instead of through the art market. In other contexts a *douceur* is not quite as naked as a bribe. Rather, it is a gift or offer of cash presented in the hope of softening up or winning over someone. A bribe by any other name, then, especially when blurred by a veil of French.

DOUCEUR DE VIVRE *doo-serr de viv're* (French)

literally 'sweetness of living'; 'very pleasant way of life':

> *God was in his heaven, Britannia ruled the waves, a sovereign was a sovereign, servants knew their place and the upper and middle classes experienced an incomparable* douceur de vivre.   (Daily Telegraph)

PRETENTIOUSNESS INDEX *!*

Douceur de vivre, not a frequently found expression, implies ease, comfort, and the absence of threat or anxiety. Its most usual application is probably to the Edwardian period which preceded World War One, as in the example.

DOYEN *doy-on* (French)

'senior member of a group':

> *…it was not in order to hear about gall wasps, on which he was the world expert (the doyen of an admittedly rather small company), that crowds flocked to his lectures.*   (The Times)

PRETENTIOUSNESS INDEX **Nil**

Doyen (feminine form, *doyenne*) tends to be used in fairly heavyweight or academic contexts. It implies expertise or knowledge in a particular field, greater than anyone else's.

DRAMATIS PERSONAE *dram-attis per-sow-nigh* (Latin)

'characters in a play', 'principal people involved in some event':

> *The dramatis personae included, besides John and Hughes himself […],*

the beautiful fiery Caitlin Macnamara and the not-wholly-sober Dylan Thomas. (Guardian)

<small>PRETENTIOUSNESS INDEX</small> **Nil**

As a formal term in the theatre, *dramatis personae* has gone the way of stage directions like 'exeunt'. But the expression still has some use to describe the participants in an event, particularly one with a dramatic or artificial quality.

DRAMATURGY *dramma-turjee* (French)

'dramatic art':

Unlike more prominently acknowledged exponents of the new wave of dramaturgy [...] he could not help bringing characters to life on stage.

(The Times)

<small>PRETENTIOUSNESS INDEX</small> **Nil**

A somewhat specialist term, *dramaturgy* applies to the more intellectual side of theatre writing, and is as much to do with dramatic theories and principles as with actual productions. The noun *dramaturge* may sometimes be used to mean 'playwright', particularly one who selects or edits plays for a company. There is something rather lumbering about *dramaturgy* and the *dramaturge*, although this may be no more than the echo of 'turgid'.

DROIT DE SEIGNEUR *drwa de sehn-yerr* (French)

literally the 'right of the lord' and describing the supposed prerogative of a feudal lord to have sex with a tenant's bride on her wedding night; by extension, the phrase is sometimes applied to any high-handed action committed by a powerful authority against the wishes of its 'inferiors':

By protesting against the US's droit du seigneur, developing nations may provoke a backlash by the neocons and backwoodsmen of Congress.

(Guardian)

<small>PRETENTIOUSNESS INDEX</small> **!!** <small>IF USED IN A NON-SEXUAL CONTEXT.</small>

The limited and historical application of *droit du seigneur* hasn't prevented the use of the phrase in other contexts – the *Guardian* quotation above is to do with the presidency of the World Bank. There is an entire drama encapsulated here, to do with an arrogant master and the outraged vassals. It's not about historical accuracy, it's about attitude. There is a Latin equivalent in *jus primae noctis*.

DU JOUR *doo jorr* (French)

'of the day', 'of the moment':

> *Scarlett Johansson was last year's babe du jour.* (The Times)

PRETENTIOUSNESS INDEX *!*

Du jour seems a newish import and a very popular one. It describes anything or anybody which is fashionable at this very moment. The difference between *du jour* and *de nos jours* is time, with the second expression taking the longer view.

D'UN CERTAIN AGE *d'ern certay'n ahj* (French)

'of a certain age', 'middle-aged', 'oldish':

> *Trouble is, while the nation's hairdressing salons will always be full of ladies d'un certain age hoping that their crimper is going to make them look a few years younger, it seems to be changing for men.* (Observer)

PRETENTIOUSNESS INDEX *!!*

D'un certain age is a slightly coy, nudging phrase which, while appearing not to to specify a person's (invariably a woman's) age, actually skewers it quite precisely to those tricky middle years when youth is no more than a wrinkle on a receding horizon.

E

ECHT   *ekht*   (German)

'authentic':

Morton has an echt star quality: a screen presence that won't let you take your eyes off her.   (Guardian)

<small>PRETENTIOUSNESS INDEX</small> ❗

There are several English equivalents for *echt* ('real', 'genuine') but the German word has a guttural, no-nonsense ring to it which may help to emphasise what's being stated.

ÉCLAT   *eh-kla*   (French)

'glittering success', 'great acclaim':

I responded to the éclat of John F. Kennedy, to the modesty and gentle-manliness of Ronald Reagan, to the sheer goodness of Jimmy Carter, however boring he seemed at times.   (Daily Telegraph)

<small>PRETENTIOUSNESS INDEX</small> ❗

Eclat can describe both a person or performance which shines and the acclaim which follows. As with *élan* (see below), there is no precise English equivalent – a good enough argument for allowing the word through immigration control even if we're not quite sure what we're getting.

E.G.   (Latin; standard abbreviation of **exempli gratia**)

literally 'for the sake of an example'; 'for example':

Have there been any high-profile players who have scored with obscure parts of their body on purpose (e.g. buttocks, shoulder, groin)?   (Guardian)

<small>PRETENTIOUSNESS INDEX</small> **Nil**

This invaluable abbreviation never appears in full, and is frequently written as *eg*, without full stops. It shouldn't be confused with *id est* or *i.e.* (see entry) which provides an explanation of whatever has preceded it. All that *e.g.* indicates is an example or two.

ÉLAN *eh-lan* (French)

'confidence and energy':

> *'I did not shag Brad Pitt. No, absolutely not,' she reportedly told one red-topped newspaper, with a fair measure of élan and a suspicious understanding of tabloidese.* (Independent)

PRETENTIOUSNESS INDEX **!**

This simple four-letter term has quite a number of English equivalents ranging from 'enthusiasm' to 'vitality'. This suggests that there's no precise translation for *élan* but rather that it embodies a number of associated qualities, all to do with confidence and dash and zip and so on…

EMBARRAS DE CHOIX *ombarrah de chwa* (French)

literally an 'embarrassment of choices'; 'more choices than one can deal with':

> *Or they get sent to school in England, where there is, as a baffled French parent might put it, an embarras de choix.* (Spectator)

PRETENTIOUSNESS INDEX **!**

Like *embarras de richesses* (see below), *embarras de choix* describes a situation where the sheer range or abundance of items produces uncertainty. There's no great difference between the two expressions although I suppose that *embarras de choix* is marginally more active in its implications, since a decision actually has to be made.

EMBARRAS DE RICHESSE *ombarrah de ree-shess* (French)

literally an 'embarrassment of riches'; 'more wealth than one can handle', 'confusing abundance':

> *Far from it: the chancellor now has an embarras de richesses, including the £22bn windfall raised by his recent auction of mobile phone licences.*
>
> (Guardian)

PRETENTIOUSNESS INDEX **!**

Embarras de richesse(s) doesn't usually refer to money, despite the

Guardian quote. Rather it can be applied to a profusion of anything which, in smaller quantities, would be desirable.

EMBONPOINT *om-bonn-pw'n* (French)

Embonpoint literally means 'stoutness'. But in practice, it has a different application for men than for women. When applied to males and their problematic stomachs, its associations tend to be negative, though humorous:

> *But Mr James's egoism is tempered by self-awareness: as he positioned himself prominently, his book displayed against his embonpoint, he murmured, 'The poor photographer doesn't realise that he's publicising my book.'* (Daily Telegraph)

But when applied to women, the word usually appears in a more positive context and is a humorous/euphemistic way of referring to 'breasts':

> *Concerned doctors have reputedly warned the show's organisers that should determined jungle leeches attach themselves to Jordan's embonpoint, the results could be even more explosive than the viewing figures.*
>
> (Daily Telegraph)

PRETENTIOUSNESS INDEX **!!**

Embonpoint is a nudge-nudge term, although journalists and others may find it genuinely handy as offering a middle way between breasts/bosom and something more colloquial.

ÉMIGRÉ *eh-meeg-ray* (French)

'emigrant':

> *Many of the English émigrés complained of English tourists and said that they did not want to live anywhere near other English people.* (The Times)

PRETENTIOUSNESS INDEX **!**

There is no substantial difference between an *émigré* and an emigrant, although one could claim that the former is an upmarket version of the latter. Originally describing the Royalist supporters who fled France during the Revolution, *émigré* tends to be used about anyone who has left his or her country to escape persecution, for greater intellectual freedom – or, in the *Times* example above, presumably to get away from the entire English population. Although the motives for leaving may be the same, *émigré* lacks the negative connotations that frequently attach themselves to 'refugee'.

ÉMINENCE GRISE   *eh-mee-n-onse greez*   (French)

literally 'grey eminence' and applied to a 'person who wields power away from public view':

> *The counter-argument runs that European wine-makers must adapt to survive in an increasingly competitive market, where the standard is set by the* éminence grise *Robert Parker, an American wine critic whose nose and palate are insured for $1 million.*   (Independent)

PRETENTIOUSNESS INDEX **Nil**

This expression is so well established in English that its oddness and origins may go unnoticed. *Éminence grise* derives from the Capuchin monk who was secretary to the French statesman Cardinal Richelieu (1585–1642). A Capuchin's robes were brown rather than grey, but they might have seemed colourless by comparison with Richelieu's red Cardinal's robes. The 'grey' also conveys the unobtrusive quality which is central to the meaning of *éminence grise*. 'Power behind the throne' is the closest English equivalent but, although expressive, it doesn't have quite the sinister overtones of *éminence grise*.

EN BLOC   *on blok*   (French)

'all together', 'as a unit':

> *Year after year, Disney shareholders en bloc were content for Eisner to continue in post on terms that were making him richer than some Third World countries.*   (Daily Telegraph)

PRETENTIOUSNESS INDEX **Nil**

En bloc emphasises the solid, undifferentiated quality of whatever word it qualifies. There is no great distinction between this term and *en masse* (see entry), both having the sense of 'all together'. However, *en masse* is perhaps more often applied to people and *en bloc* to things, unless the user wants to imply an automatic quality to human behaviour (as in the quote above). But I may be splitting hairs here.

ENCEINTE   *on-sent*   (French)

'enclosure'; 'expecting a child':

> *There was another and much more precise test called 'CVS' – chorionic*

villus sampling – which meant an enormous needle going into Clare's precious enceinte.   (Daily Telegraph)

PRETENTIOUSNESS INDEX *!!*

In its noun form *enceinte* describes an enclosure (as on a racecourse) or, as in the example above, the 'bump' of pregnancy. In its adjectival form it means 'pregnant'. In both cases there is a coy or euphemistic quality to the term.

EN CLAIR   *on clare*   (French)

'not in code':

Tony Blair can at last say out loud and en clair what he believes in.

(Observer)

PRETENTIOUSNESS INDEX *!*

An expression from the world of codes and espionage, *en clair* can be used literally to apply to messages which do not require deciphering. When used in a figurative sense, as in the *Observer* quote above, it's an alternative to English terms such as 'straightforwardly', 'unambiguously'.

ENCOMIUM   *enco'mee'um*   (Latin)

'formal commendation', 'high praise':

Take yesterday's prime minister's questions. It began with Nigel Beard [...] standing up to deliver an encomium about the skills of women and their value to the economy.   (The Guardian)

PRETENTIOUSNESS INDEX **Nil**

This widely used term (plural *encomiums* or *encomia*) tends to apply to speech rather than writing, and characterises praise which is quite formal and elaborately expressed. To refer to something as 'nice work' does not make an *encomium*.

EN FAMILLE   *on fa-mee*   (French)

'at home', 'in the company of one's family':

Trips to the cinema en famille are something of an ordeal (for the rest of the audience). When we saw ET, a flood warning was issued.   (Guardian)

PRETENTIOUSNESS INDEX **Nil**

This handy and versatile phrase, with its implications of cosiness and informality, can apply to the family outside the home (for example, on holiday together) or to individuals secure inside their domestic set-up. Politicians are fond of being pictured *en famille*, usually a sign of an impending election or an upcoming scandal.

ENFANT TERRIBLE *onfon tereeb'l* (French)

literally a 'terrible child' and so a 'person whose behaviour is embarrassing' or an 'unconventional person':

Although the young Hirst established his reputation as a radical innovator, apparently flouting tradition with the gusto of an enfant terrible, *he feeds off an awareness of the past.* (The Times)

PRETENTIOUSNESS INDEX *!*

This is one of those phrases whose literal translation gives little or no idea of its standard application. *Enfant terrible* tends to characterise not children but youngish adults (generally men) who may go out of their way to shock or embarrass others but who are regarded as having some talent, especially if it's of a very showy or undisciplined kind. The arts – particularly the visual ones – are a breeding ground of enfants terribles. When they grow up and then grow old they sometimes become *monstres sacrés* (see entry).

EN MASSE *on mass* (French)

'all together', 'in a body':

Politicians from Dublin and Belfast decamp en masse to the US capital where Ireland's national day is marked with arguably greater ceremony than anywhere else. (The Times)

PRETENTIOUSNESS INDEX **Nil**

En masse is one of those imports so well established in English that we hardly notice its origins in French. It has a useful shade-of-meaning difference from English equivalents like 'all together' or 'in a body' since these may suggest that whatever is being referred is actually together in a physical sense.

ENNUI *onwee* (French)

'weariness', 'boredom':

Her idle rich heroines suffered little more than the brief guilt of an afternoon's adultery and a migraine brought on by ennui. (Daily Telegraph)

Ennui is a more serious and resonant term than English equivalents like 'boredom' or 'tedium'. Sufferers may like to think of it as a condition related to *malaise* and *weltschmerz* (see entries), something endured by Europeans or by the more sensitive of the British. It certainly sounds more impressive than 'fed up'.

EN PASSANT   *on pa-sson*   (French)

'in passing', 'by the way':

> *The technicalities aren't skimped by Updike, who has done his research, and who offers, en passant, a short history of computer science from 1950 to 1990.*   (Guardian)

Pretentiousness Index *!*

En passant doesn't achieve anything that English equivalents like 'in passing' or 'incidentally' fail to do. On the other hand, there's nothing particularly pretentious or showy about the term. (*En passant* is also a term for a move in chess.)

ENTENTE   *on-tont*   (French)

'formal understanding between states', 'friendly relations':

> *The Churchill-Roosevelt entente eventually deteriorated, and Margaret Thatcher had disputes with Ronald Reagan.*   (Independent)

Pretentiousness Index **Nil**

Entente, like a number of other diplomatic expressions, derives from French. Not quite characterising a special relationship nor exactly a friendship, it is a conveniently vague term. The best known *entente* is that between Britain and France, known as the *Entente Cordiale* and dating back more than a hundred years. *Ententes* should be cordial by definition but perhaps – given the often fraught nature of Anglo-French relations over the centuries – it was necessary to add the extra word so as to leave no doubt.

ENTRÉE   *ontray*   (French)

'dish served between fish and meat courses'; in US the 'principal course in a meal'; 'right of admission':

> *...the chav, the stye-challenged British social grouping for whom she has*

71

emerged as a champion, fronting a programme on the social phenomenon by way of an entrée into a new career as a television presenter.

(Independent)

PRETENTIOUSNESS INDEX *!*

There are two distinct meanings for *entrée* in general use, one to do with food and the other having almost the sense of 'ticket'. Having an *entrée* somewhere implies that you have gained access to a restricted or privileged world.

(*Entrée* can also apply to the first appearance of characters on stage or any stylised entrance.)

ENTRE NOUS   *on-tre noo*   (French)

'between us' and so 'privately':

Meanwhile, in Coronation Street, Audrey has, strictly entre nous, agreed to coif the corpses in the undertaker's.   (Guardian)

PRETENTIOUSNESS INDEX *!!*

There are perfectly acceptable English equivalents for *entre nous* from 'between the two of us' to 'within these four walls', so it is not the lack of any phrase of our own that accounts for its popularity. *Entre nous* can be employed seriously for a proper confidence or secret, but most of the time the phrase will be ironic (as above) or camp (also as above).

ÉPATER LES BOURGEOIS   *eh-pat-ay lay bor-jwa*   (French)

'To shock middle class/conventional attiudes':

The Turner [Prize], celebrating its 21st birthday, has come of age. But, without any desire to épater les bourgeois by desecrating Goya's etchings or refusing to make up a messy bed, what is the visitor left with?   (The Times)

PRETENTIOUSNESS INDEX *!!*

The phrase *épater les bourgeois* is used – sometimes in a critical sense, sometimes with a touch of amusement – of the desire on the part of artists, etc. to shock for the sake of shocking. This might once have been seen as a good thing, but the bourgeoisie (or the middle classes) have been getting a better press recently, and so the desire to shock them is seen as childish. Or perhaps they are less easy to surprise these days.

ERGO   *pronounced as spelled*   (Latin)

'therefore', used to introduce an apparently logical consequence of a previous statement:

> *America still has capital punishment, ergo, America isn't civilised.*
>
> (Spectator)

PRETENTIOUSNESS INDEX **!**

This obscure-seeming term is convenient in certain contexts. *Ergo* has for centuries been employed in English to suggest how one 'fact' necessarily follows from a previous one. (Shakespeare put a mangled version of it, 'argal', into the mouth of one of the gravediggers in *Hamlet*.) It occurs quite frequently in newspapers. Without having done a proper survey of the question, I wonder whether the word frequently conveys the opposite of what it appears to convey. That is, *ergo* may stand for 'therefore-this-seems-to-be-the-case-but-it-isn't-really-so'. Certainly, this is its underlying meaning in the *Spectator* quote above.

ERRATUM   *errah-tum*   (Latin)

'error in a printed text':

> *They remind critics that when Sir Leslie Stephen's first edition [of the Dictionary of National Biography] (1885–1900) came out, its mistakes were later corrected in a 300-page erratum.*   (Observer)

PRETENTIOUSNESS INDEX **Nil**

This slightly specialist term (plural *errata*) applies particularly to a mistake which has been realised and corrected, sometimes by means of a separate insert into a book, etc.

ERSATZ   *pronounced as spelled*   (German)

'substitute' or 'fake':

> *With our pseudo-information, our boil-in-the-bags and our Musak, we live in a virtual, silicone-enhanced, pre-fab, ersatz world.*   (The Times)

PRETENTIOUSNESS INDEX **Nil**

This familiar term has almost passed into mainstream English, having first got a foothold here nearly a hundred years ago. Although it carries the sense of 'replacement' – during the Second World War *ersatz* coffee was made with ground chicory or roasted dandelion roots – the word always carries the implication of something inferior. In fact, it's become a shorthand term of abuse as in the *Times* quote above.

ESPRIT DE CORPS *espree de core* (French)

literally 'spirit of the body'; 'the members' sense of comradeship and loyalty towards a group or organisation':

Speaking before the meeting in the Commons, Mr Hoon said [...] that changes to regiments should not affect their local identity or 'esprit de corps' but make them stronger and more flexible. (Guardian)

PRETENTIOUSNESS INDEX **Nil**

The French expression is more economical and elegant than the long-winded definition which I have given above. The closest equivalent in English is probably 'team spirit' but that almost inevitably conjures up images of playing fields, and *esprit de corps* has a much wider application than that, from boardrooms to barracks.

ESPRIT DE L'ESCALIER *espree de l'ess-kally-eh* (French; sometimes esprit d'escalier)

literally, 'wit of the staircase', and so any 'witty response or come-back which occurs when it is too late to deliver it' (i.e. as the speaker is descending the stairs on the way out):

'Ah, 'he replied, with the thinnest gloss of humour,' so you get to lie around all day reading poetry?' With l'esprit d'escalier, of course, I wish I'd said, deadpan, 'Oh no, only half the day – the rest of the time I smoke weed and sleep.' (Observer)

PRETENTIOUSNESS INDEX **Nil**

The idea behind *l'esprit d'escalier* is genuinely useful, even if the expression isn't that widely known. This quirky phrase fits a real need to describe an experience which everyone has had, and there is no English equivalent for it – or nothing which so neatly hits the mark.

ET AL *pronounced as spelled* (Latin)

'and the rest':

Whereas to the hyper-rationalists at The Guardian et al the ideal state is like an Ikea coffee table: blandly functional and easy to assemble with the right Scandinavian components. (Daily Telegraph)

Et al is an abbreviation of *et alii/aliae/alia* (the masculine, feminine and neuter forms respectively of Latin *alius* or 'other') and is used as the tail-piece to a partial list of names, examples, and so on. *et al* is useful on several counts: it's shorter than alternatives like 'and the rest'; it saves writers or speakers from the trouble of naming (or even thinking about) the other items in their list; and finally there is a throw-away, dismissive quality to the phrase which may imply that the user doesn't care very much about the remaining, unnamed items.

EUREKA   *yew-reeka*   (Greek)

literally 'I've found it!'; an expression of delight at some discovery:

He then poured it into a much wider glass, and this was my eureka moment – it tasted like a completely different wine.   (Daily Telegraph)

PRETENTIOUSNESS INDEX **Nil**

The 2nd-century BC Greek philosopher Archimedes is supposed to have shouted out *Eureka* as, lying in his bath, he hit on a way of establishing the purity of gold. The phrase has come down to us over more than two millennia to characterise any instant of delight and revelation.

ÉVÉNEMENT   *eh-ven-eh-mon*   (French)

'event'; usually found in the plural (*les événements*) in reference to the strikes and demonstrations in France during the protests of 1968, and so a term for 'mass disorder and protest':

As last week's evenements around the Palace of Westminster showed, the future of hunting is an issue which matters very much indeed to a small, passionate minority.   (Daily Telegraph)

PRETENTIOUSNESS INDEX *!!*

References to *les événements* are quite popular in newpapers and television, or at least in the more serious quarters of them. This is most likely because those who remember the exhilarating – or the anarchic and threatening (take your pick) – days of 1968 have now reached senior positions in journalism and TV. The *Telegraph* quote above is about protests against a fox-hunting ban, probably about as far as one can get from the spirit of '68, but the writer's knowing use of *événements* indicates that this expression is a handy, shorthand way of alluding to politically inspired demos.

EX CATHEDRA *ex cath-ay-dra* (Latin)

literally 'from the chair'. The chair is the chair of office, specifically the Pope's throne, or the chair of a teacher/professor. So *ex cathedra* comes to mean 'authoritative', 'weighty':

> *Mr Lloyd recently used the pages of his magazine to make an ex-cathedra pronouncement. This was that the Guardian is poised to become the new paper of the British establishment.* (Spectator)

PRETENTIOUSNESS INDEX *!*

Although the literal meaning of *cathedra* is 'chair', the word also gives us cathedral (the 'seat' of a bishop) and the connection suggests the rather elevated quality of *ex cathedra* pronouncements. Anyone who issues such things must be *someone* (although it might also be used ironically to describe self-important statements).

EXEMPLI GRATIA (see e.g.)

EX GRATIA *ex grah-shee-a* (Latin)

literally '(done) out of grace', 'as a favour':

> *Israel's most famous human rights advocate, Lea Tzemel, appealed to the ministry of interior for a 'family reunification' for the couple, and the ministry eventually agreed to grant Fuad an ex-gratia permit to stay in Jerusalem with Ezra.* (Guardian)

PRETENTIOUSNESS INDEX **Nil**

Almost a technical term, *ex gratia* is generally followed by 'payment' and defines a sum which is paid for reasons of 'goodwill' and in settlement of some grievance. However, the term can also apply to other 'favours', as in the *Guardian* quote above. The key point is that anything offered *ex gratia* comes with a built-in rejection of any legal liability, and there's not likely to be much real generosity or good-will behind it.

EX OFFICIO *ex offish-eeo* (Latin)

'by virtue of office':

> *In the present grisly political mood, where politicians are more than ever unbelieved and untrusted, treated as dissemblers or liars as if it were ex officio…* (The Guardian)

PRETENTIOUSNESS INDEX **Nil**

The most frequent application of *ex officio* is to a right which is held on the strength of some title or position – so that a vicar might be, *ex officio*, on the PTA of the local church school. But the phrase can be used loosely to mean not much more than 'comes with the job', as in the *Guardian* quote above.

EX PARTE   *ex partay*   (Latin)

literally 'from the side'; 'in the interests of one side only', 'partial':

>...*the Home Secretary would apply for an ex parte order from a judge, meaning that the suspected terrorist, or his lawyers, would not be informed of the proposed control order in advance.*   (Daily Telegraph)

PRETENTIOUSNESS INDEX **Nil**

Ex parte is principally a legal term, indicating something which is issued for the benefit of only one side in a case. Although not often found, it can carry the general sense of 'prejudiced'.

EXPOSÉ   *expo-zay*   (French)

'exposure of something scandalous or criminal to public gaze':

>*And, lacking the magic touch that Eriksson so clearly possesses, [the play] was significantly less entertaining than many of the tabloid exposés that were its genesis.*   (The Times)

PRETENTIOUSNESS INDEX **Nil**

Exposés are the staples of the tabloids and play quite a large part in the life of broadsheets too, as well as 'hard-hitting/undercover' documentaries on telly, etc. Probably more often connected to the exposure of criminal or illicit activity than to sexual shenanigans, *exposés* nevertheless promise a thrill with their promise of uncovering, making bare. The accent should always be used in *exposé* to avoid confusion with the English verb 'expose'.

F

FACTOTUM *fac-toe-tum* (Latin)

'someone who does a variety of jobs for his or her employer':

> *...partly as a result of the Burrell trial, we've heard how Michael Fawcett (Charles's factotum) threw unwanted gifts on the fire [...] as well as performing numerous other peculiar functions.* (Guardian)

PRETENTIOUSNESS INDEX **Nil**

A *factotum* is a Jack-of-all-Trades among servants. A slightly old-fashioned expression, it describes an old-fashioned role.

FAIT ACCOMPLI *fate accom-plee* (French)

'accomplished fact', 'something done before discussion with or permission obtained from those who might be affected by it':

> *The whole European structure has been built by general aspirations backed by creeping bureaucracy. The common foreign and defence policy is likely to become a* fait accompli. (The Times)

PRETENTIOUSNESS INDEX **Nil**

Although *fait accompli* may refer to a perfectly legitimate action, it generally carries overtones of stealth and even dishonesty. The implication is that something has been rushed through to avoid proper examination or debate. Accordingly, this sometimes resentful expression is most likely to used by those on the receiving end of the *fait accompli*.

FAROUCHE *fa-roosh* (French)

'shy', 'awkward':

> *But there was always a tension. The one so fastidious a mind though so farouche in manner. The other a chronic gabbler.* (Guardian)

PRETENTIOUSNESS INDEX **!!**

Farouche is a little misleading, since in French it can mean 'wild' while, when used in English, it implies lack of sociability (the connection is between an undomesticated state and awkwardness in company). The word calls up images of a shaggy, shy creature, so perhaps 'wild' isn't so far off the mark after all.

FARRAGO *fa-rar-go* (Latin)

literally 'mixed fodder' [for cattle] and so a 'jumble' or 'confused mass':

After all the plot's farrago of fantasy and speculation about the hidden intrigues of the Church and their impact on Western history has filled many other potboilers. (Independent)

PRETENTIOUSNESS INDEX **Nil**

Farrago may sound worse to English ears than it really is – not just a 'confused mass' but a mess as well. The slight similarity to *fiasco* probably reinforces some additional sense of 'disaster'. Anyway, *farrago* is a pejorative term, implying someone's failure to organise what should be organised.

FATWA *pronounced as spelled* (Arabic)

'authoritative decision or opinion on an aspect of Islamic law':

A leading British organisation on Islamic law has issued a fatwa on Lucozade, saying Muslims can drink the soft drink despite it containing alcohol. (Guardian)

PRETENTIOUSNESS INDEX *!!* IF USED CARELESSLY (SEE BELOW).

Like a number of other terms associated with Islam (see entries for *ayatollah, jihad*), *fatwa* had no particular currency in the West until towards the end of the twentieth century. The issuing of a *fatwa* against author Salman Rushdie for the allegedly blasphemous nature of his novel *The Satanic Verses* (1988) 'popularised' the term. The *fatwa* against Rushdie, issued by Ayatollah Khomeini of Iran in the year after the book's publication, was a death sentence. This led to the assumption that the word automatically implied the threat of death – as in the following example (which is both anachronistic and inaccurate):

Elizabeth I addressed crowds when there was a papal fatwa on her head and offered to share the dangers of her troops in wartime. (Guardian)

Fatwa isn't exactly useful outside its fairly narrow and prescriptive religious meaning. But it has become part of a small battery of words imported from Arabic which are used – sometimes for dubious purposes – outside a Muslim context.

FAUTE DE MIEUX *fote de m'yeu* (French)

literally 'for want of (something/someone) better':

On his [David Seaman's] return he re-established himself as Arsenal's first choice: faute de mieux, Arsène Wenger probably said to himself, sighing over the unfulfilled promise of Alex Manninger and Richard Wright. (Guardian)

Pretentiousness Index **Nil**

This is a frequently used expression. Since it refers to a situation in which there is no choice (because there is no alternative), it may sometimes be preferred to the English equivalent, which has a harsher edge to it – as can be seen if 'for want of someone better' is substituted for *faute de mieux* in the *Telegraph* quote above.

FAUX-NAIF *foh-ny-eef* (French)

literally 'false-naive' and describing a person who 'putting on a show of being straightforward or simple':

Having reached an out-of-court settlement for previous allegations of child abuse, he [Michael Jackson] now presents himself as a faux-naif who considers sharing a bed with a child 'a beautiful thing'. (Observer)

Pretentiousness Index **Nil**

There's an English adjectival equivalent in the word 'disingenous', which exactly characterises the attitude or actions of a *faux-naif*, but since no noun exists to describe the person him or herself this French word is genuinely useful.

FAUX PAS *foh pa* (French)

literally a 'false step' and so a 'blunder of words or behaviour' (usually in a social setting):

One friend remembers being furious when he arrived extremely late and left indecently early from a function at which he was a guest of honour; and apologised for neither faux pas. (The Times)

Pretentiousness Index **Nil**

Faux pas is a useful term, since there's no English expression which combines delicacy and condemnation quite so well. 'Blunder' or 'mistake' are heavy-handed by comparison. The 'step' associations of the phrase in the original French suggest that social life is either a tight-rope or a minefield.

FEMME FATALE *fem fat-al* (French)

literally 'fatal woman'; 'attractive woman who brings trouble to men':

Long before Shakespeare portrayed her as history's most exotic femme fatale, Cleopatra was revered throughout the Arab world – for her brain. (The Times)

PRETENTIOUSNESS INDEX **Nil**

Femme fatale is a relatively recent phrase from the early twentieth century but it seems to fit one of the age-old, archetypal (male) images of woman. The term, which has a slightly literary feel to it, is both a compliment and a warning, with the closest English equivalent being 'siren'.

FENG SHUI *feng shoo-ee* (Chinese)

literally 'wind-water'; describing the network of intangible influences, positive and negative, that operate in a place, knowledge of which is necessary in discovering the most propitious site for putting up a building, staging an event, etc:

Gervais is amused that his workplace has recently been described by one journalist as 'minimalist', as if this was all deliberate, and the product of an expensive feng shui consultation. (Daily Telegraph)

PRETENTIOUSNESS INDEX *!*

Like *yin* and *yang* (see entries), *feng shui* is a new western import of an old philosophical or mythological idea from the other side of the world. In the east *feng shui* may be used in siting graves, but in the west it seems to operate mostly at the home-improvement level. A pretentious term perhaps, but that's part of its marketing appeal.

FEST *pronounced as spelled* (German)

literally 'party'; 'celebration', 'gathering'; *fest* is rarely if ever used by itself but added to many other words as a suffix:

[The films] Two Moon Junction, Wild Orchid and other tasteful bonkfests ...
(Independent)

PRETENTIOUSNESS INDEX *!*

This is a wildly popular import, with *fest* being tacked almost indiscriminately on to many phrases – 'the annual campfest', 'a king-size kitschfest', etc. – to suggest a rather hectic concentration of related things. But the key point is that anything which comes trailing a 'fest' is not likely to be taken very seriously.

FIASCO *fee-asko* (Italian)

literally a 'flask' but always with the meaning in English of 'flop', 'disaster':

... while the millennium bug may be history and nobody, ahem, brings it up any more, the fiasco goes on.   (The Times)

PRETENTIOUSNESS INDEX **Nil**

Fiasco is a frequently used term, if an odd one. In Italy a *fiasco* contains wine. But the expression *far fiasco* in the same language means to 'fail completely' (literally to 'make bottle'). So we've taken the second, metaphorical sense of the word. A *fiasco* usually implies some humiliation and particularly describes a public flop.

FIAT *fee-at* (Latin)

literally 'let it be done'; 'authoritative order':

Quite another thing is the constitutional elephant trap that the Government has unwittingly walked into with its Prevention of Terrorism Bill, which will allow citizens to be placed under house arrest by fiat of the Home Secretary.   (Daily Telegraph)

PRETENTIOUSNESS INDEX **Nil**

Fiat has a legal application, referring to a judicial decision. But – as with *diktat* (see entry) – it is more usually found in a non-legal context to characterise a high-handed order on the part of some authority.

FILM NOIR *film nwah* (French; often shortened to **noir**)

literally 'black film'; characterising a kind of crime film which first became popular in the 1940s, usually made in black and white:

In the 1950s' noir thriller Kiss Me Deadly, cited here as major Hollywood pop art, the object chased by everyone was called 'The Great Whatsit'.

(Financial Times)

PRETENTIOUSNESS INDEX **Nil**

The term *film noir* was coined by the French after the end of World War Two. Exposed once more to American films after a gap of several years, French critics and filmgoers noticed a darker tone and a cynical undercurrent which hadn't been apparent in pre-war US cinema. These were crime dramas that didn't guarantee a happy ending but rather showed men and women corrupted or destroyed by greed and sex in a world of shadows. The term *noir* has stuck and is also used now to characterise a hard-boiled style of crime writing as well as film.

FIN DE SIÈCLE *fan de see-ek'l* (French)

literally 'end of the [nineteenth] century' and so, by association, 'decadent':

> *Aubrey Beardsley holidayed here at about the time Oscar Wilde hinted at Brighton's qualities as a gay haven [...] and between the perversities of the fin-de-siècle imagination and tatty online 'Dirty Weekend' kits, something has been lost.* (Observer)

PRETENTIOUSNESS INDEX **Nil**

Fin-de-siècle has a specific historic application to describe the artistic and cultural life of the closing years of the nineteenth century, typified by writers such as Oscar Wilde and characterising an outlook that was gay but melancholy, as well as self-regardingly naughty. There was some attempt to revive the term for the end of the twentieth century but it didn't really stick.

FLÂNEUR *flan-err* (French)

'someone who strolls around', 'idler':

> *I found myself viewing Olly as a tedious flaneur because he didn't want to live and work at full throttle as I chose to do.* (Guardian)

PRETENTIOUSNESS INDEX **!**

Flâneur may suggest a dedicated idler, someone who does it by choice or as a philosophy of life. I'm not even sure whether 'idler' is pejorative, if it ever really was – there is, after all, a magazine called *The Idler* and the word has an old-fashioned charm about it. But *flâneur* sounds classier still.

FOLIE À DEUX *folly ah de* (French)

Literally 'madness of two' and so a 'shared delusion' or a 'foolish criminal action committed by two people':

> *He [Charlie Kray] was the oldest of the Krays and had it not been for the*

explosive folie a deux that followed him, he would probably have ended his days running a bar selling Carling Black Label and crabsticks on the Costa del Sol. (Guardian)

PRETENTIOUSNESS INDEX **Nil**

Folie à deux is both a specialist term in psychology describing a shared delusion and a phrase which can be applied to an act carried out by two people in which the illness or criminality of each makes worse the condition of the other. The relationship between Moors murderers Ian Brady and Myra Hindley was often characterised as a case of *folie à deux*.

FOLIE DE GRANDEUR   *folly de gron-derr*   (French)

'delusions of grandeur': applicable both to a self-important attitude which leads to blunders on a big scale and to the blunders themselves, particularly if they take the concrete form of a building or a monument:

> *P.Y. Gerbeau, the Frenchman intimately asociated with our most spectacular* folie de grandeur *[the Millennium Dome] of recent years...* (The Times)

PRETENTIOUSNESS INDEX **Nil**

Folie de grandeur is a valuable expression which establishes the user's superiority to the topic under discussion and implies that he or she has seen through the pretensions of others. It's interesting that, to describe something with which we're all familiar, we should turn to the French, who have a tradition of grand – or grandiose – buildings erected by the state. (Over there they are often dignified by the term *grands projets*, a term particularly associated with President Mitterand and the spectacular edifices created in Paris in the 1980s and '90s.)

FONS ET ORIGO   *fonz et orree-go*   (Latin)

'source and origin':

> *[Gordon] Brown was the true architect of New Labour, with far more right to be considered its fons et origo than Tony Blair.* (Observer)

PRETENTIOUSNESS INDEX *!*

Fons et origo is one of those belts-and-braces phrases, like 'law and order' or 'ways and means', in which each half means essentially the same as the other. A rather stuffy expression now but useful, I suppose, if you want to emphasise that something or somebody really is the starting-point for a later development.

FORCE MAJEURE   *force mahj-err*   (French)

literally 'overwhelming power'; applied to highly destructive events which prevent the fulfilling of a legal or commercial contract:

As it [the tidal wave] was a natural disaster, or force majeure, insurance companies do not have to offer compensation…   (The Times)

PRETENTIOUSNESS INDEX **Nil**

Force majeure is more or less what is called an act of God – a catastrophic event which couldn't have been prevented by human foresight, preparation, etc. – although the term can also cover strikes and war. Essentially a legal expression, it operates as a get-out clause for insurers and others.

FORTE   *fortay*   (French)

'strong point', 'activity or skill in which a person excels':

But screenwriting is their forte: they create thoughtful stories that connect with both heart and head.   (Daily Telegraph)

PRETENTIOUSNESS INDEX **Nil**

Forte derives from a word describing the toughest part of a sword blade. Applied to individuals, it suggests something which is as much innate as learned, and is comparable to another French term *métier* (see entry).

(LA) FRANCE PROFONDE   *la Fronse prof-ond*   (French)

literally 'deep France' and so applied to those areas of France which supposedy embody the country's most quintessential features:

To the few outsiders who stumbled across it, the village, with its spindly streets and small houses, its dilapidated cafe, boulangerie and half-shuttered mairie, appeared to be the near essence of la France profonde.

(Daily Telegraph)

PRETENTIOUSNESS INDEX **!**WHEN USED BY THE ENGLISH TO EACH OTHER.

La France profonde is a somewhat specialised term with a meaning that is half philosophical, even spiritual, as much as it is literal. Not just a question of place, then, but of atmosphere. And not just of atmosphere, but of that *je ne sais quoi* which makes the country what it is.

FRANGLAIS   *fronglay*   (French)

describing the 'use of English expressions in French':

I then grappled with a Franglais sentence construction that, like the Greek stadiums, took a long time coming. 'Qu'est ce que vous pense de Kelly Holmes?' (Daily Telegraph)

<small>PRETENTIOUSNESS INDEX</small> **Nil**

Franglais is a *portmanteau* word (see entry), combining *français* and *anglais,* and applying to expressions such as 'le week-end' where French and English elements are jumbled together. The French are supposedly sensitive about the importation of English terms, and have even tried to set up a *cordon sanitaire* (see entry) round their own language. Efforts to keep the purity of language are usually futile. Incidentally, the *Telegraph* example is *Franglais* only insofar as it mentions an English name.

FRISSON *free-sson* (French)

'thrill', 'pleasurable shudder':

To hear Julia Roberts use the expression 'do you fancy her?' adds a certain frisson. (Evening Standard)

<small>PRETENTIOUSNESS INDEX</small> **Nil**

Frisson is a very widely used expression, often thrown into a piece of prose without much thought. There may be a mild element of fear in the response, but most of the time *frisson* is used about anything which gives the person who's experiencing it an enjoyable little jolt.

FROIDEUR *frwah-derr* (French)

'coldness between people or groups':

There is also froideur between the BBC and Israel's government over an interview [...] with the nuclear weapons whistle-blower, Mordechai Vanunu. (Observer)

<small>PRETENTIOUSNESS INDEX</small> *!*

Froideur can characterise the relationship between individuals, although it is a slightly pretentious term when there are perfectly good English equivalents from 'cool' to 'frosty'. It has some value when applied to formal relations between groups or countries where it becomes the diplomatic way of saying 'we're going through a bad patch'.

FROTTAGE *frottahj* (French)

'rubbing', 'friction':

Dean, one of King's employees, is a virgin who engages in vigorous bouts of frottage with the Delirium's windscreen after liberally greasing his body with Turtle Wax (giving a new twist to the expression auto-eroticism).

(Daily Telegraph)

PRETENTIOUSNESS INDEX **Nil**

Frottage has a technical artistic sense to describe the effect produced on, say, paper laid on a rough surface and then shaded. But its standard application is to the sexual kink whereby individuals get gratification out of rubbing up against others, usually strangers, usually clothed. Again, this is something of a specialist usage.

FURORE   *few-rawree*   (Italian)

'excitement', 'fuss':

[Dave Allen] was even called the Irish Lenny Bruce, although given the furore caused by a single primetime use of the f-word, this may be a slight overstatement. (The Times)

PRETENTIOUSNESS INDEX **Nil**

There is not necessarily any anger in a *furore*, although there is generally a sense of outrage mixed in with the excitement. The word is particularly suited to describe the fuss stirred up by the press over some 'offence' against good taste, etc.

G

GALÈRE   *gal-air*   (French)

literally a 'galley'; 'unpleasant group' [usually of people], 'unpleasant situation':

On two successive Christmases, 2002 and 2003, two little books [...] dominated the stocking-filler market, vaulted up the best-seller lists, and inspired a gruesome galere of wannabees and parodies.   (Observer)

PRETENTIOUSNESS INDEX *!*

Any use of *galère* may be slightly misleading since it looks like 'gallery' and is often found in contexts where that word would fit. However, its primary meaning is 'galley', a boat in which convicted criminals provided the oar-power. By association, *galère* acquires its sense of a 'bad company or situation'. A useful term, therefore, but one whose negative meaning may sometimes be misunderstood.

GAMINE   *ga-mean*   (French)

describing a woman who looks 'boyish, mischievous':

Moody, gamine and matchstick thin, elfin face peeping out from under a mop of cropped hair, in the 1950s and 1960s she [Françoise Sagan] seemed the epitome of Parisian radical chic.   (Daily Telegraph)

PRETENTIOUSNESS INDEX *!*

The meaning of *gamine* is difficult to translate even if the result is easy to recognise. As the feminine form of *gamin*, originally meaning a 'street urchin', *gamine* characterises a style of feminine beauty which is variously described as elfin, boyish, pert, informal. Sometimes it seems no more than a matter of short hair and a striking bone structure. Famous *gamines* include the writer Françoise Sagan and film stars Jean Seberg and Leslie Caron – and, pre-eminently, Audrey Hepburn.

GAUCHE *go-sh* (French)

'uncomfortable', 'awkward':

It is 22 years since the most famous photographer in rock met the four gauche young Irishmen who were destined to become the biggest rock group in the world. (Observer)

PRETENTIOUSNESS INDEX **Nil**

Gauche always applies to people in social situations. It rarely characterises physical awkwardness and more often suggests uncertainty in knowing the right way to behave. It's a useful term because it seems less dismissive than English equivalents such as 'clumsy'.

GAUCHERIE *go-sheree* (French)

'clumsiness', 'social ineptness':

If he fails, we shall hear more of what he is not so good at: the gum-chewing gaucherie, say, that was scorned by some columnists when he collected a BBC award. (Daily Telegraph)

PRETENTIOUSNESS INDEX *!*

Related to *gauche* (see entry above) but less often found in English, a *gaucherie* is a single blunder or a piece of clumsy social behaviour, usually committed out of ignorance – not unlike a *faux pas* (see entry).

GEMEINSCHAFT *ge-mine-shaft* (German)

'society/community based on personal links':

In the same way, although [George] Eliot could endlessly ponder the need to transfer the social cohesiveness of gemeinschaft into heavily industrialised late 19th century Britain, she never managed to show it happening.
(Prospect)

PRETENTIOUSNESS INDEX **Nil**

Gemeinschaft, a sociological term usually contrasted with *Gesellschaft* (see entry), describes a society which is linked by ties of friendship and kinship and shared beliefs.

GEMÜTLICH *ge-moot-likh* (German)

'friendly', 'snug':

The drawing-room gives the same impression of gemütlich comfort –

button-back armchairs, Regency cabinets and highly polished tables covered with knick-knacks. (Observer)

PRETENTIOUSNESS INDEX **!** IF USED OUTSIDE ITS PROPER CONTEXT.

Gemütlich can be used about people and places, like the English 'congenial'. But it has additional overtones of comfort and homeliness. This is an expressive but fairly culture-specific term, which doesn't stray far beyond its middle-European home.

GENERALISSIMO *pronounced as spelled* (Italian)

'supreme commander', 'commander of combined forces':

The Home Secretary plays a central role in the 'war against terror' as well as being generalissimo of the government's 'crackdown on crime'.

(Observer)

PRETENTIOUSNESS INDEX **!**

Although *generalissimo* is a single word as opposed to its two- or four-word translations, it is not employed for reasons of economy. Nor does it often, I suspect, appear in a military context – or at least not when referring to the British army. Rather, *generalissimo* combines the suggestion of would-be authority and the faintly absurd. It conjures an image of a heavily bemedalled military leader (whose biggest battle may come when fitting his uniform round his large frame). In the *Observer* quote above, the use of the word perhaps throws doubt on the Home Secretary's role or plans, as do the speech marks round 'crackdown on crime'.

GENIUS LOCI *genius low-key* (Latin)

literally the 'genius of the place' and so the 'governing spirit of a place' or the 'associations which dominate in a particular place':

This clay is burned and compressed into 'London Stock', the particular yellow-brown or red brick that has furnished the material of London housing. It truly represents the genius loci… (Peter Ackroyd, *London*)

PRETENTIOUSNESS INDEX **!**

Genius loci can describe both a person whose presence or character 'shapes' a place, institution, etc. and also the atmosphere which is predominant.

GESELLSCHAFT *ge-zell-shaft* (German)

'group/society held together by common interests rather than personal ties':

This tension is at the heart of much political theory. It is the tension between Gesellschaft – the anonymous structure of transactions and rules in a modern market society – and Gemeinschaft – the close ties of community where understandings do not have to be explicit because they are deeply shared. (Prospect)

PRETENTIOUSNESS INDEX **Nil**

A somewhat specialist term (frequently associated and contrasted with *Gemeinschaft*, as in the example above), *Gesellschaft* is sometimes seen as the social model which has replaced the old-fashioned 'community'.

GESTALT *gesh-talt* (German)

'shape' or 'pattern'; most often used in psychology to describe a theory or approach which aims to see something as a whole rather than breaking it into separate parts:

So thorough is our dairy indoctrination that it requires a total gestalt switch to contemplate the notion that milk may help to cause the very diseases it's meant to prevent. (Guardian)

PRETENTIOUSNESS INDEX *!!* IF USED OUTSIDE A SPECIALIST CONTEXT.

Like a number of terms which derive from psychology, *gestalt* has wandered away from its specialist or technical context even if it has not entered mainstream use in the way that 'paranoid' or 'schizophrenic' have done (perhaps because it relates more to a method of approach or treatment than to a high-profile condition). However, anybody employing *gestalt* in a non-specialist field should ask whether the word does anything that couldn't be achieved by a simpler term. In the *Guardian* example above, it might be argued that *gestalt* suggests the emotional *and* intellectual switch required to think differently – in this case, that milk might be bad for you. But the sentence wouldn't really be affected if the word was left out altogether and it's difficult to avoid the impression that the writer has thrown it in to sex up the subject of milk.

GIGOLO *jigo-lo* (French)

'young male dancing partner/escort paid for his services', 'man paid by a (usually older) woman in exchange for sex':

But before he'd won he'd already signed up to work the summer PR-ing here, earning a few euros a night plus all he can drink at the bar in exchange for luring in the ladies. He doesn't like being a modern-day gigolo. (Observer)

Pretentiousness Index **Nil**

Gigolo is widely used. Although it can have the relatively innocent meaning of 'dance partner', it almost always carries sexual connotations. Not necessarily an insult – after all, Richard Gere was an American Gigolo in the film of that name back in 1980 – but the term is hardly a compliment either.

GLASNOST   *glaz-nost*   (Russian)

'openness in giving out information [particularly by a government]':

So no glasnost on the legal advice prior to the war in Iraq, no information on how much we wasted on Black Wednesday – yet. (Observer)

Pretentiousness Index **Nil** if used in a Soviet/historical context but arguably **!** when used elsewhere.

In the less repressive Soviet Union of the mid-1980s the Prime Minister, Mikhail Gorbachev, initiated a policy of *glasnost* in contrast to old-style habits of secrecy and suppression of information. For the best part of a decade that word (and *perestroika*) described the extraordinary changes that took place in Russia. Now *glasnost* can be applied to government openness elsewhere, and is an interesting example of an otherwise obscure foreign term which hops over specific boundaries of time and place and establishes itself (almost) in mainstream use.

GONZO   *pronounced as spelled*   (Italian)

'foolish', 'silly', 'crazy':

There are two types of porn: gonzo and features. Features has a storyline. Boy meets girl in a clinic for people with inhibitions and they both help each other overcome their neuroses. Gonzo is different. Gonzo is just continuous sex. (Spectator)

Pretentiousness Index **!**

Although *gonzo* originates in Italian, it is widely used in US slang to characterise a style of journalism – most notably, that of Hunter S. Thompson (1937–2005), author of *Fear and Loathing in Las Vegas* – which is extravagant and subjective. It also describes a style of porn film-making which is shambolic, no-holds-barred. *Gonzo* has got a foothold in British slang but it may be too obscure to really find a real welcome.

GÖTTERDÄMMERUNG *ger-terr-demmerung* (German)

'twilight of the gods'; 'catastrophic downfall':

> *There is at least the possibility of a horrifying siege of Baghdad. And on we go with our tinkering, our cleaning of the bilges, as though this Götterdämmerung simply wasn't happening.* (Daily Telegraph)

PRETENTIOUSNESS INDEX **!!** UNLESS THE USER IS REALLY TALKING ABOUT THE END OF THE WORLD.

Götterdämmerung is the title of the last opera in Richard Wagner's epic Ring cycle, and the term has entered the English language as cultural shorthand – and a piece of showing off – to express the idea of complete destruction. This is the way the world ends, not with a whimper but with a very loud bang and plenty of smoke and fire. Summoning up the word suggests an apocalypse, and the term will rarely be appropriate.

GOURMAND *gor-mon* (French)

'someone who eats too much', 'glutton':

> *The man-eater [crocodile] is 16ft long and weighs a ton. In his gourmand career, he developed his own special fast-food technique.* (Daily Telegraph)

PRETENTIOUSNESS INDEX **!** IF WRONGLY USED.

Gourmand is often used in the sense of *gourmet* (see below) to describe someone who has a fine appreciation of food. Its proper meaning, however, is almost the opposite since it characterises people who don't mind much what they eat as long as they get enough of it. Nevertheless, if the user means 'glutton' then it is probably better to put that word in preference to *gourmand* since the latter is very likely to be misunderstood.

GOURMET *gor-may* (French)

'person who is knowledgeable about food and drink', 'refined':

> *Most cook books now cater for after-work foodies who want to produce a gourmet meal in 30 minutes flat.* (Daily Telegraph)

PRETENTIOUSNESS INDEX **!**

There is a tinge of pretension about a person with the reputation of a *gourmet*, and he or she would be quite happy to acknowledge that. The word is both noun and adjective, and probably used too often. Like other expressions denoting quality – 'classic' springs to mind – *gourmet* has become devalued through indiscriminate application.

GOY   *pronounced as spelled*   (Yiddish)

'anyone who is a non-Jew', 'Gentile':

North of that yawned the foreign vastness, first named New York State but melting westwards into other names, other states, where the goyim farmed their farms and drove their roadsters and swung on their porch swings … (John Updike, *Bech: A Book*)

PRETENTIOUSNESS INDEX **Nil**

Goy is the singular form (*goyim* the plural and *goyish* the adjective) of a common US/Yiddish usage veering towards slang, and occasionally found in British English. Not necessarily pejorative, *goy* is perhaps dismissive in the way it parcels up the world into its Jewish and non-Jewish components – as Leo Rosten says about the second category in his book *The Joy of Yiddish*, 'This covers an enormous amount of ground.'

GRANDE DAME   *grond darm*   (French)

'great lady', 'woman of dignity and importance':

Yet a combination of family commitments and her fund-raising activities for Bramblewood Animal Hospital in Cobham have put on hold Twinkle's qualified career revival as a grande dame of the Sounds of the 60s trail…
(Guardian)

PRETENTIOUSNESS INDEX *!*

Grande dame is an expression that can be used straight, yet it is more likely to occur in an ironic or semi-ironic context (as above). It is interesting that non-English terms describing rank or status – *grandee* and *generalissimo* are other examples – are frequently used in this way.

GRANDE HORIZONTALE   *grond orree-zontahl*   (French)

literally the 'great horizontal' and so by a fairly obvious process a 'courtesan' or 'prostitute':

Never mind that grandes horizontales *throughout history have been amongst the most celebrated of* saloniers *and writers.*   (Independent on Sunday)

At first sight *grande horizontale* looks a bit euphemistic, and it is certainly not one of the more usual expressions for 'prostitute'. But since it refers to the position adopted for a living, it could be interpreted as an example of plain speaking.

GRAND GUIGNOL   *grond guee-nyoll*   (French)

literally 'great puppet [show]' and the name of a theatre in the Montmartre district of Paris which flourished between the late nineteenth century and the early 1960s. The theatre specialised in stylised horror. *Grand guignol* therefore describes a deliberately sensational, often bloody, style in theatre, film, etc:

> *The surreal interlude in a Nazi-run Belgian asylum (in which one of the inmates gets hold of a machine gun) seems like a histrionic nod to Fuller's earlier movie, Shock Corridor. These moments of grand guignol excess apart, the film plays like a ghost story.*   (Guardian)

PRETENTIOUSNESS INDEX **Nil**

Grand guignol applies to consciously over-the-top horror in works of art (or non-art). It is a useful expression but perhaps rather an insiders' one.

GRAVITAS   *grav-itass*   (Latin)

'seriousness', 'solemn manner':

> *Staff saw his departure as a consequence of falling circulation and an aggressive, sometimes sensational editorial formula that has undermined the newspaper's famed gravitas.*   (The Times)

PRETENTIOUSNESS INDEX **!**

This is a very useful or, at least, a very popular term. There are fashions in words as in everything else and *gravitas* has been having a good run recently. Two newspaper web-sites alone give more than a thousand examples. I don't quite get *gravitas*. Alternatives such as 'seriousness' perhaps sound dull, as do 'moral weight', 'imposing demeanour' etc. Yet the word doesn't mean anything more than these wrapped together. It must be the Latin itself that adds *gravitas* to *gravitas*.

GRINGO   *grin-go*   (Spanish)

literally, *gringo* has the probable meaning of 'gibberish' and so presumably describes the language/sound of a foreigner in the Spanish-speaking Americas; from this it comes to mean 'foreigner', particularly one from the English-speaking world:

> *The few people sitting on benches in the shade outside the Hotel Central pass the time of day spitting in the dust. They studiously ignore us, but everybody has clocked there is a gringo in town.* (Observer)

PRETENTIOUSNESS INDEX **!** IF USED SERIOUSLY BY NON-SPANISH SPEAKERS.

This is one of those South American local-colour terms like *mañana* or (occasionally) *cojones*, sprinkled over travel articles and similar. It's a derogatory expression, and when used by an English speaker will almost always occur in an ironic or self-deprecating context.

GULAG *goo-lag* (Russian)

gulag is made up from the first letters of a Russian title for the bureaucratic organisation which administered the system of labour camps during the Soviet era. Therefore it comes to describe the actual camps which held dissidents and political prisoners (the application was popularised in the West by the publication of Alexander Solzhenitsyn's *The Gulag Archipelago* between 1973–76). By extension, *gulag* can be used about any 'forbidding, prison-like environment':

> *The address was part of the Bemerton Estate, a vast high-rise gulag of a development built by Islington council in the late 1960s.* (Guardian)

PRETENTIOUSNESS INDEX **Nil** WHEN USED ACCURATELY IN THE SOVIET CONTEXT BUT **!** ELSEWHERE.

It is interesting to note how words lose their historical precision and power. However unpleasant a council-built estate, it cannot be properly called a *gulag* (see above) even if the intention was probably to recall the ugliness and monotony of Soviet-era building rather than a prison-camp in the Siberian wastes.

GUNG-HO *pronounced as spelled* (Chinese)

'enthusiastic' 'over-keen':

> *Enright was too sceptical, world-weary, unimpressible to feel at home in the gung-ho climate of a modern publishing house.* (Guardian)

PRETENTIOUSNESS INDEX **Nil**

Deriving from Chinese, although its precise source is disputed, *gung-ho* travelled to Britain via America, where it was adopted during World War Two as the motto of the US Marine Corps. It's an interesting reflection on the difference between the two countries that what might be seen as a desirable quality, at least in the US military, is regarded with scepticism in the UK (where its use is generally informal). A person who is *gung-ho* is just a bit too keen. Since everybody knows someone who fits that description, this is an invaluable term.

GURU *gooroo* (Sanskrit)

'spiritual teacher in Hinduism', 'revered expert':

> *For the ordinary customer the future, according to the mobile gurus, is no longer about smart phones and pushing technology.* (The Times)

PRETENTIOUSNESS INDEX IT'S NOT THE WORD SO MUCH AS WHAT THE WORD REPRESENTS WHICH IS PRETENTIOUS.

The *guru* really entered popular culture, along with much else from the east, in the 1960s. The word, once carrying religious overtones, has been so domesticated that it can describe an expert/instructor in something as unspiritual as mobile phones. Nevertheless a whiff of something dodgy can still hang about the term – as someone has remarked, people use the word 'guru' because 'charlatan' is too long.

H

HABEAS CORPUS   *hay-bee-ass corpus*   (Latin)

literally 'may you have the body'; a legal writ requiring a prisoner to be brought before a court so that the reason for his or her detention can be examined:

A supporter of President Mitterand, she began to take a more serious interest in political affairs, campaigning for French law to incorporate the principles of habeas corpus, for prison reform and against racism and war.
(Daily Telegraph)

Pretentiousness Index **Nil**

This is a familiar and long-established piece of legal terminology dating back to the Middle Ages. *Habeas corpus* is a safeguard against unjust or arbitrary imprisonment, in that the writ requires the person named to be produced in court so that the truth of any charges can be established one way or the other.

HABITUÉ   *abbit-you-eh*   (French)

'frequent visitor to a place':

Whatever you have previously thought of Oliver Letwin, I bet it hasn't been as an habitue of the gaming tables.   (Observer)

Pretentiousness Index **Nil**

The places a *habitué* goes to are for his or her amusement or gratification, although there is sometimes the hint of obsession or addiction in the term. Anyway, one cannot be a *habitué* at one's place of work.

HAIKU   *high-koo*   (Japanese)

'Japanese poem usually of three lines and words totalling seventeen syllables', 'western imitation of such a poem':

His most famous pitch, for a horror film about a dog, is the legendary Holywood haiku: 'It's Jaws with paws.'   (The Times)

The proper *haiku* is as steely and delicate as a Japanese drawing, but the word can be used very loosely, as in the *Times* quote above, to describe a short, rather enigmatic piece of 'verse' in which meaning is compressed.

HARA KIRI   *ha-ra keery*   (Japanese)

'ritual suicide (by self-disembowelling)':

> *Politically, any school remaining bog standard nowadays is committing hara-kiri.*   (Guardian)

PRETENTIOUSNESS INDEX **Nil**

As an expression to denote reckless or suicidal behaviour, *hara kiri* (literally 'belly cutting') is quite widely used and this has tended to blur the detail of a particularly grisly method of suicide.
See also *seppuku*.

HASTA LA VISTA   *as-ta la vees-ta*   (Spanish)

literally 'until the seeing' and so a form of farewell:

> *...that most threatening of film-based Spanish salutations, 'Hasta la vista, baby', used by Arnold Schwarzenegger as The Terminator, just before he despatches another victim.*   (Guardian)

PRETENTIOUSNESS INDEX **Nil**

Hasta la vista has no function at all, but is widely used as a joky way of saying goodbye, popularised by Schwarzenegger. Similarly, when other foreign until-we-meet-again expressions from Europe – *au revoir, auf Wiedersehen, arriverderci* – are used in English, it is generally tongue-in-cheek. Oddly, the Italian *ciao*, which is for both meeting and parting, is usually uttered quite straight.

HAUTE COUTURE   *ote coo-ture*   (French)

literally 'high dress-making'; noun or adjective phrase meaning the 'making of fashionable and expensive clothes' or 'high fashion':

> *...it's hard to imagine her [Nicole Kidman] ever eschewing her spot on the red carpet, looking exquisitely groomed in a succession of haute-couture gowns.*   (Independent)

PRETENTIOUSNESS INDEX *!*

Haute couture is a phrase that comes with quality (or at least cost) guaranteed. While *haute cuisine* (see below) may often be used with slight irony, *haute couture* is generally applied straight, any hints of snobbery and exclusiveness being part of the appeal.

HAUTE CUISINE   *ote cwee-zeen*   (French)

literally 'high cooking'; 'cooking of the highest quality':

> *The deep-fried Mars bar has achieved legendary status as an example of Scottish haute cuisine.*   (The Times)

PRETENTIOUSNESS INDEX *!*

Haute cuisine is something of a dated term now, having been super-seded by *nouvelle cuisine*, etc. Perhaps it is the slightly rarefied and potentially snobbish overtones of *haute cuisine* which have caused it to slip out of favour. At any rate the term can quite easily be used ironically, as above.

HAUTEUR   *oh'terr*   (French)

'arrogance', 'lofty manner':

> *With sharp eyes and a stern gaze, and at an imposing 6ft 4in, he [Rupert Everett] brings natural hauteur and authority to the role of the famed resident of 221b Baker Street.*   (Independent)

PRETENTIOUSNESS INDEX **Nil**

Hauteur suggests an attitude towards the world rather than characterising a particular action. It's looking down one's nose at things, a stance which is easier with height, the primary French meaning of the word.

HOI POLLOI   *hoy poll-oy*   (Greek)

'the many' and so 'the masses', 'the common people':

> *...the best ancestor he [Julian Fellowes] can come up with is a 19th century rear admiral, which makes him practically hoi polloi.*   (Observer)

PRETENTIOUSNESS INDEX *!!* IF USED SERIOUSLY.

This Greek phrase is generally employed with a touch of irony, as the users distance themselves from its snobbish overtones by tone of voice or by an exaggerated pretend-distaste for *hoi polloi*. Of course, underneath the pretend-distaste may lurk the real thing. And, arguably, by using the phrase in the first place you identify yourself as not one of 'them'. It's a mistake to say the *hoi polloi*, since *hoi* already means 'the' in Greek.

HOMBRE *om-bray* (Spanish)

'man':

If anyone is allowed to have dyed blond hair, snowy white tunics, intense relationships with other men, and a simply impossible mother – well, it is this highly-strung hombre. (Guardian)

PRETENTIOUSNESS INDEX **!** IF NOT USED IN A JOKEY WAY.

More often found in US English (and the title of an early Paul Newman western) *hombre* occasionally pops up in British English, but always in a colloquial and humorous context.

HOMMAGE *ommarge* (French)

'homage', 'tribute':

…in a touching act of hommage, *Gilbert has ransacked Tin Pan Alley for his chapter headings.* (The Times)

PRETENTIOUSNESS INDEX SOME WOULD SAY THAT IT IS THE VERY ACT OF *HOMMAGE* WHICH IS PRETENTIOUS RATHER THAN THE WORD ITSELF.

Not applying to any old tribute, *hommage* has a specialist application in the arts, where it describes a conscious echo or acknowledgement of a predecessor's work. The term is most often used in the context of films, so that a director who is deliberately imitating the style of one of the 'masters' like Hitchcock is performing an act of *hommage* – a intellectual tipping of the cap.

HOMME MOYEN SENSUEL *om mwoy-on sonn-sue-el* (French)

'man of average appetites', 'man in the street':

Is it any wonder that, at such moments, you stop being a rational homme moyen sensuel, at ease in salons from Mayfair to Montana, and become instead a raging animal, seeking blood, redress and the grim satisfaction of revenge. (Independent)

PRETENTIOUSNESS INDEX **!**

Homme moyen sensuel is a slightly dismissive and literary phrase, and one which is generally used in a knowing or self-deprecating way. At one time the nearest equivalent in English would probably have been the 'man on the Clapham omnibus' but this is likely to be as remote now (omnibus?) as the high-flown French expression.

HOMME SÉRIEUX *om seh-ree-eu* (French)

a 'serious man':

> *We want a prime minister who devotes such spare time as he or she can muster at university high tables, with intellectuals, artists and hommes sérieux; not scheming with red-top editors.* (Spectator)

PRETENTIOUSNESS INDEX **!**

Using the fairly rare phrase *homme sérieux* indicates that you most likely are an example of the type. There is no exact equivalent in English, since the idea of seriousness suggests a brow-furrowing earnestness rather than the intellectualism which it conveys in French. In fact, to call someone 'serious' – usually 'a bit serious' – comes close to being an insult.

HONCHO *pronounced as spelled* (Japanese)

literally a 'squad leader' in Japanese and so a 'boss or manager':

> *A spokesman for Network Rail said: 'The final head honcho, the man colloquially called the fat controller, would have to be Network Rail.'*
>
> (Daily Telegraph)

PRETENTIOUSNESS INDEX **!**

This is a business usage from Japan via the US and it is invariably coupled with 'head', not because the extra word makes much sense – a *honcho* is a head by definition – but because of the alliteration. 'Boss' or 'manager' are everyday terms but *honcho* adds a bit of a swagger. That said, most users probably assume it 'sounds' Spanish/Mexican (hence the mistake I once saw in a newspaper advertisement: *'So you want to be the head honcho?'*, above a picture of a sombrero'd Mexican). If this false 'Spanish' is the explanation for the popularity of *honcho*, then users are mistakenly looking for a testosterone top-up from that language (see also *cojones* and *macho*).

HONI SOIT QUI MAL Y PENSE *on-ee swah key mall ee pons*
(Old French)

literally 'shame be to him who thinks evil of it'; loosely a warning against a cynical or malicious interpretation of something:

> *Honi soit qui mal y pense. Gough, far from being a boozer, is a model performer.* (Daily Telegraph)

PRETENTIOUSNESS INDEX **Nil**

The historical origins of this phrase (often shortened to *Honi Soit* and now the motto of the Order of the Garter) are slightly better authenticated than the stories of King Alfred burning the cakes or King Canute sitting out the tide, but it comes from the same area of royal legend. Supposedly, while Edward the Third was dancing with the Countess of Salisbury, her garter slipped from her leg to the floor. The King picked it up and put it round his own leg, to the sniggers of his courtiers, whom he rebuked with the *Honi Soit* phrase. When used now, it is as a warning against leaping to some scandalous conclusion that will reflect badly on the onlooker rather than anybody else.

HORRIBILE DICTU *horree-billay dik-too* (Latin)

'horrible to tell':

> *And a fourth [student], horribile dictu (I love that dreaming spires jargon), 'was understood to have been sick all over the common room'.* (Guardian)

PRETENTIOUSNESS INDEX *!*

Not dating from Roman times but emerging in the nineteenth century, *horribile dictu* is the counterpart to *mirabile dictu* (see entry), and like that expression is rarely applied seriously. In fact it is rarely applied at any time and, when it is, suggests pretend-outrage or horror.

HORS CONCOURS *aw con-core* (French)

'out of competition':

> *It was as sublime a bit of cookery as I have had all year, but as I never wrote about it, it has to be deemed hors concours.* (Guardian)

PRETENTIOUSNESS INDEX *!*

Hors concours can also mean 'unrivalled', but its most usual sense is 'not in the running'. Quite useful in a context where there is no actual competition but a sense of rivalry between various possibilities.

HORS DE COMBAT *aw de comba* (French)

'out of battle', 'not fit to take part':

> *This time their schedule starts with their three toughest fixtures and many of their most experienced players are hors de combat.* (Guardian)

PRETENTIOUSNESS INDEX **Nil**

Hors de combat rarely if ever applies to someone in a genuine battle. Rather it describes those who are disqualified, usually through physical injury, from participating in a sporting or other event.

HORS D'OEUVRE *aw d'erv're* (French)

literally 'outside the work'; 'dish served as appetiser or starter', anything 'preliminary':

Similarly, the new surfeit of UFOria in the 1980s and 1990s, for which Whitley Strieber's Communion was merely the hors d'oeuvre, fed the paranoia of right-wing conspiracy theorists...

(Francis Wheen, How Mumb-Jumbo Conquered the World)

Pretentiousness Index **Nil**

Hors d'oeuvre (plural, *hors d'oeuvre* or *hors d'oeuvres*) is often replaced by 'starters' on a menu, but the expression has quite a wide application in non-food contexts, always with the implication that there is more – and probably better – to come.

HUBRIS *hew-briss* (Greek)

'overwhelming pride', 'arrogant behaviour where an individual starts to think he can act like a god':

Microbes not macrobes rule the world. What hubris to have believed they could be defeated or that the book on infectious diseases could ever be closed.   (Financial Times)

Pretentiousness Index *!*

Something of a buzzword in the last few years, *hubris* is having a good run for its money. In its original Greek sense, it indicated insolence towards the gods, an unwise attitude that would inevitably be followed by one's come-uppance (or nemesis). If used to describe someone's current attitudes or behaviour, the speaker is looking forward to saying 'I told you so'.

HWYL *hoo'il* (Welsh)

'fervent emotion, particularly in speech':

Search for the spirit, the essence of Welsh rugby and a long list of boxes can be ticked. Hwyl, choir, anthem, passion, exuberance, self-expression, creativity.   (Daily Telegraph)

Pretentiousness Index **Nil**

As a concept *hwyl* is unique to Wales. It is to do with qualities of speech and emotion and enjoyment that are seen as a defining national characteristic. English attempts to categorise *hwyl* tend to flounder a bit, as the *Telegraph* quote shows.

I

IBIDEM *ib-id-em* (Latin; usually shortened to **ibid**)

'in the same place'; used when referring to a source (for a quote, etc.) which has already been named. The example below provides two confusing statements made by George W. Bush before he became US President, both coming from the same source:

> 'Well, I think if you say you're going to do something and don't do it, that's trustworthiness.' *CNN online chat, August 30 2000*

> 'We cannot let terrorists and rogue nations hold this nation hostile or hold our allies hostile.' *Ibid* (Guardian)

PRETENTIOUSNESS INDEX **Nil**

One of a cluster of Latin abbreviations widely used in writing, particularly of the academic sort, *ibid* refers the reader to a source cited immediately before.

IDÉE FIXE *ee-day fiks* (French)

'fixed idea', 'obsession':

> As for the erosion of Right/Left distinctions causing the media to express an indiscriminate dislike of politicians as such, this is something of an idée fixe for Lloyd – and a puzzling one, at that. (Daily Telegraph)

PRETENTIOUSNESS INDEX **Nil**

An *idée fixe* can be distinguished from an obsession in that it characterises a belief which is more or less intellectual rather than describing an emotion or a pattern of behaviour. And the French expression sounds more heavyweight than a 'fixed idea', which may suggest nothing more than obstinacy.

ID EST *pronounced as spelled* (Latin; generally shortened to **i.e.**)

'that is', used to introduce an explanation or amplification of a previous statement:

Each bird is easily divided into four. First, gently pull the leg (i.e. drumstick and thigh) away from the body... (Sunday Telegraph)

Mitrevski is a Christmas present for Portsmouth, until such time that Chelsea require his services, i.e. never. (Guardian)

<small>PRETENTIOUSNESS INDEX</small> **Nil**

i.e. (with or without full stops) is a very widely used alternative to the comparatively cumbersome 'that is to say'. It can even be used to introduce a kind of comic punchline, as in the *Guardian* example above. Sometimes confused with *e.g.*, which introduces an example, *i.e.* should only be used where it operates as a full 'explanation' of whatever has come before it.

See also *e.g.*

IDIOT SAVANT   *id-io savon*   (French)

literally 'learned idiot'; 'person considered to be generally back-ward or unskilled but who possesses some particular capacity to a much higher degree than normal':

In the space of only a few episodes, his performance as the Doctor – a bumptious, wide-eyed idiot savant – is likely to be remembered as fondly as that of Tom Baker. (The Times)

<small>PRETENTIOUSNESS INDEX</small> **Nil**

This is really a technical term but it has entered popular use to characterise someone who appears inept or deficient in most areas but who has some extraordinary skill (such as memorising numbers) even if there seems no practical use for it.

IGNIS FATUUS   *ig-nis fat-ewe-us*   (Latin)

literally 'foolish fire' and applied to the light sometimes seen over marshes, a light which was produced by gas combustion and which might lead travellers astray. Therefore *ignis fatuus* comes to describe any 'delusive idea':

...wine, before the 1960s, was not considered a worthy investment vehicle. It is now a very glamorous one; underpinning which is the further ignis fatuus that, if all else fails, the wine can be drunk (and it will be gorgeous). (Guardian)

<small>PRETENTIOUSNESS INDEX</small> **!**

Ignis fatuus harks back to the days of romantic journeying. Its currency as an expression has declined along with the disappearance of horse-back travel and marshes into which the unwary might blunder. Even so, *ignis fatuus* retains a period charm and is more colourful than a term like 'delusion'.

ILLUMINATI *illoo-min-ah-tee* (Latin)

literally 'enlightened (ones)'; 'people who claim to have privileged knowledge, particularly in religious or philosophical matters':

He was the one who mattered, the one who hung out with illuminati in London, New York and Paris. (Observer)

PRETENTIOUSNESS INDEX **!!** IF USED ABOUT ANY CURRENT GROUP.

The original *Illuminati* were a society of rationalists formed in Germany towards the end of the eighteenth century. Linked with the freemasons and attacked by the church, they soon disbanded. However, their name lives on, if only in the shape of bonkers conspiracy theories about how 'they' secretly run the world. When the term is used in a non-specialist sense, as in the *Observer* example above, then it doesn't mean much more than 'cultural insiders'.

IMBROGLIO *imbro-leeo* (Italian)

'confused situation', 'tangle':

Iraq is aflame, the Prime Minister is daggers drawn with his Chancellor, the Home Secretary is in the midst of a quite remarkable imbroglio – but the Government can relax in the knowledge that only a freakish minority are really interested. (The Times)

PRETENTIOUSNESS INDEX **!**

An *imbroglio* is less severe than a *fiasco* (see entry) but sounds worse than a tangle, although that is what it means. It may give a touch of dignity to a political mess, as in the *Times* quote above, because the word is a piece of sinuous Italian rather than straightforward English.

IMPEDIMENTA *pronounced as spelled* (Latin)

'luggage'; 'things which weigh down or encumber':

Here we are again, 15 years on, looking at dot paintings and medicine cabinets, filled giant ashtrays and butterfly paintings, vitrines and surgical implements and the rest of his impedimenta. (Guardian)

Impedimenta is connected to 'impede' and was once used to describe all the equipment an army was required to carry. Now it has a general sense of 'cumbersome odds and ends' and is a slightly dismissive term, as in the example above.

IMPERIUM *pronounced as spelled* (Latin)

'overwhelming power', 'empire':

> *None of this is to suggest that we do not live in the age of the American imperium.* (Guardian)

PRETENTIOUSNESS INDEX *!*

Imperium combines the idea of power and empire in a single and economical expression. Even if it operates at an almost subconscious level, this Latin word inevitably recalls the heyday of the Roman empire, particularly its military might. So it is natural now to apply the term to US dominance of world affairs. The word is most frequently found in a negative or faintly disapproving context, and can carry a tinct of anti-Americanism.

See also *Pax Americana*.

IMPRIMATUR *im-pree-ma-tur* (Latin)

literally 'let it be printed'; in the Catholic Church, 'a licence for the printing of a (religious) book'; by extension, an 'official stamp of approval':

> *In their place come other policies: casinos, identity cards and a promise of jury-less courts, foundation hospitals, tuition fees and market-driven solutions for the public services – none of these carried the imprimatur of the shrivelled Labour party.* (Guardian)

PRETENTIOUSNESS INDEX **Nil**

Rarely used to describe a literal 'stamp of approval', *imprimatur* suggests endorsement rather than simple permission from a person or group in authority. To issue an *imprimatur* for anything said, published or done by others is to add moral or intellectual weight to it.

IN ABSENTIA *in absent-ee-ah* (Latin)

'in (someone's) absence':

> *She has just been sentenced in absentia to three years in jail after escaping from custody.* (Guardian)

In absentia almost always appears in a legal context to describe the trial and/or conviction of someone who is not present (often because they have absconded). It would be interesting to know how many acquittals have taken place *in absentia*.

INAMORATO/A   *pronounced as spelled*   (Italian)

'lover' (-o, male; -a, female):

At Vivienne Westwood's show, Dita von Teese, inamorata of Marilyn Manson and striptease artiste extraordinaire, popped up.   (The Times)

PRETENTIOUSNESS INDEX **!**

The range of terms to describe people's sexual partners stretches from the too complicated 'significant other' to the down-market 'squeeze'. *Inamorato* therefore comes in quite handy, elegantly occupying an area in between. It can be adjusted according to sex, it's very slightly tongue-in-cheek, and it is a little less direct than 'lover'.

IN CAMERA   *pronounced as spelled*   (Latin)

literally 'in the chamber'; 'in a judge's chamber', 'in private or secret':

'No, this was a private meeting in camera.' (Answer to an interview question on Radio 4)

PRETENTIOUSNESS INDEX **Nil**

If 'camera' in this expression is misunderstood as a Kodak, it implies the opposite meaning to the one intended. *In camera* primarily has a legal/judicial sense to describe a case which is held without the public being present (because originally in the judge's chamber) and also with a ban on media reporting. As part of the attempt to get away from Latin usage in English law, *in camera* has been replaced by 'in private', but the expression is still used from time to time, and could apply to any meeting which is intended to go unreported.

INCOGNITO   *in-cog-nee-toe*   (Italian)

'unknown', 'under an assumed identity':

He told them to fly to London, to mingle incognito with the tourists at Madame Tussaud's and [...] shave off a sliver of Madame T's wax, and smuggle it home in a false-bottomed suitcase...   (Independent)

Incognito is a convenient term to describe the (generally innocent) adoption of an alternative name/identity in order to protect oneself from notice or unwelcome publicity. Physical disguise is not usually involved.

INCOMMUNICADO   *in-communicah-doh*   (Spanish)

'without communicating with the outside world', 'in solitary confinement':

> *The recluse's incommunicado enigma deepens. A legend takes shape, bringing out the strangest yarns.*   (Guardian)

PRETENTIOUSNESS INDEX **Nil**

Being *incommunicado* can be a voluntary state, as in the example, but generally it entails denying a prisoner contact with the outside world in the form of visitors, etc.

INCUBUS   *in-cue-bus*   (Latin)

originally a 'devil in male guise who has sex with a sleeping woman'; by an association of ideas, the word comes to be applied to 'any nightmarish burden or deadweight':

> *Once you have children and property in common, this slob will hold you in thrall … Better no man than such an incubus.*   (Observer)

PRETENTIOUSNESS INDEX **!**

The primary meaning of *incubus* is rare, but it is in quite widespread use to describe an oppressive or troubling burden. The feminine equivalent of *incubus* is *succubus*.

IN FLAGRANTE DELICTO   *in flag-rantee di-lick-toe*   (Latin)

literally, 'while the crime is flaring' and so 'while the crime is being committed' or 'red-handed'. The expression could be related to any activity which would get the performers in trouble or cause embarrassment but is almost always used to mean 'while having sex' and often shortened to *in flagrante*:

> *In July 1882, O'Neill again caught her ladyship in flagrante, this time by spying her through the keyhole of the dining-room door, entwined with the London fire chief.*   (Daily Telegraph)

PRETENTIOUSNESS INDEX **!**

On the face of it, the relative popularity of this phrase is puzzling since shorter and simpler English equivalents exist. Why not just say 'red-handed' or, more specifically, 'during sex' since that's generally what is meant? But *in flagrante* serves as a kind of euphemistic short-hand by drawing a veil over the 'offence', and the Latin words have a legalistic ring. At the same time there's a faintly naughty overtone to them.

INFRA DIG *pronounced as spelled* (Latin – shortened form of infra dignitatem)

'beneath one's dignity', 'not appropriate to someone's status':

A man [Prince Charles] who thinks it infra dig to squeeze his own toothpaste is unlikely to forget about the importance of rank once he leaves the bathroom for the office. (The Times)

PRETENTIOUSNESS INDEX **Nil**

This quite familiar phrase (shown by its shortened form, always used) is usually applied with a mixture of impatience and amusement.

INGÉNUE *an-jhenoo* (French)

'simple, inexperienced young woman'; more usually, a woman who plays such a role on stage or film:

An ingénue loses her looks. (Actresses turning 40 always precipitates the 'Botox or Play the Maternal Roles' crisis.)

(The Times)

PRETENTIOUSNESS INDEX **Nil**

The *ingénue* role on stage is almost as fixed by convention as the pantomime dame's – or it was. It must be doubtful whether many parts are written now for 'inexperienced' young women, so the term is just as likely to have a historical application. However, it can be used to signify nothing more than a youngish actress, as in the example.

IN LOCO PARENTIS *in loh-coh pah-rentiss* (Latin)

'in place of a parent':

When your children are away at school, the teachers are there in loco parentis: to instruct, to guide and to steer. (Sunday Telegraph)

PRETENTIOUSNESS INDEX **Nil**

In loco parentis applies to those individuals or institutions (usually teachers and schools) who have parental-type responsibilties when children are in their care – in other words, to protect them, to guide them and so on. The formal Latin phrase indicates that many of these responsibilities are actually required by law.

IN MEDIAS RES *in med-ee-ass rays* (Latin)

'in(to) the middle of things':

Public silence in medias res – abandoning normal routines to remember the dead – has been a powerful tradition since the Armistice. (Guardian)

PRETENTIOUSNESS INDEX **!**

In medias res is quite a formal expression, and so appropriate for the *Guardian* example above. It can also be used to describe the way in which a story is presented, that is, when a reader or viewer is plunged straight into the narrative without introduction or preamble.

IN PROPRIA PERSONA *in pro-pre-ah persow-na* (Latin)

'in one's own person', 'as oneself':

Mae West, Alfred Hitchcock and Andy Warhol all make fleeting appearances in propria persona, *alongside a Frank Sinatra-like singer named Johnny Fontane and a family that recalls the Kennedys.* (Daily Telegraph)

PRETENTIOUSNESS INDEX **!!**

This phrase is quite handy as a way of distinguishing fact from fiction, as in the quote above. But *in propria persona* should not be used when the context requires simply 'in person'.

IN SITU *in sit-ewe* (Latin)

'in place', 'in the original location':

This is uncharted territory for a film director. No one has ever made a full-length feature of Shakespeare's cruellest 'comedy' [The Merchant of Venice], let alone had the budget to film it in situ. (The Times)

PRETENTIOUSNESS INDEX **Nil**

In situ fulfils most of the requirements of a foreign word/phrase when set beside its English equivalents. It's short and easy to say, and its meaning is generally obvious from the context. In the *Times* quote above, four English words would be needed to convey the precise meaning of *in situ*.

INTER ALIA *inter ay-lee-ah* (Latin)

'among other things':

I would say it is just possible a sincere display of respect, admiration and co-operative effort to introduce, inter alia, *foundation hospitals could see Mr Blair out of office before the next election.* (Independent)

This looks like an economical expression, two words rather than the three required to say the same thing in English. Even so, *inter alia* is not used for its brevity, I suspect, but because it gives a little more emphasis to the writer's pronouncements. In speech it can sound pretentious.

INTERREGNUM *pronounced as spelled* (Latin)

'interval between two governments', 'period of interruption in normal rule':

Victory for Mr Kerry would entail different kinds of uncertainty. A sort of interregnum would ensue until his inauguration next January. (Guardian)

PRETENTIOUSNESS INDEX **Nil**

Interregnum is not much used outside a political/historical context, but it can characterise the period between the stepping-down of one authority and the arrival of another in an area such as business.

INTIFADA *in-tiff-ahda* (Arabic)

literally a 'shaking off', *intifada* was first used in 1987 to describe the 'Palestinian protest and action against the Israeli presence in the Gaza Strip and the West Bank'. The term has been in constant use since then:

In the past two intifadas, or 'uprisings' during which time Palestinians have fought against what they see as Israel's occupation of their land, almost 1,000 Israelis and over 3,000 Palestinians have died. (Guardian)

PRETENTIOUSNESS INDEX **Nil**

From a linguistic point of view, *intifada* is an interesting example of a word that has entered English usage quite abruptly and which has very precise origins in a particular place and time. If the word begins to shed its sensitive associations – something which seems very unlikely at the moment – it may come to mean simply 'uprising' without respect to the Israeli-Palestinian conflict (but I could find only one example of this among several dozen uses).

IN UTERO *in you-terr-o* (Latin)

'in the womb':

After the proto-Google was conceived in 1996, it was known in utero *as BackRub.* (Daily Telegraph)

In utero is generally used in a literal sense rather than a figurative one (as in the example). The Latin term perhaps gives a euphemistic colour to the otherwise straightforward 'in the womb'.

IN VINO VERITAS   *in vee-no veritas*   (Latin)

literally 'truth in wine' and so a reference to the fact that people are more likely to speak their mind when drunk:

> *Geoff was a striking instance of in vino veritas. There was enough said and he said it all.*   (Guardian)

PRETENTIOUSNESS INDEX **Nil**

In vino veritas is one of the few Latin tags which have survived into modern English, perhaps because it wraps up a universal observation in three words where English requires a whole sentence. An irritating phrase if you are on the receiving end of someone else's smug delivery of it, but acceptable when accompanied with a wry shrug.

IN VITRO   *in vee-tro*   (Latin)

literally 'in glass', 'in a test tube':

> *Only two of the 10 or so embryos created in a Petri dish during each episode of in vitro fertilisation will be implanted back in the woman who hopes to become a mother.*   (Daily Telegraph)

PRETENTIOUSNESS INDEX **Nil**

There are other procedures which are carried out in the laboratory and *in vitro* but the only term in widespread use is *in vitro fertilisation*, describing the fertilisation of the egg outside the womb. The expression is rather clinical, but that may be the point. And the Latin is certainly more dignified than 'in a test tube'.

IPSO FACTO   *pronounced as spelled*   (Latin)

'by that fact itself', 'as a consequence of that':

> *They do not see these proposals as ipso facto undesirable simply because they are usurping individual rights.*   (Daily Telegraph)

PRETENTIOUSNESS INDEX **Nil**

Ipso facto is an economical term – although it can sometimes be substituted by the single word 'thereby'. It's also a widely used one, but only in fairly formal English.

J

J'ACCUSE   *jaccooze*   (French)

literally 'I accuse':

Well, sorry, but I'm not one of those stabbing the air, shouting 'J'accuse'.
(Daily Telegraph)

PRETENTIOUSNESS INDEX **!!**

The words are the opening of a letter written by author Emile Zola (1840–1902) to a French newspaper accusing the authorities of falsely condemning Alfred Dreyfus, a Jewish army officer, for treason and then their later attempts to prevent the truth emerging. The phrase therefore signals a formal denunciation of some wrongdoing, usually on the part of those in authority. *J'accuse* isn't exactly a phrase that trips casually off the lips or the pen. Rather it is a trumpet call or a drum-roll, demanding attention. (The novelist Graham Greene used it as the title for a booklet published in 1982, attacking organised crime in the South of France which, he claimed, flourished under police protection.) It's one thing for distinguished, crusading novelists to choose to shout *J'accuse* or not. Whether it's appropriate for journalists and hacks is another question...

JE NE SAIS QUOI   *je ne say kwa*   (French)

literally 'I don't know what' and so applied to 'anything indefinable', 'a quality or experience impossible to express':

I cannot deny that there is a certain je ne sais quoi *about floating around in mid-air with Belgian physicists.*   (The Times)

PRETENTIOUSNESS INDEX **Nil**

One of the most frequently found of foreign expressions, *je ne sais quoi* is used to describe the indescribable. The context tends to be humorous, or at least not too serious (as in the example). It is a useful phrase because English equivalents such as 'indefinable' or 'indescribable' tend to sound ponderous.

JEU D'ESPRIT *je d'espree* (French)

literally 'game of wit'; 'light, humorous (artistic) work':

Many years later Valerie Eliot was invited to Andrew Lloyd Webber's country home to hear his ideas for a musical based on her late husband's jeu d'esprit. She returned won over. In 1981 Cats opened in London, where it played 8,940 consecutive performances. (Guardian)

PRETENTIOUSNESS INDEX **!**

A *jeu d'esprit* is normally literary. It characterises a piece of work which has been done as a joke or tease, often as a break from an author's more serious output. In the case of T.S. Eliot, *Cats* was a very lucrative *jeu d'esprit*.

JEUNESSE DORÉE *jherr-ness daw-ray* (French)

literally 'gilded youth'; 'group of young, wealthy and sophisticated people':

During the winter months he [Ian Fleming] skied competitively with the local jeunesse doree at Megeve and, closer to the capital, at St-Cergue.
(Andrew Lycett, *Ian Fleming*)

PRETENTIOUSNESS INDEX **!**

The *jeunesse dorée* have been around since the time of the French Revolution (they were against it). This is a phrase which hasn't quite reached its sell-by date even after more than two centuries of use but it is unlikely to be applied to a contemporary group, except with a slight irony or a faint sneer.

JIHAD *jhee-had* (Arabic)

'holy war', 'passionate crusade':

For the current jihad against hunting cannot be viewed in isolation from the other injustices being visited on non-metropolitan Britain. (The Times)

PRETENTIOUSNESS INDEX **Nil** WHEN APPLIED IN A CORRECT HISTORICAL/ POLITICAL CONTEXT BUT **!** WHEN USED MORE GENERALLY.

Jihad is a word that has come barrelling into the headlines in the last few years, and particularly since 9/11. One newspaper web-site alone gives over 2,000 occurences. At one level, the reasons for this are obvious since *jihad* describes a war waged on behalf of Islam (either in defence of it or for its propagation). Like 'crusade' – although this is not always a PC expression now – the term *jihad* has slipped so that it can encompass any very fervent campaign against something. It may seem odd that *jihad* should be used to characterise the policy or the supposed attitude of a British political party, as in the *Times* quote above. But the writer is trying to scare us, of course, with his suggestion of an aggressive fanaticism on the part of the government.

JOIE DE VIVRE   *jwah de veev're*   (French)

literally 'joy of living'; 'exuberance':

This mesmerising performance, a maelstrom of human energy and joie de vivre, was out of the very top drawer.   (Daily Telegraph.)

PRETENTIOUSNESS INDEX **Nil**

'Exuberance' doesn't always cover *joie de vivre*, although it is the nearest English equivalent. But the French expression can convey a state of mind and feeling which is steadier and less hectic than simple high spirits.

JOLIE LAIDE   *jho-lee layd*   (French)

literally 'attractive-ugly' and so 'attractive in an unusual way'. A contradictory expression to describe the style of looks in which standard 'non-prettiness' or 'ugliness' becomes enticing:

She isn't just plump, she's almost obese, and her face – jolie laide at the best of times – looks like the American advertising character the Pillsbury Doughboy.   (Guardian)

PRETENTIOUSNESS INDEX **Nil**

There is no English expression for this and it is perhaps typical – of us and them – that we have to go to the French for a term that expresses an unusual style of physical attraction, particularly a female one (although there is a rare maculine equivalent in *joli laid*).

JUNTA   *hoon-ta*   (Spanish)

'small, tight-kit group', '(military) group controlling a country, usually after seizing power':

If the government banned British subjects and residents from engaging in any foreign conflict, no one would be able to assist the armed opposition to the Burmese junta.   (Guardian)

Although *junta* can be applied generally to a secretive and powerful group, it is almost always used in the military sense given above. Whatever the context, the connotations of the word are exclusively negative – as borne out by the rule of *juntas* (in Greece in the 1960s, and in Chile and other South American countries in the 1980s).

K

KAIZEN *ky-zen* (Japanese)

'continuous improvement in business practices':

*No one believed him either, which is why Voda shares are still sliding.
'Kaizen' it ain't.* (Daily Telegraph)

<small>PRETENTIOUSNESS INDEX</small> *!*

This relatively obscure word tends to be confined to the business
sections of the newspapers, where it is sometimes accompanied by an
explanation of its meaning (although not in the *Telegraph* quote
above). *Kaizen* seems unlikely to gain much of a foothold in British
culture, not necessarily because ideas of improvement are looked on
with suspicion but because of a justified scepticism about business
'philosophy' and the associated jargon.

KAMIKAZE *kammi-karz* (Japanese)

**literally 'divine wind'; used of the Japanese pilots in World War Two
who carried out suicide missions by crashing explosive-loaded
planes onto an enemy target; by extension, 'anybody who behaves
in a reckless or suicidal way' or used to describe behaviour which
is 'reckless and self-destructive':**

*Combining kamikaze odds with those times when we are chasing money is
a recipe for wipeout – punters lose more in later races as they desperately
bet on longer-odds horses to get back into profit before the day ends.*

(Observer)

<small>PRETENTIOUSNESS INDEX</small> **Nil**

Kamikaze – the 'divine wind' connection is a reference to a storm that
destroyed an invading fleet in the twelfth century – is a very popular
import from Japan. Not often used to describe a suicide mission, it
is loosely applied to any form of reckless behaviour or even, as in
the *Observer* quote above, to something as everyday as long odds in

betting. An interesting example of how a word can get watered down as it moves away from its historical context.

KAPUT *kah-put* (German)

'smashed', 'done for', 'broken', 'exhausted':

It is game over for Tony Blair. This must be true because I've read it in so many newspapers of such different political complexions. He's kaput.

(Observer)

PRETENTIOUSNESS INDEX **Nil**

This is a widely used colloquial expression to describe anything which is ruined beyond repair, from a gear-box to the career of a politician. The popularity of *kaput* must surely be because of its brisk, no-nonsense sound.

KARMA *pronounced as spelled* (Sanskrit)

'destiny based on previous actions', 'fate':

Shanghai is slowly sinking. It is, you might be forgiven for thinking, karma. For the past 15 years it has been rising faster and higher than any city in the history of the world. But the city's greedy appropriation of the air is proving too much for the ground beneath to bear. (Guardian)

PRETENTIOUSNESS INDEX AS WITH SOME OTHER TERMS IN THIS BOOK, IT'S NOT SO MUCH THE USE OF THIS WORD WHICH IS PRETENTIOUS (ALTHOUGH IT MAY BE) BUT THE SLOPPY THINKING THAT LIES BEHIND ITS USE.

Karma is a difficult concept to grasp, and the term tends to be employed very casually in the west ('It's *karma*, man.') to mean, more or less, fate. But in Buddhist or Hindu belief, *karma* implies that actions in an individual life determine a person's status in their next, a concept which is far from the idea of an impersonal destiny over which one has no control. More generally, *karma* stresses a law of cause-and-effect (which is how it used in the *Guardian* quote above). Or, as they say, what goes around comes around.

KISMET *kizmet* (Turkish)

'fate', 'destiny':

Call it kismet, or just canny merchandising, but when I left the casino that night, poorer but none the wiser, I came across a shop with a window full of books promising to teach me to control the dark arts that had just emptied my wallet of its contents. (Guardian)

Kismet has been used in English since the middle of the nineteenth century. Perhaps a little dated now, it is the title of a 1950s' musical and film (most famous song: *Strangers in Paradise*), and sounds more benign than terms like 'fate' or 'providence'. Accordingly, *kismet* is used – half jokingly – when people are quite happy at some turn of events, or at least not too unhappy about it.

KITSCH   *kitch*   (German)

'cheap and showy':

A kitschy little garden of waterfalls and lights is enlivened by a nerdy-looking fellow with rucksack, anorak and vacuum flask.   (The Times)

PRETENTIOUSNESS INDEX **Nil**

There are some terms which really are more or less beyond translation and *kitsch* is one of them. Even though we may not be able to define it, however, we can't do without it. One reason is that all of the English equivalents – 'tacky', 'sentimental', 'flashy', 'naff', 'without taste' and a dozen more – are too dismissive. There is a knowing quality to *kitsch*, or at least to the appreciation of *kitsch* items, and the expression can be used with a kind of affection. As with the term 'camp', with which it has affinities, *kitsch* is far easier to recognise than it is to define.

KLUTZ   *klutts*   (Yiddish)

'clumsy person', 'fool':

At first I thought the trouble might be caused by too many dimethyl-polyethylamines in the water, but I didn't really know what that meant (I'm such a klutz when it comes to that sort of thing).   (Guardian)

PRETENTIOUSNESS INDEX **!**

Klutz isn't that familiar and so may appear slightly pretentious. But, as with many Yiddish terms, the meaning is apparent from sound (it is related to 'clot') as much as context. It is perhaps surprising that the term is not more widespread in British English.

KOSHER   *ko-sher*   (Hebrew)

'(of food) prepared according to Jewish religious laws'; 'genuine', 'proper':

Chelsea's decision to sack the player following the revelation of his non-kosher extra-curricular activities was a means by which Mourinho could simply wash his hands of a player. (Guardian)

<small>PRETENTIOUSNESS INDEX</small> **Nil**

Kosher has its proper religious and cultural context – its *kosher* context, one might call it – in the area of Jewish dietary laws which lay down what foods may be eaten, how meat should be prepared, and so on. But *kosher* has a very widespread, colloquial use in a sense which combines 'acceptable' and 'authentic'. The nearest single English equivalent is probably 'right', but this lacks the special flavour of *kosher*.

KOWTOW   *both syllables to rhyme with 'cow'*   (Chinese)

Derived from words meaning 'knock' and 'head', *kowtow* relates to the one-time practice in China of touching the head to the floor as a mark of extreme respect in the presence of a superior; hence it means to 'show sycophancy', to 'grovel':

French critics have accused their own government of simply kowtowing to Beijing. (Guardian)

<small>PRETENTIOUSNESS INDEX</small> **Nil**

The origins of this familiar term are either forgotten or not known, so it lacks the critical sting it would have if the action of *kowtowing* was visualised literally. All the same, it is a useful term when the context is too dignified for 'crawling' or other colloquial expressions.

KUDOS   *cue-doss*   (Greek)

'credit', 'renown':

Yet the bank's presidency offers the Bush administration a painless and cost-free way of setting out some multilateral credentials, and gaining kudos in the developing world. (Guardian)

<small>PRETENTIOUSNESS INDEX</small> **Nil**

Kudos is a frequently used term, and fills a gap which no English word is quite equipped to do. It is not so straightforward as 'credit' or 'acclaim', which may be won incidentally rather than being a principal aim. *Kudos* is generally acquired in a calculated way – brownie points on a grand scale, if you like.

KVETCH   *pronounced as spelled*   (Yiddish)

'complain', 'whinge':

A glorified version of the factory canteen, studio commissaries were once the noisy hub of the lot, 500-seat arenas for producers and talent to schmooze and kvetch, often while still in costume. (The Times)

PRETENTIOUSNESS INDEX *!!*

A *kvetch* or *kvetcher* is someone who looks for faults, and *kvetching* is what they do when they've found them. This is a US colloquial term – the example above describes the old-style Hollywood canteen – but the word is occasionally found in British English.

L

LACRIMAE RERUM   *lac-rim-eye rare-um*   (Latin)

literally the 'tears [because of the nature] of things' and so 'sadness at life':

Our experiences during life help us to understand more fully the lacrimae rerum – the tears that are at the heart of the human condition.

(Daily Telegraph)

PRETENTIOUSNESS INDEX *!!*

It can't really be claimed that the phrase *lacrimae rerum* (from the Roman poet Virgil) is a common expression, but it memorably describes a sense of sadness which is almost philosophic, built into life itself. Useful perhaps to those looking for an alternative to terms such as *weltschmerz* (see entry).

LACUNA   *la-coona*   (Latin)

'blank', 'gap':

The [honorary Oscar] institution is usually a way for the Academy to fill embarrassing lacunae in its voting. Neither Newman nor O'Toole had won any of their nominations.   (Independent)

PRETENTIOUSNESS INDEX **Nil**

Lacuna (with plural forms *lacunas* or *lacunae*) has a specialist application to describe a missing portion in a text, particularly a maunscript. The word suggests that something ought to be in the blank space and so has a slightly different meaning to the simple 'gap' (which does not necessarily imply an absence).

LAISSEZ-FAIRE   *laysay-fair*   (French; also **laisser-faire**)

literally 'let do' and applied particularly to a 'policy of non-interference by a government' in business and industry; more generally, describing an attitude which is 'tolerant' or 'indifferent':

He is pretty laissez-faire about London's development, and pooh-poohs the idea that St Paul's should dominate the skyline. (Daily Telegraph)

<small>PRETENTIOUSNESS INDEX</small> **Nil**

Laissez-faire is principally associated with government policy, especially in the field of economics where it is the opposite of *dirigisme* (see entry). But the term is also useful to describe a style of management or, at a stretch, an attitude to life.

LAMA *larma* (Tibetan)

'Bhuddist monk in Tibet or Mongolia':

Readers of Cosmopolitan who seek the serenity of a Buddhist lama but can't be fagged to put in hours of meditation each day for years can expect to be disappointed. (Daily Telegraph)

<small>PRETENTIOUSNESS INDEX</small> **Nil**

A specialist religious term, *lama* is most often found linked to Dalai Lama (the head of Tibet's Bhuddists).

Lama should not be confused with llama, a Spanish/Peruvian word describing the 'four-legged beast of burden' which is the South American equivalent of the camel.

LARGESSE *lar-jess* (French)

'giving of gifts', 'generosity':

Christmas is coming, and so Band Aid is here again to spread Western largesse to the most benighted parts of the globe. (The Times)

<small>PRETENTIOUSNESS INDEX</small> **Nil**

Largesse isn't exactly straightforward generosity, and the French term fills a genuine gap in English. The word almost always implies the superiority of the givers, not only in financial terms but also in a vague moral sense. The distributors of *largesse* are well aware of what they are doing and will probably welcome the publicity that comes with it. Perhaps this is why the word often occurs in an ironic or sceptical context, as in the quotation above.

LEBENSRAUM *lay-benz-rowm* (German)

'living space':

But so long as the beneficial or neutral members of the bacterial cast [in the human stomach] are there to compete for lebensraum, the bad ones can't multiply to cause a problem. (Daily Telegraph)

PRETENTIOUSNESS INDEX ❗ IF USED OUTSIDE THE CONTEXT OF WORLD WAR TWO HISTORY.

Lebensraum is the space or territory required not merely to live in but to live well in. Originally found in an academic context, the expression is now tainted by its association with the Nazis – the doctrine of *Lebensraum* was used to justify the occupation and settlement of territories neighbouring Germany before and during World War Two. Using the word in an everyday context, as in the example above, inevitably implies a conflict over the 'living space'.

LEGERDEMAIN   *le-jair-dermann*   (French)

'sleight of hand', 'trickery':

As any three-card-trick hustler knows, legerdemain depends for its success on fooling all the audience all the time. (Francis Wheen, *How Mumb-Jumbo Conquered the World*)

PRETENTIOUSNESS INDEX **Nil**

Legerdemain implies a deceptive manoeuvre more often than it refers to actual conjuring. As such it's a valuable term when the user wants to hint at dishonesty or trickery rather than employ those terms explicitly.

LEITMOTIV   *light-mo-teef*   (German; also **leitmotif**)

'principal and repeated theme', 'recurrent idea or image':

…when he double-faulted, the Centre Court expelled that soft moan of disappointment which has been a leitmotiv of so many of Henman's matches here. (Guardian)

PRETENTIOUSNESS INDEX ❗

Originally applied in classical music to a recurring theme which is identified with an idea or character, *leitmotiv* can now be used more generally to describe anything whose repetitions seem to amount to a pattern. The background of some performance is implied, whether on stage, screen or tennis court.
See also *motif*.

LÈSE MAJESTÉ   *lez mahj-estay*   (French)

literally 'hurt majesty'; 'insult to authority', 'disrespectful behaviour':

You cannot see any of Tony Blair's world peer group putting themselves in

the stocks and inviting the public to chuck rotten eggs. Jacques Chirac, of
the imperial French presidency, would not allow such lèse majesté.

(Observer)

PRETENTIOUSNESS INDEX **Nil**

Lèse majesté is a convenient phrase when the user wants to put a gap
between himself and whatever authority is being dissed, as some
would say now. In other words, the use of *lèse majesté* may suggest that
the object of disrespect is not quite as worthy of reverence as he or she
may think. It is a term that comes tongue-partly-in-cheek.

LIBIDO   *li-beedo*   (Latin)

'desire', 'sex impulse or drive':

He put on 25lb, suffered from depression and, as his girlfriend [...]
immodestly tells the camera, struggled to perform in bed despite no prior
libido problems.   (The Times)

PRETENTIOUSNESS INDEX **Nil**

A specialist term deriving from psychology, *libido* is on the margin of
mainstream use. It sounds more technical than 'sex drive' and may
have therefore have some value as a euphemism.

LINGUA FRANCA   *lin-gwah frank'ah*   (Italian)

literally 'Frankish language', and describing a mixture of languages
once spoken in the eastern Mediterranean ports; now applied to a
'language generally understood across a wide stretch of the globe':

English is the lingua franca of scientists, of air pilots and traffic controllers
around the world, of students hitchhiking around Europe, and of dropouts
meditating in India or Nepal.   (Robert Claiborne, *English*)

Lingua franca also describes any system of communication which is
readily understand between a group:

I wondered whether the relentlessly upbeat lingua franca of American life
– 'How are ya today?' [...] 'You're welcome', and always ending with either
'Have a great day!' or 'Have a wonderful day!' – far from being casual,
throwaway phrases, were intended to provide mutual reassurance that the
American dream is alive and well.   (Daily Telegraph)

PRETENTIOUSNESS INDEX **Nil**

This is an interesting term as well as a widely used one. A *lingua fran-*
ca may be both a language with an extensive reach around the world,

as well as describing a set of 'specialist' terms which are understood by people operating in a particular field or united by a particular culture (as in the second example).

LITERATI *litter-ah-tee* (Latin)

'educated and cultured people'. *Literati* is the plural form of the Latin *literatus* ('literate').

> *But even so, I predict that it will take at least a year or so for any self-respecting member of the literati to recover from [the film] The Hours.*
> (Spectator)

PRETENTIOUSNESS INDEX *!*

This is an expression which is quite often found, and generally in a disparaging or faintly ironic sense. Even when the writer/speaker is a member of the *literati* – and, let's face it, only those who are themselves *literati* are likely to be caught using the word – there is a suggestion of over-refinement or preciousness. The negative colouring of *literati* can be seen more plainly in fake-Latin derivatives like *glitterati* or *chatterati*.

LOCUM (TENENS) *low-cum (ten-enz)* (Latin)

'substitute covering work and duties during temporary absence of doctor or clergyman':

> *It has emerged that the trust [...] has not kept separate figures for the operations carried out by visiting locums, covering for holidays.* (Guardian)

PRETENTIOUSNESS INDEX **Nil**

Locum applies only to two professional areas, medicine and the church. It seems almost anorakish to point out that this very familiar abbreviation means in full (someone) 'holding a place'.

LOCUS CLASSICUS *low-cuss classic-us* (Latin)

literally 'classical place'; 'passage in a book, etc. which is the best illustration of some idea or theme', 'defining example':

> *A surprising number of writers, however, have soulmates encounter each other at parties. Helen Fielding's Bridget Jones's Diary provides the locus classicus, the Alconburys' New Year Turkey Curry Buffet.* (Guardian)

PRETENTIOUSNESS INDEX *!!*

Locus classicus is not a widely used expression, and it doesn't do a great deal that is not achieved by a more straightforward English equivalent such as 'defining example'. However, it has its place in the more academic prose or, as in the *Guardian* quote above, can be used to mildly ironic effect.

LONGUEUR *lawn-gurr* (French)

'boring passage in a book', 'long and tedious period of time':

There are many longueurs ahead for the men and women on the jury: hours of incarceration in the jury room while silks argue points of law and admissibility of evidence. (The Times)

PRETENTIOUSNESS INDEX **Nil**

Longueur is a handy single-word term which requires a whole phrase in English translation. Quite often used at the heavyweight end of book-reviewing, *longueur* can also apply to other kinds of production and performance, even a court case (as above).

LOUCHE *loosh* (French)

'shady', 'disreputable':

While an errant text message might smack of the technologically-savvy young playboy, the Viagra packet reeks of something louche and faintly clammy: the ageing dilettante who can't quite get it up in those sweaty liaisons with his 23-year-old mistress. (Guardian)

PRETENTIOUSNESS INDEX **Nil**

There's no real equivalent for *louche* in English. Words like 'disreputable' or 'shifty' are intrinsically disapproving, but to term someone *louche* occasionally indicates that there's something to be attracted by, as much as condemned.

M

MACHO   *matcho* (Mexican/Spanish)

'virile', 'ostentatiously masculine':

> *The International Conference was a fairly macho negotiating forum, with a great deal of banging of fists on tables and ripe language...*

> (Independent)

PRETENTIOUSNESS INDEX **Nil**

Everybody knows what *macho* means. The interesting thing is that, at least in British English, the word appears more frequently in a negative than in a positive context. This is not just a question of language. English equivalents such as 'virile', or the rather dated 'manly', also tend to cause ripples of unease – or laughter. Anyone wanting a relatively unencumbered term should use 'masculine', which still carries undertones of exclusivity, etc., but largely avoids the swagger of *macho*.

MAESTRO   *my-strow*   (Italian)

literally 'master'; 'high-profile musical composer or conductor'; 'very notable performer in any field':

> *...talent comes in all sorts of packages, and it was Terry, not the Brazilian maestro, who had the concluding word in this seething passion play.*

> (Daily Telegraph)

PRETENTIOUSNESS INDEX **Nil**

There is a suggestion of physical performance and showmanship in what the *maestro* does, which is why its standard application is to conductors rather than composers. Outside music, the most usual context is probably in sport rather than the other arts.

MAFIA   *maff-ia*   (Italian/Sicilian)

used in two ways: to describe the 'secret criminal society originating in Sicily':

...the Mafia is an apolitical leech on any ideology that indulges or fears it enough to give it space. (Observer)

and (usually with a lower-case spelling) to apply to any 'secretive organisation that may use violence or cunning to gain its ends':

Opus Dei, the charitable Catholic organisation depicted by Mr Brown [in The Da Vinci Code] as a self-flagellating religious mafia, has been forced to issue a 127-page response pointing out 'it is a work of fiction'.

(The Times)

PRETENTIOUSNESS INDEX **Nil**

Everybody knows the Mafia. The term has become so much part of everyday speech that it is applied to groups which have nothing criminal or even underhand about them, but are simply tight-knit and private – and which are regarded with suspicion by the person who uses the term.

See also *Cosa Nostra*.

MAGNIFICO   *mag-nifficko*   (Italian)

originally a 'Venetian nobleman'; 'person of high rank or importance':

They sit there, these craggy magnificoes, each thinking that he or she is a combination of Woodward and Bernstein, waiting to growl out their questions. (Daily Telegraph)

PRETENTIOUSNESS INDEX *!*

I doubt that this word (plural *magnificoes*) ever appears without irony – the disparaging reference in the *Telegraph* quote above is to political correspondents. What *magnifico* really describes is someone who is self-important. Compare with *generalissimo* and *politico*, also Italian terms that are more than half-mocking when applied in English.

MAGNUM OPUS   *pronounced as spelled*   (Latin)

'great work', the 'most important work produced by a writer, artist, etc.':

In the 19th century, those who failed to produce their promised magnum opus ranged from Coleridge and de Quincey (both of whom suffered an opium habit) to Casaubon in George Eliot's novel Middlemarch, with his grandiose plans to write a scholarly Key to All Mythologies. (Guardian)

PRETENTIOUSNESS INDEX *!*

Magnum opus could be used about someone's recent artistic production, although it would take a very confident critic or reviewer to apply it. Generally it's safer to wait until the artist is dead. In any case, the era of the *magnum opus* seems properly to be in the past.

MAÎTRESSE EN TITRE   *mayt'ress on tit'r*   (French)

literally 'mistress in name' and so a man's 'officially acknowledged mistress':

> *[Virginia] Carrington – daughter of the Tory statesman Lord Carrington – is a close friend (and former flatmate) of the Prince's* maitresse en titre, *Camilla Parker Bowles.*   (Independent)

PRETENTIOUSNESS INDEX **!**

There isn't much call to employ the rather dignified term *maître en titre* on an everyday basis. In fact, during the last few years in Britain, there was only one woman with a real claim to this title (see above) and even that is history now.

MALAISE   *mah-laze*   (French)

'feeling of sickness', 'unease':

> *If Chelsea's success has been built on their granite defence, Almunia's jitters have been a contagous malaise for the Arsenal rearguard.*   (The Times)

PRETENTIOUSNESS INDEX **Nil**

Malaise is a handy catch-all term. Rarely if ever employed to describe a physical condition, it describes a state of mind and feeling, the sense that something indefinable is about to go wrong. It's as intangible as an atmosphere, and so defies explanation.

MALAPROPOS   *mal-ah-prop-oh*   (French)

'clumsy', 'inappropriate':

> *The phone is ever peremptory, and Franzen exploits its capacity to insist on dialogue that is ill-timed, to demand family 'communication' that is* malapropos.   (Guardian)

PRETENTIOUSNESS INDEX **!**

The opposite of *apropos* (see entry), *malapropos* applies particularly to social situations where an intervention or a comment, which might be perfectly acceptable in other circumstances, strikes the wrong note. Characterising something less cringe-making than a *faux pas* (see entry), *malapropos* is a refined term for a subtle fault.

MAÑANA   *man-yah-na*   (Spanish)

'tomorrow', 'sometime in the future':

According to the Rough Guide to a Better World, they [British tourists] should leave their watches, their personal organisers, and their attitude, at home, and switch to 'mañana mode'.   (The Times)

PRETENTIOUSNESS INDEX **Nil**

More than a word, *mañana* is a way of life, at least to the thinking of clock-watching, work-driven northern Europeans. Associated with Spain and Spanish-speaking countries – warmer climes, as they say – it embodies the attitude of 'why do it today if you can put it off until tomorrow?' This may not seem fair to the dynamic economy which Spain has enjoyed for the last quarter century but the word is an example of an entire culture being caricatured in a single word or phrase, like the *dolce far niente* of the Italians.

MANO A MANO   *ma-no ah ma-no*   (Spanish)

literally 'hand to hand', and so meaning 'confrontation' or 'head to head':

That means either you pretend these insults don't hurt, or you settle the matter mano-a-mano behind the bike sheds at four o'clock.   (The Times)

PRETENTIOUSNESS INDEX *!*

Like other Spanish terms (*macho, cojones*), *mano a mano* conjures up a world where men prove their masculinity with a set of flying fists. In fact, it is often used figuratively to describe rivalry or confrontation in business. I suspect that the British aren't hot-blooded enough to treat the phrase with the seriousness it deserves.

MANQUÉ   *monkay*   (French)

describing something or somebody as 'having a particular potential which has not been fulfilled'; 'would-be':

Heylin, thankfully, is no therapist manqué, and eschews mist and mythology in favour of the historical record.   (The Times)

PRETENTIOUSNESS INDEX **Nil**

Manqué – deriving from a French word meaning to 'lack' – is a genuinely useful term, and one which is not quite covered by the English definitions given above. To describe someone as a 'therapist manqué', for example, is to imply that he or she might have the capacity or the vague wish to act as a therapist but that this has not been achieved for some reason. The simplest English equivalent, 'would-be', tends to be forward-looking while *manqué* refers more to the past.

MANTRA   *pronounced as spelled*   (Sanskrit)

'sacred text or phrase repeated in prayer or meditation', 'frequently repeated sentence or idea':

And yet, a decade and a half after the Berlin Wall came down, most comedians have yet to come to terms with the death of the ancient left-wing mantras. (The Times)

PRETENTIOUSNESS INDEX **Nil**

Like *karma* and *guru* (see entries), the *mantra* entered popular usage during the 1960s. Its religious associations haven't altogether been lost but instead have been turned against it. That is, any use of the word tends to be critical, suggesting a mindless clinging to formulaic ideas which are endlessly repeated in the style of spells or prayers.

MARGINALIA   *margin-ay-leeah*   (Latin)

'marginal notes':

The particular attraction for Cure-spotters here is the extra CD of rare demos dating from their early years that – mostly – augments rather than duplicates the haul of Cure marginalia already available. (Observer)

PRETENTIOUSNESS INDEX **Nil**

In general, *marginalia* is used literally to apply to scribblings on the edge of a page, but it can describe collected material which is interesting but shapeless and casual (as in the *Observer* quote).

MARIAGE BLANC   *mah-ree-ahj blonk*   (French)

literally a 'white marriage'. Not a reference to a white wedding but to a marriage which is never sexually consummated:

Sonia's second marriage, to the homosexual Michael Pitt-Rivers, was as quixotic as her first. He had been the victim of a notorious prosecution, and their mariage blanc was meant to restore him to his rightful place in society.
(Daily Telegraph)

PRETENTIOUSNESS INDEX **Nil**

Mariage blanc is not a widespread term (or experience) but there is no precise equivalent in English to describe this relationship. Marriages

134

may be *blanc* by accident, so to speak, or by design. If it's the latter it may also be a *mariage de convenance*. (An example of one which was both – that is, simultaneously sexless and convenient – occurred in 1935 when the poet W.H. Auden married Erika Mann, daughter of the German writer Thomas Mann, because she required a British passport to get out of Nazi Germany. Both husband and wife were gay.)

MARQUE   *mark*   (French)

'commercial make or brand', particularly of cars:

At 20, Stephen had bought himself the first of several Rolls-Royces; the marque's first sale to someone so young.   (The Times)

PRETENTIOUSNESS INDEX **Nil**

Marque is the verbal equivalent of a logo, something that applies to the entire brand rather than a specific model. It could be used of other products, even of people, but its general application is to cars.

MATÉRIEL   *matay-r-i-ell*   (French)

'military equipment, usually of a standard sort':

...the Allied advantage in materiel soon proved irrelevant: this was a soldier's battle supported not so much by tanks as by pack mules.

(Daily Telegraph)

PRETENTIOUSNESS INDEX **Nil**

Matériel distinguishes the equipment from the personnel of an army. A technical term, it has an oddly reassuring ring to it, subliminally conveying the idea that the writer or speaker is well versed in military matters.

MAUVAIS QUART D'HEURE   *moh-vay carr d'urr*   (French)

literally a 'bad quarter of an hour', this expression applies to any 'short but disturbing experience', usually one in which a person's outlook or expectations are threatened:

Given Gore Vidal's recent anointment of [Christopher] Hitchens as his earthly successor, that may make you wonder about the perceived drift of Hitchens's own politics. (Many Guardian readers will have suffered a mauvais quart d'heure when they found out that their views on the Gulf war were closer to Peter's than Christopher's.)   (Guardian)

PRETENTIOUSNESS INDEX *!*

Although there are plenty of ways of saying more or less the same thing in English – a sticky moment, a bad patch, etc. – none of them quite have the elegance of this French phrase. For all that, there's a slightly self-conscious sophistication to it when used by English speakers/writers.

MAVEN   *may-ven* (Yiddish; also **mavin**)

'expert':

The horribly positive and bouncy stop-smoking maven Allen Carr tells us that there is no pleasure in smoking a cigarette; that all it does is temporarily still the craving it itself inspires.   (Independent)

PRETENTIOUSNESS INDEX *!*

Maven, not a term which has yet achieved widespread circulation, derives from a Hebrew word for 'understanding'. Like other expressions which are Yiddish or Jewish in origin it has arrived here from the US. My impression is that it is mildly pejorative, carrying the suggestion of 'self-appointed' to go with 'expert'. There seems no reason why the expression shouldn't catch on in British English, since there are so many *mavens* around.

MAZELTOV   *pronounced as spelled*   (Yiddish)

'good luck', 'well done!', 'congratulations!':

The Beckham 'brand' might now, we are told, be damaged beyond repair. Mazeltov! One day, but one day, we might be able to watch Beckham the footballer and forget about Beckham the icon.   (The Times)

PRETENTIOUSNESS INDEX *!*

Although the literal meaning of *mazeltov* is to do with luck ('good star'), it is an exclamation of congratulation and thankfulness. Not in mainstream use, it may look incongruous, as it surely does in the *Times* quote above.

MEA CULPA   *may-ah cul-pah*   (Latin)

literally '(through) my fault' and so an 'admission of guilt or responsibility':

Judging by the experiences of others, it probably also wanted a grovelling mea culpa from the company, and widespread compensation.   (Daily Telegraph)

PRETENTIOUSNESS INDEX **Nil**

The Latin *mea culpa*, which comes from a prayer of confession, is an often used expression probably because it handily combines the admitting of a fault together with the implication that one is sorry for it, yet without actually using the word 'sorry'. The term has largely lost its religious overtones, and there is often a perfunctory quality about a *mea culpa*, whether it is an individual admission or a corporate one.

MÉLANGE   *may-lonj*   (French)

'mixture':

> At my little girl's school, the holiday concert is a mélange of multicultural dirges that are parcelled out entirely randomly.   (Daily Telegraph)

PRETENTIOUSNESS INDEX *!*

Mélange sounds a bit more dignified than 'mixture' and may imply a deliberate variety rather than a casual selection (though not in the quote above). However, there are English equivalents like 'miscellany' or 'medley' which will do the job just as well.

MÊLÉE   *mell-eh*   (French)

'muddle', 'scrum':

> In a mêlée of television crews, fans and sheriff's deputies, the defendant [...] climbed out of the back of a stretched black sports utility vehicle.
> (The Times)

PRETENTIOUSNESS INDEX *!*

A *mêlée* implies physical contact and confusion. Not quite a fight, it could become one at any moment.

MEMBRUM VIRILE   *membrum vir-ee-li*   (Latin)

literally the 'male member', 'penis':

> For ages, the gallery curators could not work out how the marble youth with the enormous right hand and the cocktail-sausage membrum virile became covered in dirt and grime shortly after being restored and cleaned.
> (Independent)

PRETENTIOUSNESS INDEX *!!* UNLESS USED AS A JOKE.

Membrum virile can only be used for comic effect, as in the example above, or as a self-conscious archaism. The term is a reminder of an era when the genitals had to be veiled in the modesty of Latin.

MEMENTO MORI *meh-men-toe morree* (Latin)

'reminder of death':

The story begins with awestruck visitors to Rome during the Middle Ages. For these pilgrims, the city was either a gigantic memento mori – a solemn reminder that everything is transient – or it was rock-solid evidence of the triumph of Christianity over paganism. (Daily Telegraph)

PRETENTIOUSNESS INDEX **Nil**

The standard *memento mori* is a skull, supposedly kept at one time by monks in their cells as a symbol of mortality, ever-present. But anything that points to decay and death will do, even an entire city as in the example above.

MEMORABILIA *mem'rahbilli-ah* (Latin)

'memorable or notable items', 'souvenirs':

Royal enthusiasts were already snapping up memorabilia with the April 8 date yesterday in the belief that they could become collectors' items.

(Daily Telegraph)

PRETENTIOUSNESS INDEX **Nil**

Memorabilia, often deliberately manufactured, seem to commemorate a person or event rather than a place, and this is perhaps one of the slight differences between the Latin word and 'souvenir'. Of course, it may be that *memorabilia* is simply a more dignified – or salesworthy – expression than souvenir.

MÉNAGE *maynahj* (French)

'household' 'management of a household':

He refuses to budge until he's paid; he and the girl become part of the ménage for the rest of the day. (Observer)

PRETENTIOUSNESS INDEX *!*

Ménage is often used to stand in for the longer phrase *ménage a trois*, and here it will generally carry the sexual sense (see below). However, the expression can simply mean 'household', not so much in the sense of a family but of a collection of people living under one roof and sharing domestic arrangements.

MÉNAGE À TROIS   *may-nahj ah twah*   (French)

literally 'household for three' and used to describe any arrangement of 'three people living together, usually a married couple together with the lover of one of them':

Pat and I began to see each other without Barrie on occasion. We finally confessed our love for each other, but we did not want to hurt Barrie, who also loved Pat, nor did we wish to fracture the magical ménage à trois, so we kept it secret. (John Boorman, Adventures of a Suburban Boy)

PRETENTIOUSNESS INDEX **Nil**

The French provide quite a few terms to do with sexual behaviour or arrangements, and *ménage à trois* is one of the most convenient. It would take us at least a sentence to explain what they can sum up in three words. A *ménage à trois* may not always be sexual but that is generally implied.

MENSCH   *mench*   (Yiddish)

'honest person', 'decent individual':

Or is he more of a mensch *than his eye for a good sale [...] and his reputation in Trivia City will allow him to admit?*   (Independent)

PRETENTIOUSNESS INDEX *!*

Mensch is a term of high praise, even though in its original sense it conveys nothing more than 'human being'. This is less familiar in English than some other Yiddish terms, and it may be necessary to clarify its meaning through context.

MÉTIER   *met-ee-eh*   (French)

'trade', 'business', 'area of skill':

In the 1980s he founded the Chelsea Wharf restaurant [...] But business was not really his metier and he found the minutiae of running it something of a drudge after a while.   (The Times)

PRETENTIOUSNESS INDEX **Nil**

The closest equivalent to *métier* is another Fench term, *forte*, which could be substituted in the *Times* quote above. But a *métier* involves the idea of working for a living (which *forte* does not), while implying skill and almost a sense of vocation. So there is no precise English equivalent. See also *forte*.

MIRABILE DICTU *mi-rah-billay dik-too* (Latin)

'wonderful to tell':

> *The eldest of Brendel's four children is, mirabile dictu, a rock musician.*
>
> (Daily Telegraph)

PRETENTIOUSNESS INDEX *!*

A little rhetorical flourish, *mirabile dictu* tends to be used ironically or sarcastically to indicate that whatever is being referred to isn't unexpected or wonderful at all – it's the equivalent of 'how true'. In the *Telegraph* example above, however, it appears to be used straight (unless it's natural that the daughter of a classical pianist becomes a rock musician).

MISE-EN-SCÈNE *meez-on-senn* (French)

'setting or staging of a scene':

> *Last year, for example, a man was shot dead while sitting in a barber's chair, a typical Mafia* mise-en-scene. (Independent)

PRETENTIOUSNESS INDEX *!*

Mise-en-scène, often associated with the way a film or play is presented, describes the 'framing' of an event, the detail and overall look designed to enhance the action. Arguably, a slightly pretentious term if applied to events in real life.

MODUS OPERANDI *mow-duss opper-andee* (Latin)

'way of operating':

> *Police believe that he actually raided more than 40 McDonald's restaurants across America, gaining entry by drilling holes through the roofs – a modus operandi that earned him the nickname Roofman.* (The Times)

PRETENTIOUSNESS INDEX **Nil**

Modus operandi can be used about anyone's way of setting about a task or approaching a problem, etc. Supposedly revealing of individual character, the most usual application of *modus operandi* is probably to criminal behaviour (as above), popularised through frequent references in TV and fiction and often abbreviated to MO.

MODUS VIVENDI *mow-duss viv-endee* (Latin)

'compromise', 'way of living':

> *We seem to be living in what might be termed the culture of Having A*

Laugh, where everything's a joke, nothing is serious and the only accepted modus vivendi is to treat life as a perpetual giggle-athon.   (Daily Telegraph)

PRETENTIOUSNESS INDEX **!**

The literal sense of *modus vivendi* is 'mode of life', the sense in which it appears in the quotation above. However, a more frequent application describes a compromise whereby two people or groups come to an arrangement which allows them to get on together, usually before some final settlement.

MOI   *mwah*   (French)

'me':

Superficial, moi? 'I like to be considered a pin-up,' says Gotscho.
(Independent)

PRETENTIOUSNESS INDEX **!!!** – BUT THAT'S THE POINT, OF COURSE.

When did (some) people start using this? *Moi* is not exactly a useful import but is widely found in a self-mocking context. The little word is almost always followed by a question mark and is a camp, self-deprecating way of undermining a pretentious statement or claim.

MONSTRE SACRÉ   *monst're sacray*   (French)

literally 'sacred monster'; a 'well-known person, part of whose public appeal lies in their odd or controversial manner and behaviour':

Long life, coupled with a virtuoso instinct for self-publicity, made her [Barbara Cartland] into an upper middle-class monstre sacrée.   (Guardian)

PRETENTIOUSNESS INDEX **!**

This is one case where a literal translation from the French might be misleading. There is nothing truly monstrous about a *monstre sacré* but there is likely to be something eye-catching, and probably not to everyone's taste. There may be plenty of these creatures in British public life, but there's no equivalent in our language.

MONTAGE   *mon-tahj*   (French)

'arrangement of separate shots on film or television to produce a themed sequence'; 'any art-work where differing elements are placed together':

As for those of us in the new front line, I don't want to end up in some weepy CNN montage of dead commuters.   (Spectator)

Montage is something of a technical term but it sums up in a single word what requires a sentence of English.

MORATORIUM   *morra-taw-ree-um*   (Latin)

'stretch of time when some process or activity is halted':

There has been little support from the conservation community for the Botswana government's four-year moratorium on lion hunting.   (Guardian)

PRETENTIOUSNESS INDEX **Nil**

Moratorium – deriving from the Latin for 'delay' and with the plural forms *moratoriums* or *moratoria* – is often applied to the suspension of debt-payment. In a wider sense it describes any temporary ban on an activity. (*Moratorium* is sometimes confused with 'amnesty', probably because both words refer to a specified period in which some normal process is suspended.)

MORES   *more-ays*   (Latin)

'customs of a group', 'rules of behaviour':

Elton [...] can now squeeze a cheap laugh at the uncomplicated mores of an earlier generation ...   (The Times)

PRETENTIOUSNESS INDEX **Nil**

Despite the echo of 'morals' in the word, there is nothing necessarily moral about the *mores* of a group if viewed from the outside. But members will see them as embodying something valuable – if they see them at all, that is, since *mores* are often the unspoken assumptions which guide behaviour. This is a useful and familiar term, often appearing without italics.

MOTIF   *mo-teef*   (French)

'pattern', 'theme':

In Pinter, rooms conjure up two of the recurring motifs of his plays – isolation, when an individual is alone, and conflict, when he finds himself visited by an outsider.   (Daily Telegraph)

PRETENTIOUSNESS INDEX **Nil**

You can have a *motif* on a piece of clothing or anything manufactured, but the word is most often found in the context of music and the other arts. The difference between this term and the similar German term *leitmotiv* (see entry) is that the latter applies only to music, etc. rather than the decorative arts.

MOT JUSTE *mow joost* (French)

'exactly appropriate word or phrase for the occasion':

> *[Prime Minister Harold] Wilson was a brilliant exam-passer, not to say a train-spotter (mot juste: he had a lifelong obsession with railway timetables).*
> (Spectator)

PRETENTIOUSNESS INDEX **Nil**

The punchy economy of *mot juste* does the job better than rather flat English equivalents such as 'the right word'. Besides, *mot juste* conveys that extra something, it's *precisely* the right word.

MUFTI *pronounced as spelled* (Arabic)

an 'official who expounds Islamic law'; outside the Muslim world, used to describe the 'clothes worn by someone who usually wears a uniform' and so 'everyday wear':

> *So the vast majority are following the hints on the Unicef website, which suggests that schools host dress-down days (children come to school in mufti and bring a donation).* (Daily Telegraph)

PRETENTIOUSNESS INDEX **Nil**

The connection between the two meanings of *mufti* seems to be obscure – one suggestion is that it refers the dressing-gown-and-slippers garb worn by someone portraying a *mufti* on stage and which could be seen as a form of everday wear rather than 'costume'. Whatever the origin, the term is widely used in schools or in a military context.

MUTATIS MUTANDIS *mew-tah-tees mew-tan-dees* (Latin)

'with the appropriate changes being made'; this expression is used when, in order to compare two similar situations or products, sur-face differences have to be altered or overlooked:

> *Yet the Catcher [in the Rye] is one of those books, like [The Great] Gatsby, which are almost word perfect; they are, mutatis mutandis, like certain three-minute songs in which you wouldn't wish to change a note.* (The Times)

Mutatis mutandis is a convenient term when two or more things are being compared and the writer wants to avoid the accusation that they don't have much in common because they occupy different categories. But this is one of those phrases only to be used if you're sure of your ground.

MYSTIQUE   *miss-teek*   (French)

'deliberately cultivated air of mystery':

> *With his generally astute grasp of politics, Hitler realised that it was essential for people in his position to preserve some kind of mystique.*   (Observer)

PRETENTIOUSNESS INDEX **Nil**

Mystique is more to do with the appearance of mystery than its substance (if mystery can have substance). Above all, it's about impressing others with a consciously calculated effect. Despite this, the word is not usually found in a negative context, and may even be a selling point.

N

NABOB *nay-bob* (Portuguese/Spanish from Hindi)

originally a 'Moghul ruler', then a 'European who returned from India with a fortune' and now a 'person (who makes a show) of wealth and importance':

The Hours is exactly the kind of dull, drab, pseudo-literary movie – with contributions from posh Brits such as Daldry and Sir David Hare – for which vulgarian Hollywood nabobs are such suckers. (Spectator)

PRETENTIOUSNESS INDEX **Nil**

The overtones of this word are entirely negative, presumably because the 18th-century *nabobs*, returning to England after a profitable period in India, flashed their money around and made themselves into objects of ridicule. It's interesting to speculate whether the sound of the word, with its ducking little 'bob' at the end, contributed to the overall effect. Anyway, the word now suggests self-importance as much as it does wealth.

NADA *nah-dah* (Spanish)

'nothing':

…we aren't paying overtime, so in the first two hours of your shift you'll be working for nada. (The Times)

PRETENTIOUSNESS INDEX *!*

Every language has a word for 'nothing', so there is no practical reason for importing *nada*. But variety adds spice to a sentence, and it's possible that some users feel the Spanish word is more emphatic than the plain old English alternative. For extra emphasis, *nada* is sometime combined with the US slang term 'nix', with the same meaning.

NAIF *nigh-eef* (French)

'naive person':

Those few critics who do not regard him as the incarnation of evil, generally dismiss him as a dreamy naif, a man wedded to the palpably fantastic notion that democracy can take hold anywhere in the world … (The Times)

<small>PRETENTIOUSNESS INDEX</small> **Nil**

To refer to someone as a *naif* sounds more damning than to call them a 'naive person', perhaps because it implies that naivety is so fundamental a part of their character that no change is possible. It's not so far from 'simpleton'. See also *faux-naif*.

NÉE   *nay*   (French)

'born (under the name)'

Fancourt, who died on Thursday, married Lillian Marion Osborne (née Parkin) in 1921, whom he divorced in 1960 (Daily Telegraph)

<small>PRETENTIOUSNESS INDEX</small> **Nil**

Née – like a reference to someone's 'maiden name' – is a rather courtly usage that is on the way out now, not necessarily because women don't change their names when they marry as because it seems part of a time when such a change was automatic and unquestioned. Its place will therefore be in the older-style obituaries. An obvious alternative is 'born –'.

NEBBISH   *nebb-ish*   (Yiddish)

'hapless person', 'incompetent individual':

The result, a constant series of humiliations for Stiller (as is customary for most of the nebbishes he plays), was rackety fun. (Observer)

<small>PRETENTIOUSNESS INDEX</small> *!*

Not very common in British English, *nebbish* is part of an armoury of Yiddish terms characterising the doltish, the accident-prone and the brainless. Not as emphatic as *klutz* or *schmuck*, and sometimes conveying a touch of pity, the *nebbish* deserves to be better known.

NEM CON   *pronounced as spelled*   (Latin)

'with no one disagreeing' (*nem. con.* is a shortened form of *nemine contradicente*):

At that year's (1997) general election Central Office had kept him [Michael Howard] away from the cameras, such, it was felt, was his lack of appeal to undecided voters. Now, everything points to his being elected nem con. (The Times)

PRETENTIOUSNESS INDEX **Nil**

Nem. con. (with or without the full stops which indicate an abbreviation) is a borrowing from Latin which most frequently appears in a business or 'political' setting, and applies to a decision or contest where there has been no opposition. Although having a rather formal quality, *nem con* may be useful as an alternative to the more whole-hearted 'unanimous(ly)'.

NE PLUS ULTRA *nay plus ultra* (Latin)

literally 'not further beyond'; 'furthest or highest point':

Melissa P is the ne plus ultra of an eye-watering literary phenomenon. Women have taken to writing, with what one can only describe as complete and utter candour, about their sex lives. (Daily Telegraph)

PRETENTIOUSNESS INDEX *!*

The expression *ne plus ultra* was imagined by the early inhabitants of the Mediterranean world to be inscribed on the Pillars of Hercules (or Strait of Gibraltar) as a warning that sailors could go no further west. Current applications of the term are usually less romantic, and frequently describe an extreme point in some artistic production.

NIL DESPERANDUM *pronounced as spelled* (Latin)

literally 'nothing is to be despaired of'; 'don't despair':

Loads of green waste sitting on the chopping board? Nil desperandum. Wash well, chop, and use with celery, carrots, garlic and herbs to make vegetable stock. (Guardian)

PRETENTIOUSNESS INDEX *!*

This cheerful, if erudite, bit of encouragement comes from the opening of a poem by the Latin author Horace. The context is generally not too serious, as in the *Guardian* example above.

NIRVANA *nur-va-na* (Sanskrit)

in Bhuddism, 'release from cycle of life and death and absorption of individual into the divine'; by extension, a 'blissful state':

The Premiership's glass ceiling continues to offer a tantalising glimpse of nirvana to the have-nots. (Guardian)

PRETENTIOUSNESS INDEX *!*

Like *karma* (see entry), *nirvana* has been watered down and secularised for daily use so that it is sometimes synonymous with 'heaven' and sometimes means not much more than a 'nice place to be in'.

NOBLESSE OBLIGE *no-bless obleej* (French)

'status carries obligations':

But UK senior partner Mike Rake also feels a sense of noblesse oblige; he described in a newspaper diary how the firm had recently set up a charity for deprived children. (Guardian)

PRETENTIOUSNESS INDEX **Nil**

Quite a complicated web of ideas is contained in this straightforward French expression. The principle is that birth and social position (and, often, money) confer on the person possessing them the duty to use their advantages in a way that will benefit others who aren't so fortunate. *Noblesse oblige* can apply to a deliberate act of charity (as in the *Guardian* example above) but it also describes less tangible but more personal acts of kindness or attention. For all that, the person who shows *noblesse oblige* never forgets his or her position.

NOLI ME TANGERE *no-lee may tan-gerree* (Latin)

literally 'don't touch me'; a warning not to touch:

Interestingly, only two of them aren't dressed or posed like prostitutes; Cate Blanchett, wearing a smoking jacket and a stern gaze, and Kate Winslet, in head-to-toe Boho chic and noli me tangere air. (Guardian)

PRETENTIOUSNESS INDEX *!*

Noli me tangere is Biblical in origin, being the Latin version of the words spoken by Christ to Mary Magdalene when he appears to her outside the tomb after the Resurrection. Contemporary applications of the expression don't amount to much more than equivalents of 'disdainful' or 'stand-offish', as in the *Guardian* quote above. *Noli me tangere* is also the name of a chronic skin condition and of a plant.

NOM DE GUERRE *nomm de gairr* (French)

literally 'name of war'; 'pseudonym adopted by someone involved in warfare or other activity':

Lukovic, who gained the nom de guerre 'Legija' after serving with the French Foreign Legion, rose to infamy with the brutal 'Tiger' paramilitaries

led by Serbian warlord Arkan in Croatia and Bosnia in the early 1990s.
(Daily Telegraph)

PRETENTIOUSNESS INDEX **Nil**

A *nom de guerre* may be taken by or applied to someone whose business is not actual warfare. But the context will generally involve a struggle or campaign of some kind.

NOM DE PLUME   *nomm de ploom*   (French)

'pen-name', 'writer's assumed name':

   ...'Belle de Jour', the nom de plume of a working girl whose blog has just landed her a five-figure book deal.   (Independent on Sunday)

PRETENTIOUSNESS INDEX *!*

Oddly, *nom de plume* does not actually appear in French and it tends not to be used about serious writers – writers, that is, such as Eric Blair, who took the name George Orwell, or Mary Ann Evans, who wrote under the male pseudonym of George Eliot. There's something slightly frivolous about a *nom de plume*. It therefore seems appropriate in the *Independent* example above to describe the assumed identity of the web woman (who might be a man) who might be a call-girl (or not).

NOMENKLATURA   *pronounced as spelled*   (Russian)

at one time the 'senior and influential officials in the Soviet Union' and, by extension, an 'elite group':

   Here she is, a member of the middle-class nomenklatura, the kind of person who might well find herself sitting next to a top dermatologist at a dinner party.   (Daily Telegraph)

PRETENTIOUSNESS INDEX *!* WHEN USED OUTSIDE THE SOVIET CONTEXT.

Nomenklatura derives from a Latin term meaning 'list of names'. With the disappearance of the Soviet Union, the expression has lost its historical moorings. However, *nomenklatura* can still be applied to any influential group – almost invariably with the implication that such a group is self-important and perhaps corrupt.

NONPAREIL   *non-parray*   (French)

'someone or something having no equal':

   ...a crossroads night for [Lennox Lewis] the World Boxing Council's *nonpareil, who was 38 on Sept 2 and has been fighting for money for 14 gruelling years.* (Daily Telegraph)

PRETENTIOUSNESS INDEX **Nil**

Nonpareil is only used in a positive sense – unequalled or unrivalled because the best in the field – and more often applied to people than to objects or ideas. Not a very common term in English but a handy noun/adjective alternative to its 'translated' definitions.

NON SEQUITER   *non seh'quitter*   (Latin)

(statement or response which) 'does not follow' (from what went before), and so applicable to any remark or reaction which, in its context, seems illogical or simply irrelevant:

...a chapter about this [homosexual] aspect of his life in his autobiography, An Inspector Calls, is enlivened by the memorable non sequitur: 'I suppose I might never have recognised myself as being gay if I had never joined the Georgian Group trip to Edinburgh in 1953.' (The Times)

PRETENTIOUSNESS INDEX **Nil**

Non sequitur is genuinely useful, since it requires only a handful of syllables to describe what would otherwise take a sentence of English. Most conversation is full of *non sequiturs*, and the term should really be used only about arguments or otherwise fairly formal statements.

NOSTALGIE DE LA BOUE   *nostal-ghee de la boo*   (French)

literally 'desire for the mud'; 'desire for things which are degrading':

There is also a tendency to laddishness, even if it is self-critical, and too many references to football teams, punk bands, run-down pubs, and an occasional sense of nostalgie de la boue (a peculiarly masculine literary affectation), which some may find off-putting.

(Independent)

PRETENTIOUSNESS INDEX **!**

Nostalgie de la boue is a fairly elegant and refined phrase for something which is the opposite – the desire to get more than one's hands dirty, to revel in things which are degrading. It doesn't occur very often and I suspect that on most of its outings *nostalgie de la boue* means no more than 'slumming it'.

NOSTRUM *nosstrum* (Latin)

'quack medicine', 'favourite cure for some social problem':

We bring the successful nostrum home and put it in the medicine cupboard, or, even better, leave it in the travel bag and take it on holiday again every year. (Independent)

PRETENTIOUSNESS INDEX **Nil**

Nostrum is a shortened form of *nostrum remedium* (remedy of ours), a reference to the home-made quality of quack medicines. Despite its application to an actual cure in the *Independent* example above, *nostrum* is more usually applied now to pet remedies for political or social ills, and the word comes with an in-built scepticism.

NOTA BENE *no-ta ben-eh* (Latin; generally abbreviated to **NB**)

'note well':

This room [...] last week rose to fame for the nota bene that graces [the] website, 'We will only allow heterosexual couples and singles to occupy our double bedded rooms' (Observer)

PRETENTIOUSNESS INDEX **Nil**

Nota bene alerts the reader to something he or she ought to be aware of before proceeding any further. Particularly when spelled out in full – rather than shortened to the more usual *NB* – it can carry the overtone of an order, which is probably why more tactfully phrased qualifications, prohibitions, etc. tend to be preceded by some expression like 'please note that ...' *NB* is for putting one's foot down and used in fairly formal or official prose.

NOUS *nauss* (Greek)

'intellect', 'common sense':

...this woman knows exactly what she wants and how to get it. This nous comes in handy for seducing the young gardener or spending even more of her financier husband's money. (The Times)

PRETENTIOUSNESS INDEX **Nil**

The distinction between *nous* and common sense is narrow, perhaps almost non-existent, but general usage seems to suggest that it's a sharpened 'native wit', especially where one's own interests or advantage are concerned.

NOUVEAU PAUVRE *noo-vo porv're* (French)

literally 'new poor' and applying to someone who has abruptly become 'poor':

> *Suddenly nouveau pauvre, the manager who seemingly could not stop buying players in Yorkshire has also reinvented himself as O'Leary the asset stripper.* (Guardian)

PRETENTIOUSNESS INDEX *!*

Nouveau pauvre is a recent expression, formed by analogy with *nouveau riche* (see below). I don't think the phrase would be used by or about anyone who had become genuinely impoverished. Rather, it is a humorous or rueful way of referring to the fact that one has much less money than one used to have, probably because of new financial commitments (mortgages, children, etc.).

NOUVEAU RICHE *noo-vo reesh* (French)

literally 'new rich' and so describing someone whose taste are 'flashy or vulgar':

> *Of course, it's hypocritical of me to moan about the invasion of the nouveau riche dotcommers and the expulsion of the hardy pioneers and ex-hippies who founded this rural community.* (Daily Telegraph)

PRETENTIOUSNESS INDEX *!*

It's interesting that *nouveau riche*, sometimes shortened to the single word *nouveau*, is a quite widely used expression. Older terms such as *arriviste* and *parvenu* (see relevant entries) sound snobbish, but for some reason this one is perfectly acceptable, as long as you pick the right company.

NUMERO UNO *numero oo-no* (Italian/Spanish)

'number one', 'most significant person':

> *The final straw was the case of Britain's numero uno lady (golf dept), Laura Davies, who has been permitted to enter the ANZ championship in Sydney.* (Guardian)

PRETENTIOUSNESS INDEX **Nil**

This humorous or slightly disparaging way of referring to the 'most important person' in some set-up is a useful alternative to the altogether more mocking 'big cheese' (or in the joke-French version, *grand fromage*).

O

OBITER DICTUM *o'bitter diktum* (Latin)

literally 'something said by the way' and so an 'off-the-cuff remark':

One of Haldane's obiter dicta, delivered in Bloomsbury pubs in the Fifties, was that a man would lay down his life for two brothers, four nephews or eight cousins. (The Times)

PRETENTIOUSNESS INDEX *!*

Obiter dictum – more often found in the plural, *obiter dicta* – also has a legal application to describe a judge's comment on the law which does not have immediate relevance to the case in hand. The average pub conversation is unlikely to throw up many *obiter dicta* unless the speaker is someone distinguished like the now-forgotten scientist J.B.S. Haldane, as in the *Times* example above. Plain English equivalents such as 'incidental remark' will generally be good enough. Only those people who have their biographers to hand are going to deliver *obiter dicta*.

OBJET D'ART *ob-jhay d'ah* (French)

literally 'object of art'; 'item of some artistic value':

So if you have a brass, bronze or copper objet d'art, think carefully before you get the Brasso out. (Daily Telegraph)

PRETENTIOUSNESS INDEX *!*

Objet d'art can sound a bit precious in English, and there may be a lurking humour in its use, as in the quote above. However, the expression could quite innocently be used about any smallish object which has artistic merit and, probably, no other reason for its existence.

OBJET TROUVÉ *ob-jhay troo-vay* (French)

literally 'found object'; anything which has been discovered by chance but is then given artistic importance by being displayed, incorporated into a work of art, etc:

153

Tolkien described the genesis of hobbits as if they were objets trouvés, thrown up on the shore of his unconscious. (Rick Gekoski, *Tolkien's Gown*)

PRETENTIOUSNESS INDEX *!*

An *objet trouvé* usually crops up in an artistic context. It often describes something which has literally been found and then turned into an art-object – a piece of driftwood, junk metal transformed into a sculpture – but it can also be used figuratively, as in the example above.

ODALISQUE *o-dal-isk* (French)

originally a 'female slave in a harem'; now an 'alluring, exotic-seeming woman':

At Byron Bay, a famous New South Wales beach and hippie time-warp, where barefoot and patchouli-scented odalisques still loiter, I found an authentic Irish witch … (Spectator)

PRETENTIOUSNESS INDEX *!*

This elegant word, which seems to curl up like cigarette smoke, derives prosaically from a Turkish word for 'chamber'. Any use of *odalisque* will tend to be self-consciously exotic, however.

OEUVRE *erv're* (French)

'work of art', 'collected body of work':

Should this vaguely crackpot behaviour colour our view of Eastwood's screen oeuvre? (The Times)

PRETENTIOUSNESS INDEX **Nil**

A versatile word, *oeuvre* can refer to a single work or the whole lot. It tends to give seriousness and dignity to an artist's output, and although – like almost any term – *oeuvre* can be used ironically, this is a word that tends to be played straight.

OMBUDSMAN *om-bhudzman* (Swedish)

literally a 'representative'; 'person officially appointed to look into complaints against government departments or other organisations':

The financial ombudsman service has grown rapidly, and now handles more than 30,000 cases a year. (Guardian)

PRETENTIOUSNESS INDEX **Nil**

Fortunately we have a single Swedish word for what would otherwise occupy a whole line of English. Although the very concept of the *ombudsman* seems quintessentially Scandinavian, other nations have adapted to it very happily, and the term is almost as universal and popular as that other great Swedish export, Abba.

OMERTÀ *o-mer-ta* (Italian)

originally a dialect form of the Italian term *umilta* (humility) and now referring to the 'Mafia code of silence, which threatens death and dishonour to an informer'; more generally, any 'conspiracy of silence':

I vowed ten years ago that I would rather sleep with the fishes than write about Hugh Grant again. My omertà *on the subject of my old school colleague was prompted not so much by pride as by guilt.* (Observer)

PRETENTIOUSNESS INDEX *!*

Omertà is a specialist term, indeed a criminal one. It's quite often used to describe a no-talking policy on the part of those engaged in some activity which they want to keep confidential, and fits well into the closed world of politics, etc. Nevertheless, there's something slightly self-conscious and pretentious about the use of this Mafia expression outside its 'proper' area.

OMNIUM-GATHERUM *pronounced as spelled* (Latin/English)

'mixed collection':

It [the menu] was an omnium-gatherum of contemporary table-top favourites, garnered, as you might say, from the four corners of the globe.
(Guardian)

PRETENTIOUSNESS INDEX *!!*

Omnium-gatherum is an invented piece of Latin from the sixteenth century, with 'gather' being given a Latin-style ending. The *omnium* – from *omnis* or 'all' – may mislead too, if it suggests that the collection is complete or comprehensive. In fact, an *omnium-gatherum* is a bit of a rag-bag.

ON DIT *on dee* (French)

literally 'one says'; 'hearsay', 'gossip':

The on dit is that it hasn't been a vintage year, despite some wonderful films. (Guardian)

PRETENTIOUSNESS INDEX *!*

On dit is perhaps a little stronger than rumour, with the closest English equivalent being 'the word is …'. The use of the impersonal *on* neatly suggests the anonymous nature of such comments.

OUBLIETTE *ooblee-ett* (French)

'a place of imprisonment only accessible through a hole in the roof' and so 'a place in which someone or something can be dropped and forgotten about'. The word comes from the French *oublier*, to 'forget':

In my line of business you often hear interesting gossip about people's private lives, and I mentally classify each nugget into those which have the ring of truth, and those to be filed in the oubliette called nonsense.

(Guardian)

PRETENTIOUSNESS INDEX *!*

This slightly obscure word recalls medieval and later punishments. Any current use is likely to be metaphorical (one hopes).

OUTRÉ *ootray* (French)

'unconventional', 'mildly shocking':

'In the last 10 years there has been an explosion of selling sex as lifestyle. Agent Provocateur used to be outré, but now their half-cut bras are in M&S.'   (Quoted, Daily Telegraph)

PRETENTIOUSNESS INDEX **Nil**

Outré is a fits-all-sizes term, applicable to almost anything which strikes the user as eccentric or mildly improper (I have even seen it used to describe beetroot cake). It registers a civilised surprise, and has no precise equivalent in English – a useful expression, therefore.

P

PACE *pa-chay* (Latin)

shortened form of 'pace tua' and meaning 'by your leave'; 'with due respect to (another's point of view)' :

> *Furthermore,* pace *Antony Worral Thompson, who writes critically of the Government's plans on page 25, the Health Secretary's reluctance to legislate is to be applauded.* (Independent on Sunday)

PRETENTIOUSNESS INDEX **!**

Pace is almost invariably used to introduce an opinion expressed by someone else with whom the writer disagrees. It's a courteous nod and an economical four-letter word, but its meaning is equally well conveyed by an English phrase such as 'whatever X may say'. Even so, it's quite often used. *Pace* should be italicised or underlined when written or it risks being confused with 'pace'.

PANACHE *pan-ash* (French)

'swagger', 'flamboyant style':

> *She [Ute Lemper] became a star here after her incandescent portrayal of Velma in* Chicago, *a demanding physical role in which she sang show-stoppers such as* All That Jazz *with utter panache.* (Daily Telegraph)

PRETENTIOUSNESS INDEX **Nil**

Originally meaning a 'feathered plume', *panache* characterises any performance carried off with confidence, style and showiness. The word itself is exuberant; it sounds like a cymbal being hit.

PAPABILE *papa-bill-ay* (Italian)

'eligible to become a pope'; 'fitted for high office':

> *If by the week's end Mr Hague does not seem papabile, his opinion-poll position could rapidly deteriorate.* (Spectator)

PRETENTIOUSNESS INDEX **!!** IF USED ABOUT ANYBODY WHO IS NOT IN THE RUNNING TO BECOME POPE. IN OTHER WORDS, ALMOST ALWAYS PRETENTIOUS.

Papabile can be used literally about those cardinals in the Catholic Church who are regarded as suitable candidates for the papacy. By extension, the term can be applied to anybody aspiring to some exalted position, usually in government. It suggests not just that they are senior and capable enough but that they have some aura of leadership. But, away from a Catholic context, the term seems a bit forced.

PAPARAZZO *pronounced as spelled* (Italian)

'freelance photographer who specialises in catching celebrities, particularly during off-guard moments':

> *So before we know it, the subject of screen nakedness has suddenly exposed itself. It is a topic that has, over the years, followed [Helen] Mirren like an especially persistent paparazzo.* (Independent)

PRETENTIOUSNESS INDEX **Nil**

Paparazzo is the surname of a fictional free-lance photographer in the 1960 Italian film, *La Dolce Vita*. The word now applies to a whole class of contemporary villains. A *paparazzo* (plural, *paparazzi*) is likely be a hate figure for the celebrity, unless his/her career is flagging or unless there is some other, tortuous reason for publicising that 'indiscreet' moment. From the opposite side, the *paparazzi* can get a lot of stick from the public for hounding celebs, as shown by the uproar following the death of Princess Diana in 1997. Yet everyone knows the world would be a duller place without them.

PAR EXCELLENCE *par ex-cell-onss* (French)

literally 'by excellence'; 'pre-eminently', 'supreme':

> *Alistair Cooke may have retired last week, but he remains, for Americans, the Briton* par excellence: *witty, eloquent – and steeped in nostalgia.*

> (Observer)

PRETENTIOUSNESS INDEX **Nil**

Par excellence, quite often used in English, is perhaps not such an assertive term as 'supreme' or other near-equivalents. The expression also contains the idea of 'quintessential', as in the reference to Alistair Cooke above.

PARI PASSU   *pary pass-oo*   (Latin)

literally 'with equal step'; 'at the same time and rate':

The consumption of antidepressants rises pari passu with that of single person households.   (Daily Telegraph)

PRETENTIOUSNESS INDEX *!*

Though not a widely used expression, *pari passu*, neatly combining time and speed, can stand in for longer English phrases.

PARTI PRIS   *party pree*   (French)

literally 'side taken'; 'with a preconceived position', 'biased':

Partisanship is not necessarily wrong for a newspaper. The tradition of parti pris papers is strong in Europe and well known in Britain.

(Daily Telegraph)

PRETENTIOUSNESS INDEX *!*

Parti pris can be used about individuals or groups, institutions, etc. Not a particularly common expression, it is useful for anyone wanting to avoid a more negative term such as 'prejudiced' or 'one-sided'. Editorial columns in newspapers are inevitably *parti pris* and so, frequently, is the slant given to the news.

PARVENU   *par-venoo*   (French)

describing someone with 'newly acquired wealth or status' and so 'lacking taste':

A ruined castle built at Wimpole Hall, near Cambridge, was intended not only to assert the ancient ancestry of its parvenu owner, but also to claim for him allegiance with the barons who had drawn up Magna Carta.

(Daily Telegraph)

PRETENTIOUSNESS INDEX *!*

Parvenu – describing both a person and his or her attitudes, tastes, etc. – is a word that comes with an inbuilt sneer, like *arriviste* (see entry). These are two terms which can safely be used about people who are dead, preferably long dead. Applying *parvenu* or *arriviste* to individuals now can look snobbish and silly – but you would get away with *nouveau riche* (see entry).

159

PAS DE DEUX *pah-de de* (French)

literally 'step of two'; 'dance involving two people':

Ten days in January saw the French judiciary and press locked in an intriguing pas de deux. (Observer)

<small>PRETENTIOUSNESS INDEX:</small> **Nil**

Although *pas de deux* is used literally in the context of classical ballet, it also appears in a figurative sense when two individuals or groups are involved in a complicated manoeuvre, during which one step is taken in response to another. Oddly, the expression may hint at competition or hostility rather than the co-operation which is presumably required in ballet.

PAS DEVANT LES ENFANTS *pah de-von laze on-fon* (French)

literally 'not in front of the children', and applying to any remark or behaviour which it is considered unsuitable for children (or some other specific audience) to hear or see:

She also told the News of the World, which went very pas devant les enfants *on the garlicky details of Christine Hamilton's alleged involvement.*
(Daily Telegraph)

<small>PRETENTIOUSNESS INDEX</small> *!!*

Pas devant les enfants implies that children need to be sheltered from something shocking, explicit, etc., not so much on television but in real life conversation. The French phrase, which is spoken aloud on the grounds that children won't understand the warning, may be patronising but it has a certain period charm.

PASSÉ *passay* (French)

'dated', 'out of fashion':

Imagine how comforting it would be for men like me to crack open Alan Clark's Diary and read about how, time after time, women refused to sleep with him on the grounds that he was too much of a male chauvinist pig. 'Sorry, Alan, but that whole arrogant, rightwing bastard thing is just so passé.' (Guardian)

<small>PRETENTIOUSNESS INDEX</small> **Nil**

Passé is more expressive than its English equivalents. The open-ended sound provided by the accent on the 'e' (passay) gives the word a casual, throw-away quality that suits its meaning.

PASSEGGIATA *pass-edjarta* (Italian)

'walk', 'stroll':

Wouldn't it be nicer if our town centres, on a Saturday night, were thronging with people of all ages dressed up to the nines doing passeggiata, rather than being a no-go area for anyone over 21 who doesn't want to drink until they lose control of their oesophagus. (Guardian)

PRETENTIOUSNESS INDEX *!!* IF USED TO DESCRIBE AN EVENING STROLL ROUND, SAY, WOLVERHAMPTON.

The *passeggiata* is much more than a stroll. It's an opportunity to socialise, to see and be seen. Describing the leisurely evening walk enjoyed by southern Europeans, particularly the Italians, the *passeggiata* is an essential part of town life. Whether it could ever be properly imported to Britain is not just a matter of climate but, as the writer of the *Guardian* piece indicates, also a question of culture.

PASSIM *pa-sim* (Latin)

literally 'scattered'; 'in many places', 'throughout':

Few things are less funny than 'comedy' (telly passim). (The Times)

PRETENTIOUSNESS INDEX **Nil**

Passim frequently appears in a glossary or footnote as an indicator that some topic or reference is to be found at many places in a text. But it can also be used as a shorthand way of saying, in effect, 'wherever you look'.

PATERFAMILIAS *pay-ter fam-millee-ass* (Latin)

literally 'father of a household'; 'male head of a family':

I still needed his permission for quotation, especially crucial since the evidence of Gill's sexual aberrations was potentially so explosive and likely to be challenged in Catholic circles where his reputation was still that of revered paterfamilias. (Guardian)

PRETENTIOUSNESS INDEX *!* IF USED WITHOUT IRONY ABOUT THE MALE HEAD OF ANY HOUSEHOLD NOW.

Paterfamilias is a historic term in a double sense. It can be used about the (male) head of a household in any century until the early twentieth, although its most common application is probably to fathers in the Victorian or Edwardian era. Otherwise it is a term whose day has

161

passed. That is, *paterfamilias* couldn't be used in any contemporary context except with a touch of irony. Males don't have to be heads of households; heads of households aren't necessarily male; in fact, the whole concept of a 'household head' looks antiquated.

PAX AMERICANA   *packs americarna*   (Latin-derived)

'American peace':

> *Ultimately it was America that came out on top during the Second World War, by building enough aircraft carriers to overwhelm the Japanese. Pax Britannica was replaced by Pax Americana.*   (Daily Telegraph)

PRETENTIOUSNESS INDEX *!*

Quite a widely used phrase now for obvious reasons, *Pax Americana* derives ultimately from *Pax Romana*, a phrase coined by the Latin author Pliny to describe the peace and stability imposed by the Romans on the various parts of their empire. As with *imperium* (see entry), there is a tendency to return to the best-known of the early empires to characterise any very powerful and influential nation which seeks to shape the world.

PECCADILLO   *peck-a-di-yo*   (Spanish)

'little sin', 'trivial offence':

> *Similarly, this week's investigations did not take into account the delightful peccadilloes of living, breathing sexuality, but instead gave us hard and fast rules as titillating as algebra.*   (Guardian)

PRETENTIOUSNESS INDEX **Nil**

Peccadillo (plural *peccadillos* or *peccadilloes*) is almost always applied with an indulgent smile. Although deriving from the Spanish word for sin, *pecado*, this is such a minor slip that, when reference is made to someone's *peccadilloes*, it can seem more a defining feature of personality than a criticism.

PEON   *pe-on*   (Spanish)

'labourer', 'low-grade worker':

> *'He only beats up on his managers now. He leaves us peons alone.'*
> (Quoted in The Times)

PRETENTIOUSNESS INDEX *!* IF USED OUTSIDE ITS PROPER CONTEXT

Peon is a culture-specific word, not often applicable outside South

America or South-east Asia. A disparaging term, akin to 'peasant', if found in a western context.

PER CAPITA   *pronounced as spelled*   (Latin)

'by each person':

French and German visitors consistently spend more per capita in the US than their British and Japanese counterparts.   (The Times)

PRETENTIOUSNESS INDEX **Nil**

One of those invaluable nuts-and-bolts phrases, particularly where statistics are concerned, *per capita* is a way of expressing the averaging-out of a figure across a specified group, nationality, etc.

PERESTROIKA   *peri-stroyka*   (Russian)

'restructuring' (of an economic/political system):

It was August 1991 and the people had taken to the streets to protest against an attempt by hardliners to overthrow Mikhail Gorbachov and put an end to the sweeping changes being brought about by his perestroika.

(Guardian)

PRETENTIOUSNESS INDEX **!** IF USED OUTSIDE ITS RUSSIAN/HISTORICAL CONTEXT.

Perestroika is indelibly associated with changes encouraged by Prime Minister Gorbachev in the Soviet Union of the 1980s. On the crest of the wave of Gorbymania which swept the world at the time, *perestroika* with its sister word *glasnost* entered general usage and the two terms were widely applied in other, non-Soviet contexts. Most uses now are likely to relate to the historical situation in the USSR a couple of decades ago. See also *glasnost.*

PERPETUUM MOBILE   *perpet-ewe-um mo-bill-ee*   (Latin)

'perpetual motion', describing a 'machine that would go on for ever':

It could be that in the longer-run, the fuel cell itself would generate the electricity to produce the hydrogen to run the fuel cell, even recycling the water which the fuel cell creates to be re-used for further hydrogen: the dream of perpetuum mobile realised at last.   (Spectator)

PRETENTIOUSNESS INDEX **Nil**

Perpetuum mobile describes both the fact of perpetual motion and the imaginary machine which would never need refuelling, wear out, etc. This is a rarely used phrase but not quite as elusive as the thing itself.

PER SE   *per say*   (Latin)

'in itself', 'intrinsically':

But observers of the Indian TV market point out that it is hard to establish how much of the success of these formats was down to James per se.

(Observer)

PRETENTIOUSNESS INDEX **Nil**

This widely used phrase is still with us because it is handy and space-saving. It frequently introduces or implies some sort of qualification – 'I don't object to this scheme *per se* but...'

PERSIFLAGE   *per-siff-lahj*   (French)

'mockery', 'flip talk':

The pipe-smoking, the persiflage, the laughter, the steps on to and up the English literary ladder [...]: terrible, terrible scenes, and with variants that will always be with us.   (Guardian)

PRETENTIOUSNESS INDEX **!!**

Persiflage is a variant on 'banter'. It doesn't add much to that word or other English equivalents and has a slightly twee or over-literary quality.

PERSONA   *persow-na*   (Latin)

'public image', 'assumed personality'

Her sexually predatory stage persona can become perilously edgy – in a recent show in New York she walked off with a businessman's tie and credit card after flirting with him and announcing, 'I'm for sale after the show.'

(Daily Telegraph)

PRETENTIOUSNESS INDEX **Nil**

This is a widely used term. *Persona* suggests the mask adopted for public display but even though an individual many have more than one of them (plural: *personae*) there is rarely the idea of deliberate deception behind it.

PERSONA GRATA   *persow-na grah-ta*   (Latin)

'acceptable person':

The Italian president Giancarlo Dondi called Pugh a 'persona grata' who had played a crucial part in Italy's incorporation into the Six Nations, for which 'we are eternally grateful'.   (Guardian)

Persona grata is found infrequently compared to its opposite (see below) and has a specialist and diplomatic sense to describe someone who is 'acceptable' to a foreign government (as ambassador, etc.). Otherwise, it describes a person who is not merely acceptable but liked and welcomed.

PERSONA NON GRATA *persow-na non grah-ta* (Latin)

'someone who is not welcome':

…such a visit [by the American President] would prove deeply uncomfortable for Michael Howard, who is persona non grata *at President Bush's White House.* (Independent on Sunday)

PRETENTIOUSNESS INDEX **Nil**

Persona non grata can be used in any context, although it tends to apply to formal settings or situations in which a person might be refused admission to an institution or establishment.

PETIT-BOURGEOIS *petty-bor-jwa* (French)

'lower middle class' and so by implication 'conventional':

Leitch regarded his adoptive parents as petit-bourgeois and limited – although he was very fond of his adoptive father. (The Times)

PRETENTIOUSNESS INDEX **Nil**

Petit-bourgeois is not generally a neutral, sociological description but, like other expressions involving the *bourgeoisie*, is the equivalent of a slur or an accusation since it suggests small-mindedness, etc. But it's a rather dated term now.
See also *bourgeois*.

PETITE *peteet* (French)

'small', 'delicate':

Presumably because of her petite size, her big brown eyes, and general air of vulnerability, Portman has most often been compared with Audrey Hepburn. (Independent)

PRETENTIOUSNESS INDEX **!**

Petite is a term of approval where 'small' may not be. It carries overtones of daintiness and grace.

PICAYUNE *pee-k e-yoon* (French)

originally, in the US, a 'small coin', and so something 'of little value', 'insignficant':

> *Great-uncle Mick was a socialist firebrand in the East End, a union official caught between the universal cause of workers' revolution and the picayune needs of Jewish solidarity.*   (Independent)

PRETENTIOUSNESS INDEX *!*

Picayune carries the implication of 'petty', 'not worth bothering with'. Occasionally found in British English and more frequently in the US.

PIÈCE DE RESISTANCE *pee-ess de rezistonse* (French)

literally 'piece of resistance'; 'main dish in a meal', 'best item in a collection':

> *The* piece de resistance *of the set are the two 'lost' John Lennon tracks, Free As A Bird and Real Love …*   (Daily Mail)

PRETENTIOUSNESS INDEX **Nil**

Although *pièce de resistance* can be used to describe the highpoint of a meal it is more frequently applied in English to the best of any bunch. In its original context, presumably what one is enabled to 'resist' by eating the big dish are the pangs of hunger until the next meal.

PIED-À-TERRE *pee-ed-ah-terr* (French)

literally 'foot to earth'; applying to a 'house or flat, particularly in a city, used from time to time as a second home':

> *…the reformed Commons does not sit late and unpredictably into the night as it did before 'family friendly' hours were introduced, removing some justification for a handy pied a terre*   (Guardian)

PRETENTIOUSNESS INDEX **Nil**

Pied-à-terre is a long-established term, and not just with estate agents. It sounds more elegant than the slightly long-winded equivalents in English.

PIQUANT *pee-kont* (French)

'sharp', 'stimulating':

> *It is piquant that walkabout, originally used in Australia for an Aborigine going wandering the bush, has come to be used as the easygoing word for*

royalty, prime ministers and presidents putting on a democratic act by strolling among the crowds.   (Godfrey Howard, *The Good English Guide*)

<small>PRETENTIOUSNESS INDEX</small> **Nil**

Piquant applies both to food and taste (a *piquant* sauce) and also to remarks, observations, quirky facts, etc. which are curious or noteworthy. The key point is the appetising sharpness of both uses of the word. *Piquant* is the opposite of bland or dull.

PIQUE   *peek*   (French)

'bad feeling', 'wounded pride':

In their pique at being excluded, Italy, Spain and Poland have conjured up a fantasy of the Big Three sitting down together in confident intimacy.

(The Times)

<small>PRETENTIOUSNESS INDEX</small> **Nil**

Deriving from a French word for 'pike', *pique* is an umbrella term sheltering a bundle of emotions ranging from irritation to resentment to anger – but always in response to something done to the sufferer. *Pique* is also a verb with the same meanings (to wound or irritate) as well as the more positive sense of 'stimulate'.

PIS ALLER   *peez al-eh*   (French)

literally 'worse to go'; 'last resort':

Like most one-nation Tories they actively disliked their own party and put up with it as a pis aller.   (Guardian)

<small>PRETENTIOUSNESS INDEX</small> *!*

One of those phrases which may be misunderstood in English, a *pis aller* is the option you must take because all others are closed. It's Hobson's choice.

PLACEBO   *pla-see-boh*   (Latin)

literally 'I shall please'. *Placebo* describes a medicine or treatment which has no effect on a medical condition, but which is provided to a patient either as a psychological comfort or as part of an experiment in which others are given the genuine medicine and the difference in reaction assessed. *Placebo* also describes any procedure, system etc. which may reassure those undergoing it but which has no real substance:

Top neurologists, pharmacologists, anatomists, ethicists and theologians are to examine the scientific basis of religious belief and whether it is anything more than a placebo. (The Times)

<small>PRETENTIOUSNESS INDEX</small> **Nil**

Placebo is a genuinely valuable term, expressing in a single word what takes a sentence of explanation in English.

PLUS ÇA CHANGE   *ploo sa shonge*   (French)

literally 'the more things change'. In full, the expression is *plus ça change, plus c'est la meme chose* ('the more things change, the more they stay the same') but the sentence almost always appears only in its first half, the reader or listener supplying the rest:

…the new owners seem to think that whatever their paper may say or do, they will respond to any attack on themselves with an immediate writ. Plus ça change. (Observer)

<small>PRETENTIOUSNESS INDEX</small> **Nil**

The fact that this saying can be cut in half without its meaning being impaired or lost shows how familiar it is. The general meaning of the saying – that however much things may appear to change on the surface, the underlying reality stays the same – is comforting or cynical depending on one's viewpoint.

POINT D'APPUI   *pwa-n d-appwee*   (French)

literally 'point of support'; 'support', 'fulcrum':

Her previous book, Restoration London, drew heavily on Pepys's diaries. Where the eighteenth century is concerned, there is no such obvious point d'appui (Guardian)

<small>PRETENTIOUSNESS INDEX</small> *!*

Point d'appui, sometimes used within a military context, suggests something on which an argument or a case pivots. The phrase is more elegant than 'prop' but rather less likely to be understood.

POLICIER   *polisi-yeh*   (French)

'police/detective novel or (more usually) film':

This is his kind of city: raw, louche and a bit anarchic, with the cinematic energy of a French policier and scarcely a tourist in sight. (Daily Telegraph)

PRETENTIOUSNESS INDEX **Nil**

There are plenty of police procedural stories on British television but they don't quite fit the French term *policier*, which summons up a world of flics, Gauloises and shadowy streets.

POLITICO   *pronounced as spelled*   (Italian/Spanish)

'politician' or 'would-be politician' or 'political':

I cannot see any of the contestants in last night's talent show for budding politicos succeeding.   (The Times)

PRETENTIOUSNESS INDEX **Nil**

One of those cases where using the 'foreign' expression is intrinsically disparaging (see also *generalissimo*). A *politico* is unlikely to be a serious contender, or is so only in his own eyes, and the expression suggests play-acting, lack of gravitas and all the rest of it.

PORTMANTEAU   *port-mon-tow*   (French)

literally 'carry-coat' and so a 'travelling bag for clothes'. Also a term to describe the blending of two or more words to form a new word (such as 'brunch' for breakfast+lunch):

I have heard some people refer to this time of year, perhaps half in jest, as 'Chriskwanukkah', an unlovely portmanteau of Christmas, Chanukkah and Kwanzaa, the African-American winter festival.   (The Times)

PRETENTIOUSNESS INDEX **Nil**

Portmanteau is a neat way of describing the combining of two words to form something which is new or partly new.

POST HOC   *post hock*   (Latin)

'after this', 'after the event':

The post hoc justification for the 1990–92 period of ERM membership is that it enabled the UK to get inflation out of the system.

(Observer)

PRETENTIOUSNESS INDEX **Nil**

A handy phrase since it implies, with a hint of criticism, that whatever is *post hoc* is being done afterwards with the benefit of hindsight rather than having been foreseen.

POULE DE LUXE   *pool de loox*   (French)

literally 'hen of luxury' (!); 'prostitute':

What a scene it must have been for the immense army of journalists, lobbyists and poules de luxe who follow the Euro parliament's caravanserai from Brussels to Strasbourg.   (Daily Telegraph)

PRETENTIOUSNESS INDEX **!**

There are several euphemistic terms for 'prostitute' (e.g. call-girl, working girl), but *poule de luxe* is one of the more rarefied and sophisticated, albeit in a self-conscious way. It looks appropriate in a European context, as in the *Telegraph* example, but is probably too roundabout to find more than a cultured toe-hold in English.

POURBOIRE   *poor-bwar*   (French)

literally 'for drinking'; 'tip', 'gratuity':

…at one congested entrance to the arena [in Paris], stewards sought tips for directing customers to seats. Pourboire: poor taste in the mouth.

(Daily Telegraph)

PRETENTIOUSNESS INDEX **!**

Translated literally, *pourboire* indicates the use to which the money will probably be put. When used in an English context the term can sound a bit twee. There's nothing wrong with the plain 'tip' or – if one wants to draw a veil over the naked gift of cash – a 'gratuity'.

POUR ENCOURAGER LES AUTRES   *poor ankoor-ahjay laze oh-tr*   (French)

literally 'to encourage the others':

Only 346 of the 3,080 death sentences were actually carried out, mostly 'to reinforce discipline in a particular unit or at a particular time'. In other words, pour encourager les autres.   (Daily Telegraph)

PRETENTIOUSNESS INDEX **!** IF USED AS A STRAIGHTFORWARD ALTERNATIVE TO 'ENCOURAGE'.

When this phrase is used it quite often has a military context but any application of *pour encourager les autres* ought to acknowledge its original irony. The expression comes from the French writer Voltaire who used it in his satirical novel *Candide*, published in 1759. Three years earlier, British naval forces under Admiral Byng had been defeated off

Minorca by the French. Byng was executed by firing squad for 'cowardice'. Voltaire's comment was that the English believe 'it is a good thing to kill an admiral from time to time to encourage the others'. Voltaire didn't actually approve of the execution of the English admiral, who, he said, was being shot 'for not having killed enough people [in battle]'. In other words, the expression reveals a distaste for military methods as well as cynicism about motives.

PRÊT-À-PORTER *prett-ah-portay* (French)

'ready to wear':

How can you indulge your junk food craving while still boasting the wash-board stomach and pert buttocks that the Zeitgeist, kings of pret-a-porter and advertisers demand? (The Times)

PRETENTIOUSNESS INDEX **Nil**

This is a widely used phrase, as shown by its adoption/variation by the Pret-a-Manger chain. *Prêt-à-porter* sounds slightly more glamorous than its English translation, which is presumably the main reason for importing it from Paris.

PRIMA DONNA *preema donna* (Italian)

literally 'first lady'; 'principal female singer in opera'; 'someone (particularly in the arts or entertainment world) who is touchy and self-important':

...the queue to sign the petulant prima donna for £6m and pay him the £2m a year he is getting at present has been slow to form. (Guardian)

PRETENTIOUSNESS INDEX ANY PRETENSION IS LIKELY TO BE FOUND WITH THE *PRIMA DONNA* HERSELF (OR HIMSELF)

Prima donna is rarely if ever used in its operatic sense. Rather it describes woman – and men – who are demanding, sensitive, self-centred, etc. For some reason, showbiz is full of them. Even supposedly macho activities like professional football have their share of *prima donnas* (see above).

PRIMA FACIE *pryma fay-shee* (Latin)

'at first sight':

'If he makes a run for it, we'll have prima facie *evidence – but we'll still need the hard stuff.'* (Graham Greene, *The Human Factor*)

Prima facie is most frequently linked with 'evidence' and has legalistic overtones. In law, it indicates a strong case.

PRIMUS INTER PARES *preemus inter pah'rays* (Latin; also in feminine form **prima inter pares**)

'first among equals':

> *According to population and economic growth projections, by mid-century the US will be one power among equals, perhaps 'primus inter pares', perhaps not.* (Spectator)

Pretentiousness Index **Nil**

This is a older and less cynical version of George Orwell's 'All animals are equal but some are more equal than others'. The person or group or country which is *primus inter pares* is the 'senior partner'.

PRO BONO PUBLICO *pro bone-oh publico* (Latin)

literally 'for the public good'; generally shortened to *pro bono* and used (especially in a US legal context) to describe 'work for poor clients undertaken by lawyers who do not charge their normal fees':

> *'...and I've been doing a lot of* pro bono *work, and I've done some "regular lawyer stuff", real estate mostly ...'* (Eric Kraft, *Reservations Recommended*)

Pretentiousness Index **Nil**

This is a technical term and is, in effect, the equivalent of charity work on the part of lawyers.

PRO FORMA *pronounced as spelled* (Latin)

an 'invoice'; 'as a matter of form':

> *That appears to have paid off, with LRC expected to record a small profit of £290,000 this year, against a pro forma loss of £800,000 in the previous year.* (Guardian)

Pretentiousness Index **Nil**

Pro forma has a double sense – as a noun meaning 'invoice' and as an adverbial or adjectival phrase meaning 'as a formality'. In this second definition it may mean no more than 'appearing on paper' as opposed to 'actual'. An additional meaning, when applied to someone's behaviour or actions, is 'perfunctory'.

PROLETARIAT *pro-leh-tariat*   (French from Latin)

'working class':

And to round the evening off, an extract from the musical Les Misérables, with its heart-warming depiction of an impoverished 19th-century Parisian proletariat.   (Guardian)

PRETENTIOUSNESS INDEX **Nil**

Although once part of Marxist terminology, *proletariat* has generally been applied in a dismissive way (in George Orwell's *1984*, *prole* is the term for the lowest and slowest members of society). Indeed, the Latin origins of the term reflect the fact that members of the *proletariat* were expected to serve the state only by providing it with their offspring or 'proles', the civilian equivalent of cannon fodder. The term 'working class' still has a certain resonance in British English but *proletariat* is hardly found now except in a historical context. (The pejorative term *lumpenproletariat* was sometimes used to characterise the underclass beneath the labouring class, *lumpen* being German for 'rag'.)

PRO RATA *pro rah-ta*   (Latin)

'proportionally':

…it is a truism that the British book trade produces, pro rata, far more new titles each year than even its American counterpart.   (Observer)

PRETENTIOUSNESS INDEX **Nil**

This is an expression which has surely survived because of its convenience and simplicity – two short words as against the five-syllabled 'proportionally'.

PROTEGÉ *protay-jhay*   (French)

'person who is under another's patronage/protection':

Following Ramsay's success, Marcus Wareing, another celebrity chef and one of Ramsay's protegés, was installed to run the famous Savoy Grill at that hotel.   (Daily Telegraph)

PRETENTIOUSNESS INDEX **Nil**

There is no exact English equivalent for *protegé* or at least not without resorting to roundabout phrasing. It combines the ideas of teaching, guiding, nurturing, etc. and comes with suggestions of protection and favouritism too. A valuable word therefore.

PRO-TEM   *pronounced as spelled*   (Latin)

'for the time being':

> *The dress, the ring, the television coverage, even Mrs Parker Bowles's future title – Duchess of Cornwall pro-tem, Princess Consort in due course – minor details like that, were all that was left to sort out.*   (Guardian)

PRETENTIOUSNESS INDEX **Nil**

Rarely if ever spelled out in full (the complete expression is *pro tempore*), the abbreviated *pro-tem* is an alternative to 'temporary/temporarily'. Presumably all of the English equivalents were considered slightly inappropriate in the example from the *Guardian* above.

PUDEUR   *poo-derr*   (French)

'ready sense of shame', 'modesty':

> *If there was one thing you could always rely on the French for, it was a healthy attitude to sex. Not for them the furtive fumblings, the embarrassed embraces, the puritan pudeur, the shamefaced shambles that constitute – in French eyes, at least – the Anglo-Saxon idea of romance.*

> (Guardian)

PRETENTIOUSNESS INDEX **!**

Not an expression which is widely used, *pudeur* describes not so much the experience of being ashamed after the event as sensitivity to situations in which shame might arise.

PUKKA   *pronounced as spelled*   (also **pucka** and **pukkah**)   (Hindi)

'very good', 'proper':

> *But there are sausages and there are sausages: pukka sausages, stuffed with good meat and in natural casings, properly seasoned and made with care; and debased sausages for which even the treatment suggested by Cathalina is too good.*   (Guardian)

PRETENTIOUSNESS INDEX **Nil**

This term is a imported relic of British rule in India, where a *pukka sahib* was a 'true gentleman'. Its current popularity is mostly the responsibility of über-TV-chef Jamie Oliver, who peppers his speech with *pukkas*. The little detonation of this word, the way it puckers the lips, registers the speaker's approval and enthusiasm.

PUNCTILIO *punctil-ee-o* (Spanish/Italian)

'small point of etiquette', 'over-fine detail':

Every councillor in Britain had teams of people breathing over his shoulder, checking every tiny thing he did, wasting time on unnecessary punctilio.

(Guardian)

PRETENTIOUSNESS INDEX **Nil**

This is a more pejorative term than it may at first appear. Not to be confused with 'punctuality' (although both derive from the Latin word for 'point'), *punctilio* is a fussy bothering over detail.

PUNDIT *pronounced as spelled* (Sanskrit)

'knowledgeable person', 'expert':

The greatest anxiety gnawing at the guts of the government is that too many people, voters and pundits alike, take it for granted that Labour is cruising to a comfortable third term. (Observer)

PRETENTIOUSNESS INDEX **Nil**

Older dictionaries have *pundit* down as a jocular usage when meaning an 'expert' (rather than its earlier and specific sense of a 'Hindu learned in Sanskrit'). In current usage, the word isn't quite complimentary – the *pundit* generally has a well-developed taste for making public pronouncements on his or her area of expertise – but nor is it insulting.

PURDAH *pronounced as spelled* (Persian/Urdu)

Originally deriving from a word for 'curtain', *purdah* describes the practice in some Islamic and Hindu cultures of preventing women being seen by outsiders; by extension, it means a 'state of seclusion or isolation':

The doom and gloom has been encouraged by the fact that in the run-up to Christmas the good retailers tend to keep their heads down. They do not want to tempt fate and go into corporate purdah. (Observer)

PRETENTIOUSNESS INDEX ARGUABLY **!** IF USED OUTSIDE ITS ORIGINAL CULTURAL CONTEXT.

Purdah is in quite widespread use outside its original religious/cultural setting and is a convenient term if one wants to describe how a person or group has withdrawn temporarily from society.

PUTSCH *put'ch* (Swiss German)

'sudden and violent uprising':

On Easter Monday 1916, a band of republican idealists tried to overthrow British rule in Ireland and were executed after the putsch failed.

(Observer)

PRETENTIOUSNESS INDEX **!**

There are several words to choose from, both home-grown and imported, to describe the attempt to overthrow a ruling authority or state, ranging from 'rising' to 'revolt' to 'coup d'etat'. Of these, *putsch* tends to be reserved for the attempt by a smallish group to seize control of the levers of power. The sound of the word, originally meaning 'thrust', seems to hint at its aggressive meaning.

PUTZ *putts* (Yiddish)

'stupid person':

'What happened?' asks Washington's bedraggled Everyman, to which Schreiber's pitiful putz replies: 'Mother happened.' (Observer)

PRETENTIOUSNESS INDEX **!**

Putz (with the slang sense of 'penis') is more contempuous than equivalent Yiddish terms of abuse such as *schlemiel* (see entry).

Q

QED   see quod erat demonstrandum

QUARTIER   *cart-ee-ay*   (French)

'district in a (French) town or city'

> *...he vowed he was going to open up the Barbican to the neighbouring 'quartier' of Clerkenwell and Smithfield.*   (The Times)

PRETENTIOUSNESS INDEX *!!!* IF USED ABOUT ANY URBAN AREA IN BRITAIN.

Quartier, suggesting a self-conscious area with artistic or low-life aspirations, sounds ridiculous or precious if applied to any district of a British city. We have suburbs.

QUASI   *kwah-zee*   (Latin)

'as if', 'almost':

> *She finds herself in a rather mysterious and sinister home for pregnant girls. It is a quasi-thriller.*   (The Times)

PRETENTIOUSNESS INDEX **Nil**

Quasi – generally hyphenated before a noun or adjective – is a handy way of hedging around a description or a piece of categorisation. It suggests that something or someone has aspirations towards a particular status without quite having reached it.

QUID PRO QUO   *pronounced as spelled*   (Latin)

'something given in exchange for something received':

> *The current situation is the result of an unhealthy carve-up, between the Europeans (mainly, the French, Germans and British), who get to choose the head of the International Monetary Fund, and the US, which gets to name the bank president in a quid pro quo.*   (Guardian)

A *quid pro quo* is not an exchange of Christmas presents, but a hard-headed transaction of the 'you-scratch-my-back-I'll-scratch-yours' variety, a mutually advantageous swapping of favours, etc. In fact, the term is so devoid of friendly associations that it can describe an act of revenge.

QUI VIVE   *key veev*   (French)

literally '(long) live who' – the challenge issued by a sentry to discover the loyalty of someone approaching; by extension the phrase comes to mean 'on the lookout':

> *Naturally, in the absence of a free press, and with Gadafy's 'purification committees' ever on the qui vive for seditious thinking, it is hard to know just how far Libya has moved away [...] from being a pariah.*

(Guardian)

PRETENTIOUSNESS INDEX **!**

This long-lived phrase goes back five centuries to a time when the appropriate respose to the question might have been 'Vive le roi!'. Now *qui vive* operates as an expressive substitute for 'on the alert', 'lively and watchful'.

QUOD ERAT DEMONSTRANDUM   *pronounced as spelled*   (Latin; usually abbreviated to **QED**)

literally 'which was to be proved' and put at the closing point of an argument:

> *Reason with a physical cause is not true reason at all. Therefore true reason does not emerge from our bodies, but is a gift from beyond the frontier. Therefore there is a world beyond Nature to give such gifts. QED.*

(Francis Spufford, The Child That Books Built)

PRETENTIOUSNESS INDEX **Nil**

QED, originally connected to a proof in mathematics, is a familiar enough term to have been used as the title of a long-running BBC science series. The abbreviation sometimes comes up in a half-humorous context to suggest that the user has 'proved' something, at least to his own satisfaction if no one else's. It may also be used straightforwardly to signal the clinching point in an argument.

QUOD VIDE   *quod veeday*   (Latin; generally abbreviated to **q.v.**)

literally 'which see' and used to refer a reader to a point elsewhere within the same text or to a different text:

Or that their evolutionary hierarchy (q.v. The Life of Mammals) is most valuable demonstrating how superior our particular branch is in life's web.
(Guardian)

PRETENTIOUSNESS INDEX **Nil**

As with several of the Latin abbreviations in English use (others include *e.g.*, *i.e.*, *cf*), the job of *q.v.* – rarely found in its full form of *quod vide* – is to help prop up a statement or argument by referring readers to another example or source of information. Its function is essentially rhetorical. Not many readers are going to rush off and look up the reference, but they will be reassured that they could if they wanted to.

QUONDAM   *pronounced as spelled*   (Latin)

'former', 'sometime':

The Bayleys were eccentric – 'out of centre' – in their complementary brilliance (he is a novelist, a quondam poet, a literary critic of effortless fluidity).   (Guardian)

PRETENTIOUSNESS INDEX *!*

Quondam is occasionally used as an alternative to 'former' or other English equivalents. It doesn't carry any additional shade of meaning, and its use may seem slightly pretentious.

R

RACONTEUR *ra-con-terr* (French)

'teller of stories and anecdotes':

> *Pete King – raconteur, sometime fiction writer and one of two House Republicans with the nerve to vote against the impeachment of Bill Clinton – has a great story about the former First Couple.* (Independent)

PRETENTIOUSNESS INDEX **Nil**

Raconteur has no precise equivalent in English. Terms such as 'story teller' or 'teller of tales' may suggest a writer or, at worst, a liar. But a *raconteur* (feminine form *raconteuse*) is a person who has a fund of anecdotes at his or her disposal and who is skilled at telling them, almost as a profession. With their stories refined through repetition and often delivered in a variety of accents, *raconteurs* are always welcome on the fustier chat shows.

RAISON D'ÊTRE *raison det'r* (French)

'reason for being', 'purpose for which something exists':

> *As a result, we now have a vast plethora of competing charities whose raison d'etre seems to be survival at the expense of the others, rather than relieving people's poverty and want.* (Guardian)

PRETENTIOUSNESS INDEX **Nil**

Raison d'être is very widely used, perhaps because, with the English equivalents being slightly more cumbersome, it's the first expression to hand.

RAPPORT *ra-poor* (French)

'harmonious understanding', 'sense of emotional and mental connection':

> *Telling the story in [the book] Paper Lion (1966), he revealed both his respect for the players as individuals and his strong rapport with the team.*
> (Guardian)

Rapport describes a relationship which is instinctive and unforced. Combining notions of harmony, sympathy, being on the same wavelength, etc., the word is usually found in contexts where good relations aren't automatic – among work colleagues, say, or between two people who occupy the same position in different and competing organisations.

RAPPORTEUR   *ra-poor-terr*   (French)

'individual who investigates and reports back to an organisation':

> *Syria [...] is part of the five-person bureau (headed by the chairman) which runs the business of the [United Nations Commission on Human Rights]. It is the bureau's responsibility to decide which countries, or subjects, should be subject to investigation by a UN rapporteur.*   (Guardian)

Pretentiousness Index **Nil**

Something of a specialist term, *rapporteur* is almost always used in the context of United Nations business.

RAPPROCHEMENT   *ra-prosh-mon*   (French)

'coming together', 're-establishment of good relations, particularly between countries':

> *Dinner with Jacques Chirac will start the rapprochement with Old Europe while other leaders wait in line, olive branch in hand.*   (Spectator)

Pretentiousness Index **Nil**

Rapprochment is generally applied to the situation in which nations edge towards each other after a frosty period in their relationship and describes the stage before a reconciliation. It may also be used of individuals.

RARA AVIS   *rare-ah ay-viss*   (Latin)

a 'rare bird' and so an unusual person or event:

> *Most people seem remarkably ignorant about the very existence of the inner-city bungalow, but this rara avis of the urban property scene is suddenly making a bit of a splash – though not necessarily under its original name.*
> (Daily Telegraph)

Pretentiousness Index *!*

Since the English equivalent of *rara avis* conveys the meaning just as well there seems no reason not to prefer 'rare bird'. But *rara avis* sounds a bit more exotic and so better reflects its meaning, although there is sometimes a faintly absurd aspect to the term.

REALPOLITIK   *ray-al-politeek*   (German)

literally 'practical politics' (as opposed to political policies which are based on moral principles):

> *The days are over when America, out of hardheaded realpolitik, would underwrite a Noriega in Panama, or a Diem regime in South Vietnam, as a gambit in the great international chess game with the Communist enemy.*
>
> (Daily Telegraph)

PRETENTIOUSNESS INDEX *!*

Realpolitik is a term which can either be brandished defiantly by those who practice it or, as in the *Telegraph* quote above, used as shorthand condemnation of those same people. It characterises the politics of expedience – and specifically a foreign policy – in which actions that are convenient or handy for your cause or side take precedence over ethical considerations.

RECHERCHÉ   *reshershay*   (French)

'carefully sought out' and so 'obscure':

> *[Christmas book-list] choosers are becoming wary of highlighting obscurities. Novelist Philip Hensher used to be wonderful at this – no 13th-century Lithuanian poet was too recherché to be recommended as a stocking-filler.*
>
> (Guardian)

PRETENTIOUSNESS INDEX *!!*

One of those terms which occur in contexts that suggest both admiration and irritation. The user is commenting on the industry and knowledge of the person who's searched for that unusual word, book, fact, etc. But *recherché* also carries a hint that such knowledge may be just too specialised or self-advertising. Indeed there is something *recherché* about the very word *recherché*.

RÉCLAME   *reklamme*   (French)

'fame', 'self-advertisement':

> *He [Richard Perle] is a leading Jewish neo-conservative of considerable reclame, for whom the invasion of Iraq was a priority.*   (Daily Telegraph)

Réclame neatly suggests in a single word the kind of fame and acclaim that come about through a shrewd manipulation of the media. The publicity involved is self-publicity.

RECULER POUR MIEUX SAUTER *reh-coo-lay poor mi-yer sortay* (French)

literally to 'move back so as to jump better' and describing a tactical withdrawal or stepping-back so as to give a better chance of progress or success later on:

Rather than going ahead with Emu [Economic & Monetary Union] with all the attendant risks […] Europe will, I believe, take the alternative route reculer pour mieux sauter (Prospect)

PRETENTIOUSNESS INDEX *!*

The expression is proverbial – in full it is *Il faut reculer pour mieux sauter* ('It's necessary to …') – and there's no near equivalent in English. This is surprising, maybe, since the idea behind the phrase is both practical and face-saving. Stepping back can indeed provide a better opportunity to tackle a problem – a longer run-up? – or at least this can always be the explanation for the manoeuvre.

REDUCTIO AD ABSURDUM *reduct-ee-oh ad absurd-um* (Latin)

'ridiculous conclusion':

Here, taken to its reductio ad absurdum, is the principle beloved of progressive educationalists, that studying historical documents is more conducive to empathy, and thus to understanding, than reading the history books that draw on them. (Daily Telegraph)

PRETENTIOUSNESS INDEX **Nil**

Strictly speaking, *reductio ad absurdum* is a term from logic used to demonstrate the falsity of an argument. But almost always the term is used more casually to indicate some foolish end-point in a process, and so to cast doubt on the whole process. – as if the speaker is saying, 'This is where we'll get to if we follow this road. Don't let's start.'

REDUX *pronounced as spelled* (Latin)

'restored', 'brought back to life':

'This isn't the return of the boom, it is the [dot-com] bubble redux and it is likely to end in tears once again.' (quoted in Daily Telegraph)

Redux is a slightly rarefied way of describing the reappearance/revival of something or somebody. Placed Latin-style after the noun to which it applies, the term occasionally crops up in titles. Examples include John Updike's novel *Rabbit Redux* (1972) and the reissue, many years after its 1979 appearance, of Francis Ford Coppola's epic Vietnam film as *Apocalypse Now Redux*, the *redux* part being justified by the extra footage.

RENTIER   *ronti-yay*   (French)

'person who lives on investments':

> *Oil also encourages the emergence of a rentier class of leaders – Saudi Arabia has 3,000 princes – who need do nothing more than grant a licence to a foreign company to get rich.*   (Daily Telegraph)

PRETENTIOUSNESS INDEX *!*

Rentier, originally an example of late nineteenth-century economic and social categorisation, is a rather dated and specialist term now. It's to do with those who make money not so much on 'rents' as on big returns (*rentes* in French) from their investments.

REVENANT   *revennon*   (French)

'someone who returns' (particularly from the dead), 'ghost', 'spirit from the past':

> *With his ironed-down hair and his rimless glasses, looking eerily like a revenant from the Vietnam War era, Mr Rumsfeld has been glaring out from the pages of the Paris press every day since he denounced France and Germany as 'old Europe'.*   (Sunday Telegraph)

PRETENTIOUSNESS INDEX **Nil**

The comparative rarity of *revenant* and its sense (from the original French) of 'one who comes back' perhaps give the word a sinister edge over the familiar English 'ghost', with which it is more or less synonymous.

RISORGIMENTO   *risawjimen'toe*   (Italian)

'revival', 'renewal':

> *Fortunately, that wasn't all there was to the American risorgimento of the 1980s.*   (The Times)

Risorgimento (usually capitalised) refers to the specific historic events which led to the unification of Italy in 1870. More generally, it can describe any process of spirited revival although there are a number of Englands words which can do the job just as well.

RISQUÉ   *riss-kay*   (French)

'sexually suggestive':

> *In a world where lap-dancing bars have become the fashionable form of risque entertainment for businessman, there's a danger that the bunny girl with her tail and floppy ears will seem tame, if not ridiculous.*
>
> (Scotsman)

Risqué comes from the French *risquer*, which (surprise) translates as 'risk'. But the risk is a safe one, skirting the borders of offence and outrage but never crossing them. The term has a slightly dated hint of ooh-la-la naughtiness about it, which is obviously what English speakers once liked to associate with the French.

RODOMONTADE   *rodo-montahd*   (French)

'ranting', 'bragging':

> *I can only admire his courage in volunteering to suffer O'Connor's mood swings and his tolerance for the semi-coherent rodomontades of his conversation. (No doubt it helped to be drunk.)*   (Observer)

PRETENTIOUSNESS INDEX *!!*

Rodomontade is a fairly rare term (it derives from the name of a pagan king in a sixteenth-century Italian epic poem). Its meaning can usually be guessed from the context, but it does not really achieve anything that the simpler 'boasting' would not.

ROMAN FLEUVE   *romon flerv*   (French)

literally 'river novel'; 'series of novels which chronicle history of a group of characters'; 'slowly unfolding narrative':

> *And of course the two years he [Jeffrey Archer] is likely to serve are really just another chapter in the long and thrilling roman-fleuve which is his life.*
>
> (Guardian)

PRETENTIOUSNESS INDEX **Nil**

There's something leisurely about the *roman fleuve*, as it takes the reader on a meandering course from source to estuary, beginning to end. This expressive term is usually applied to novel sequences like John Galsworthy's *The Forsyte Saga* or Anthony Powell's *A Dance to the Music of Time*, but it can equally well be used of the slowly developing narrative of someone's life, particularly if it's full of incident (as in the *Guardian* example).

ROMAN À CLEF   *romon ah klay*   (French)

literally 'novel with a key' and used to describe any work of fiction in which the characters and narrative are thinly disguised versions of real people and events:

This acerbic novel [My Name is Legion] provided Fleet Street with one of the year's best guessing games. To what extent was A.N. Wilson's book, about the British tabloid press, a roman à clef recording the author's sharp recollections of his years as a newspaper pundit?

(Daily Telegraph)

PRETENTIOUSNESS INDEX **Nil**

The English language produces *romans à clef* (one of the best examples of recent years being *Primary Colors*, based on Bill Clinton's campaign for the White House in the early 1990s), but we need the French phrase. There is no English equivalent. Presumbly the 'key' refers to the reader's insight or intuition, required to understand what the closed world of the novel is really about.

ROSBIF   *ros-beef*   (French)

'roast beef'; and so, in honour of the one-time national dish, 'English':

France had never conceded as many points in a championship match and their coach Bernard Laporte reacted by demanding his side give up wine and cigarettes in order to compete with les rosbifs.   (Guardian)

PRETENTIOUSNESS INDEX **Nil** WHEN USED BY THE FRENCH, PERHAPS **!** WHEN USED BY THE ENGLISH.

French dictionaries will claim that *rosbif* is a pejorative term for 'English', like 'limey'. If so, it is one that has been taken up with enthusiasm by some on this side of the Channel, particularly sports writers (as above), probably because there are associations of beef with strength, appetite, etc.

ROUÉ *roo-eh* (French)

'dissolute person', 'rake':

Still, old roue Sven is not entirely averse to clasping the bosom of the establishment, according to the testimony of a comely Telegraph journalist.

(Guardian)

PRETENTIOUSNESS INDEX **Nil**

The origins of *roué* are grim, since one of the meanings of the verb *rouer* is to 'break on the wheel', probably the most agonising form of public execution ever devised. The term was used by a French nobleman about his debauched companions, as if they were deserving of such a punishment. Applications of *roué* now tend to be milder, indeed almost affectionate and often preceded by 'old'.

RUSE DE GUERRE *rooz de gerr* (French)

'one-off plan or action to trick the enemy in wartime':

Flying the American flag as a ruse de guerre, Fancourt hoped to delay any French response until he had landed some 700 American rangers.

(Daily Telegraph)

PRETENTIOUSNESS INDEX **Nil**

The *ruse de guerre*, a justified piece of trickery, tends to be confined to genuine warfare but the phrase might be used in contexts where military terms are thought suitable (e.g. an election campaign).

RUS IN URBE *roos in ur-bay* (Latin)

literally the 'country in the city' and so describing the attempt to produce a countryside atmosphere in an urban setting:

The answer is to take a leisurely stroll through London's verdant royal parks [...] Throw in a little boating, add a few ice creams and a snooze in a deckchair, and this could be the perfect rus in urbe short break.

(Daily Telegraph)

PRETENTIOUSNESS INDEX *!*

Rus in urbe goes right back to the first century AD, showing that the desire to pretend you're in the country while enjoying the benefits of the city is nothing new. The phrase can apply to a building, an atmosphere, etc. and, while relatively rare, does convey an old idea in an economical way.

S

SALON *sahlon* (French)

originally a 'drawing/reception room' and then used to describe the 'group (artistic/political) which a fashionable woman gathers round her':

> *It's always a bit of a downer to describe a social circle around a woman as a salon.* (Daily Telegraph)

PRETENTIOUSNESS INDEX *!*

The *salon* might have once been something quite grand, whether it designated a room or an artistic circle. Now the term is more often associated with hair care and beauty maintenance.

SALON DES REFUSÉS *sahlon day refu-zay* (French)

'collection of those who have been refused elsewhere', 'display of rejects':

> *I am delighted to report that the backbenchers, the huge salon des refuses, hot, cross and resentful, are finally rebelling.* (Guardian)

PRETENTIOUSNESS INDEX *!!*

Salon des refusés has a specific historical reference. The Salon in nineteenth century Paris was an annual exhibition of works by living artists. In 1863 Napoleon III demanded another exhibition to accommodate those who'd been turned down by the Salon – hence *salon des refusés*. The expression is not widespread but it's a nice way of conjuring up a bunch of vaguely discontented individuals, as in the *Guardian* quote above.

SAMIZDAT *pronounced as spelled* (Russian)

'self-published literature'; in the former Soviet Union, 'texts which were produced and circulated privately because of political censorship'; any 'privately circulated material which may incur disapproval':

My sexual fantasies were sustained by magazines that were risibly chaste by today's standards, passed furtively from hand to hand like samizdat.

(Guardian)

PRETENTIOUSNESS INDEX *!* IF USED ABOUT ANYTHING WHICH IS NOT REALLY CENSORED OR SUPPRESSED.

The era of *samizdat* in the USSR came before the time of *glasnost* and *perestroika* (see entries). These publications were not for the public, but produced on secret presses and passed from hand to hand for fear of political persecution. The term can be used out of context to describe any text which is distributed surreptitiously, although there's a worthiness about true *samizdat* material which doesn't really apply to sex mags, despite the *Guardian* example above.

SANCTUM SANCTORUM   *pronounced as spelled*   (Latin)

'holy of holies (in a temple)', 'most sacred place':

This serial fibber [...] told a witting untruth in the sanctum sanctorum, the Chamber of the House of Commons.   (Daily Telegraph)

PRETENTIOUSNESS INDEX *!*

Sanctum sanctorum is sometimes used literally but is more often found with a touch of irony, as in the example.

SANG FROID   *song-fwah*   (French)

literally 'cold blood' and so 'self-possession', 'calmness in a dangerous situation':

For her brother she cycled twice to Paris, going through numerous checkpoints and heavy German formations, escaping detection even when frisked, thanks to her sang-froid.   (The Times)

PRETENTIOUSNESS INDEX **Nil**

Sang froid means 'coolness' but it lacks the ambiguity of that English term (a cool person may be 'calm' or 'aloof' – or, most likely now, 'excellent'). The French expression combines the physical and the psychological in a way that no English equivalent does.

SANS-CULOTTE   *son-koolot*   (French)

literally 'without knee-breeches'. The expression was used as an insult in pre-Revolutionary France to describe those republicans or revolutionaries who wore trousers rather than the breeches

favoured by the aristocrats. So *sans-culotte* describes a radical individual, originally of a rather unrespectable kind:

> ...*the house of English fiction [in 1970] looked like a shabby, suburban Edwardian rectory. If you wanted to find energy or originality, you had to go down the road to the pub. There, in an upstairs room, you might find contemporary playwrights at work: Pinter in his prime, or the young sans-culottes like Christopher Hampton, Trevor Griffiths and David Hare.*
>
> (Observer)

PRETENTIOUSNESS INDEX *!*

Sans-culotte has acquired a slightly romantic tinge and understanding the word may depend on a glancing familiarity with its historical origins. The term has a touch of flamboyance, which is odd when one considers that it's about preferring trousers to breeches.

SATURNALIA *satter-nay-lee-ah* (Latin)

in Roman times a 'period of three days in mid-December in honour of Saturn, the god of agriculture, and a time of festivity'; by extension any 'period of wild revelry':

> *In 1973, he relocated the review to an office in his home on 72nd Street, New York, where his parties became a preppy, literary, alcoholic, heterosexual alternative to the nightly saturnalia at Andy Warhol's Studio 54.*
>
> (Guardian)

PRETENTIOUSNESS INDEX *!*

A *saturnalia* (usually without a capital letter and treated as a singular noun) is more of an orgy than a party. The Roman *Saturnalia* (capitalised, plural) were marked by the temporary freeing of slaves which perhaps explains the anarchic associations of the word. If any condemnation is intended by a contemporary application, it's going to be of a fairly literary and obscure kind.

SAUVE QUI PEUT *sove key peuh* (French)

literally 'save who can' and so applicable to any situation of panic or disorder where every person struggles to preserve himself without regard to others:

> *All this might have put Mr Taubman in the clear, had it not been for the sauve-qui-peut climate of panic that was created by the relentless, four-year investigation.* (Guardian)

Sauve qui peut is more elegant than 'panic' or 'rout', though that is what it means. The phrase tends to be used not about literal life-or-death catastrophes (such as the sinking of the Titanic) but about situations in which, say, one person will give evidence against old associates in order to save himself from jail.

SAVANT *sa-von* (French)

'learned person':

With his groomed beard and trim physique, the American writer-director is neater and less cuddly than Silent Bob, the stoned savant he has played in each of his first five movies. (Daily Telegraph)

PRETENTIOUSNESS INDEX **!**

A *savant* – the term is often used of scientists – is more than someone who is erudite or well educated. There is the implication of charisma and cultishness about the term too. A *savant* is likely to have followers.

SAVOIR FAIRE *savwah fer* (French)

literally 'know how to do'; 'instinctive awareness of the right thing to do':

His astuteness and his political contacts brought a much needed savoir faire to the organisation. (Daily Telegraph)

PRETENTIOUSNESS INDEX **Nil**

Perhaps the key point about *savoir faire* is that it's not knowledge which has been laboriously acquired but rather an intuitive sense of what behaviour is appropriate, particularly in social situations. 'Tact' is probably the nearest and simplest English equivalent but that doesn't quite suggests the worldliness that goes with *savoir faire*.

SCHADENFREUDE *shah-den-froyde* (German)

'pleasure in the misfortunes or embarrassment of others':

It is a peculiarly British schadenfreude and it's weird that we need a German word to describe it. When we moved to Tuscany last April I was genuinely surprised at how delighted people were (not, obviously, our real friends) that we found it difficult at first. (The Times)

Schadenfreude is a very useful and very popular term, the current Chardonnay of foreign phrases imported into English – always there whether you like it or not. This one word contains so much, and encapsulates a pretty universal human response. As the writer (Anna Blundy) of the passage above says, it's odd that we possess no English equivalent. It must be British self-denial rather than niceness... The opposite of *Schadenfreude* is *Erfolgsneid* – envy/displeasure at friends' success.

SCHLEMIEL   *shle-meal*   (Yiddish; also **shlemiel**)

'foolish person', 'clumsy, bungling person':

...anyone who goes there [New York] for a weekend's shopping and thinks they're some sort of sophisticat is, as I suspected, a real schlemiel who deserves to have their passport taken away for playing Supermarket Sweep with such a complex and, after a fashion, dignified city.   (Guardian)

Pretentiousness Index **!**

Yiddish is rich in terms for 'fool', and *schlemiel* – possibly derived from an Old Testament figure – is perhaps not as expressive as *klutz* or *schmuck*. One for the connoisseur of Yiddish insults, therefore.

SCHLEPP   *shlep*   (Yiddish; also **schlep** and **shlepp**)

'drag', 'move slowly':

Dvorak's cello concerto is always exciting but we have long since stopped schlepping to the Wigmore Hall.   (The Times)

Pretentiousness Index **Nil**

Schlepp implies a journey that's tedious and made with effort. It's an oddly expressive term, perhaps because the sound of the word suggests a kind of slurred or dragged step. *Schlepp* can also take an object – that is, you can *schlepp* things about the place.

SCHLOCK   *shlock*   (Yiddish; also **shlock**)

'trashy', 'cheap, inferior goods':

Instead of critical analysis, the public is being fed self-serving affirmation: war-time schlock designed to underpin the unique calling, manifest destiny and selfless heroism of the US nation and, above all, its superhuman presidents.   (Guardian)

PRETENTIOUSNESS INDEX *!*

More frequent in US slang than British English, *schlock* is well understood on this side of the Atlantic too. Both noun and adjective (also in the form *schlocky*), *schlock* generally relates to something which is offered for public consumption, whether goods or ideas.

SCHMALTZ *shmalts* (Yiddish; also **shmaltz**)

'nauseatingly sentimental stuff':

This wasn't argument, though, but standard celebrity schmaltz, poured on in industrial quantities by everyone from Miss Piggy [...] to Billy Joel.
(Independent)

PRETENTIOUSNESS INDEX **Nil**

Derived from the German word for cooking fat, *schmaltz* is an invaluable term to describe certain pieces of music and film, celebrity bashes and so on. Straightforward sentimentality may sometimes have the excuse of naivety or innocence, but *schmaltz* is calculated and cynical. (There is also the adjectival form, *schmaltzy*.)

SCHMOOZE *shmooze* (Yiddish)

'chatter', 'talk intimately':

Seriously successful people were doing some serious schmoozing.
(Independent)

PRETENTIOUSNESS INDEX *!*

Although US/Yiddish in origin, *schmooze* is quite often found in the UK. The term may now convey more than a simple heart-to-heart talk and, as in the *Independent* example above, it can carry overtones of manipulation or networking.

SCHMUCK *shmuk* (Yiddish)

'foolish, contemptible person':

What kind of base and brainless schmucks are these people to worship somebody who, number one, never existed ...   (Philip Roth, *Portnoy's Complaint*)

PRETENTIOUSNESS INDEX *!*

Schmuck is also slang for 'penis' and an abusive term when applied to an individual as (perhaps) the sound of the word indicates.

SCHNORRER *pronounced as spelled* (Yiddish)

'beggar':

> *I haven't actually done it yet, but I am tempted to write back to these remorseless charities saying 'lay off, you schnorrer, or I'll cancel my original banker's order.'* (Guardian)

PRETENTIOUSNESS INDEX **!**

Not often found in British English, *schnorrer* conveys the sense of moral entitlement on the beggar's part – he will see himself almost as a professional, helping the fortunate donors to discharge their charitable duty.

SCHTICK *shtik* (Yiddish; also **shtick** and **shtik**)

'stage act' and so 'gimmick' or 'special routine':

> *Pierce Brosnan will discuss why he's not returning as James Bond, despite having rescued the franchise with his super-smooth schtick ten years ago.*
>
> (The Times)

PRETENTIOUSNESS INDEX **!**

Like many Yiddish terms, *schtick* resists an easy translation into an English equivalent, and has several more definitions than those given above. Also like them, it is more common in the US than in Britain. Nevertheless, we can grasp at its meaning.

SEPPUKU *sepoo-coo* (Japanese)

'suicide by cutting open the stomach':

> *The prime minister is in Japan, where a train driver once commited seppuku – self-disembowelment – after bringing in the emperor's train two minutes late.* (Guardian)

PRETENTIOUSNESS INDEX **Nil**

Seppuku is an alternative expression to the more familiar *hara kiri* (see entry), and describes a similarly ritualistic and grisly method of committing suicide.

SHAMAN *shay-man* (Russian)

'priest-healer', 'someone with spiritual powers of guidance or healing':

He truly believes that he speaks for all the forgotten people of Britain and, like all shaman, there is more than a hint of truth in what he says. (The Times)

PRETENTIOUSNESS INDEX **Nil**

There have been *shamans* in cultures as widely scattered as Siberia and the North American Indians. When the term is applied to anyone in a 'secular' western context, it suggests someone who is in touch with secret, spiritual sources. It may be hard to avoid giving the impression that the word is sometimes an alternative for 'charlatan'.

SHIBBOLETH *shib-eleth* (Hebrew)

literally an 'ear of corn' or a 'stream'. In the Old Testament book of Judges, the men of Gilead, who were at war with the men of Ephraim, used the word *shibboleth* as a means of preventing the Ephraimites from escaping across the river Jordan. The men of Ephraim couldn't pronounce 'sh', saying *sibboleth* instead (Judges, 12, 5–6). Hence *shibboleth* comes to mean a 'distinguishing mark or feature':

Clothes aside, you can tell Jonathan Meades is a dandy by his use of the word 'dandiacal', which is the dandy's shibboleth, and he exhibits all the dandiacal traits. (Daily Telegraph)

By an extension of meaning, *shibboleth* can also describe any 'old or unquestioned idea or set of beliefs':

America's centre of gravity has moved rightward, creating a set of shibboleths that cannot be challenged. (Guardian)

PRETENTIOUSNESS INDEX **Nil**

Shibboleth is a strange word, surviving thousands of years from the time of the Old Testament and still in quite widespread use. Its application seems to me to be faintly pejorative, with the second definition (of 'unquestioned belief') taking precedence over the sense of 'distinguishing mark'.

SHIKSE *shiksy* (Yiddish; also **shiksa**)

'non-Jewish girl or woman':

Dad dear, a question has just occurred to me, twenty-five years later [...]: why did you bring a shikse, *of all things, into the house? Because you couldn't believe that a gentile woman should go through life without the experience of eating a dish of Jewish jello?* (Philip Roth, *Portnoy's Complaint*)

Shikse is largely a US word which, unlike some other Yiddish expressions, has not established a foothold in British English. It is a disparaging term, as the quotation above suggests.

SHTUM   *pronounced as spelled*   (also **schtum, stumm**) (Yiddish)

'silent', 'dumb':

Andrew Sullivan, discussing why The New York Times and Washington Post both kept schtum about the relationship, opined that it was 'striking how even allegedly liberal outlets routinely excise the homosexual dimension from many people's lives – even from someone dead.'   (The Times)

PRETENTIOUSNESS INDEX **Nil**

This is a well-accepted expression deriving from Yiddish and the US. One keeps *schtum* about something which it may be compromising or even risky to reveal to anyone else. The way the mouth clamps shut when saying the word aloud is a neat reflection of its meaning.

SHTUP   *pronounced as spelled*   (Yiddish)

'have sex with':

And then there is the sexually insatiable one, Gabrielle [...], who is shtupping the gardener on a regular basis ...   (Independent)

PRETENTIOUSNESS INDEX **!**

In respectable usage *shtup* means 'push', but in what dictionaries call the vulgar vernacular it has the sexual sense given above. Although not often used in British English, *shtup* provides an easily understandable alternative to euphemisms such as 'sleep with' or the less acceptable colloquialisms which still require all those ******* stars. Let's hear it more often.

SIC   *pronounced as spelled*   (Latin)

'thus'; used (in brackets) when something is being quoted, and a writer wishes to show that a mistake in spelling or grammar, or a questionable statement, is not his but is to be found in the original:

...reports from China and Japan about something Soft Seaweed Defating [sic] Soap ...   (Independent on Sunday)

The atmosphere outside Reno's, where a green sign promised 'Entertainement' [sic] inside, was boisterous but unthreatening. (The Times)

PRETENTIOUSNESS INDEX **Nil**

Sic is immensely useful in certain contexts, and not only those where the writer wants to show he or she is more intelligent than the source which is being quoted. It is a very compact way of indicating doubt about material which is not your own.

SIC TRANSIT GLORIA MUNDI *pronounced as spelled* (Latin; generally shortened to **sic transit**)

'so passes the glory of the world':

I shall miss my readers, who wrote the most literate, courteous and inform-ative letters of any I have ever had from readers of any newspaper. Sic transit, my dears.

(Germaine Greer signing off on her last gardening column in the Daily Telegraph)

PRETENTIOUSNESS INDEX *!*

Sic transit gloria mundi was coined by the medieval Augustinian monk Thomas à Kempis to describe the inevitable transitoriness of all earthly things, however glorious and successful. As likely to be used tongue-in-cheek now as seriously, the phrase still retains a kind of melancholy. Everything must pass, even gardening columns…

SIMPATICO *pronounced as spelled* (Spanish)

'pleasing', 'easy to like':

Neither charismatic nor 'simpatico', he still managed to draw a crowd – according to his own estimate – of around 800,000 people. (Guardian)

PRETENTIOUSNESS INDEX *!*

Like the French *sympathique* (see entry), Spanish *simpatico* is different from the English 'sympathetic', since it is more to do with the feelings or responses which an individual inspires rather than those which he or she gives out. Also like *sympathique*, the word can be used of place and atmosphere.

SINE DIE *sinnee dee-eh* (Latin)

literally 'without day'; 'indefinitely':

Last week Parliament passed the new Civil Contingencies Act, which gives the government astonishing powers to declare and prolong a state of emergency sine die. (Spectator)

PRETENTIOUSNESS INDEX **Nil**

Sine die is a technical (usually legal) phrase indicating that some business has been adjourned or suspended without any date being set for its resumption.

SINE QUA NON *sinnee qua non* (Latin)

literally 'without which not' and so applying to anything which is 'vital' or 'essential':

The environmental label is the sine qua non of a successful module, degree or grant application. (Guardian)

PRETENTIOUSNESS INDEX **Nil**

Sine qua non can be used both adjectivally and as a noun phrase (as above). I suspect it has more force than 'essential', also both noun and adjective, if only because the English equivalent has been watered down through casual use ('10 essential things you'll need for a fun holiday'). But a *sine qua non* really is essential, because without it you will not get what you want.

SMORGASBORD *smawges'bawd* (Swedish)

'assortment of light dishes in a buffet meal'; 'variety', 'mixture':

…sex is portrayed in the media as some sort of enormous sensual smorgasbord … (The Times)

PRETENTIOUSNESS INDEX **Nil**

Smorgasbord is probably used less often in a literal sense than it is metaphorically to mean a 'medley'. And I would take a small bet than many of those metaphorical applications are to do with sex – it must be the Swedish origins of the term or perhaps because it contains an anagram of 'orgasm'. Seriously.

SOBRIQUET *so-bree-kay* (French; also **soubriquet**)

'nickname', 'assumed name':

Hablot Knight Browne worked as Dickens's principal illustrator for more than 20 years [...] He signed his first illustrations for Pickwick 'N.E.M.O.', but thereafter adopted the sobriquet 'Phiz', short for 'physiognomy', the popular pseudo-science of inferring character from facial features. (Spectator)

Sobriquet falls between the two definitions given above. It's a more dignified term than 'nickname' yet it does not carry the implications of deception which sometimes go with 'assumed name'. So it does a job which no English expression is quite fitted to do.

(See also *cognomen*.)

SOI-DISANT *swa-deez-on* (French)

'self-styled', 'so-called':

> *The philistines of* le nouveau monde *are ruining us by flooding the market with their execrable* soi-disant *'easy drinking' wine.* (The Times)

Pretentiousness Index **Nil**

Soi-disant applies both to a person who gives himself some inappropriate title, attribute, etc. and to anything which is misleadingly labelled or described, as in the 'easy drinking' wine above. There's an element of pretension (for people) and pretence (for things) to the term. However, it avoids the directness of 'so-called'.

SOIGNÉ *swahnyay* (French)

'well turned-out', 'elegant':

> *A tatty, claustrophobic box has been magically made over into a soigné supper club, with a mouthwatering selection of Stephen Sondheim items on the menu.* (Guardian)

Pretentiousness Index *!*

Soigné can be applied to places or people (and their clothes). One of those terms with a spider's-web of meanings, it encompasses ideas of smoothness, sophistication, etc.

SOIXANTE-NEUF *swa-sonnt-nerf* (French)

literally 'sixty-nine' or 69 – a visual/numeric way of referring to the sexual position in which a couple orally stimulate each other's genitals:

> *One wonders what the good sister would have made of the Chapman brothers' two blow-up dolls clamped in an eternal, lock-jawed soixante-neuf that sent one prominent TV correspondent spluttering from the gallery accusing the Tate of 'being party to the cynical degradation of women'.*

> (Guardian)

Once again the French come to our sexual rescue. Any dictionary definition or translation of *soixante-neuf* sounds po-faced. But the '69' formulation is both elegant and economic, as well as avoiding such clunking expressions as 'orally stimulate' (see my definition above).

SOTTO VOCE   *sot'to(w) vochay*   (Italian)

literally 'below the voice'; 'in an aside', 'in a muted way':

> *At the outset, both Palestinians and Israelis were fairly unimpressed, with officials on both sides suggesting,* sotto voce, *that it might have more to do with Mr Blair's domestic agenda post-Iraq than the future of the region.*

> (Independent)

PRETENTIOUSNESS INDEX **Nil**

Like an aside in a theatre, anything delivered *sotto voce* is meant to be heard but not necessarily by everyone. It's a more expressive way of saying 'confidentially'.

SOUPÇON   *soup-sonn*   (French)

originally 'suspicion' and so 'trace', 'tiny amount':

> *It's [environmental science] got everything: business, politics, economics, love and hate, rich and poor, science and art, and also, for comic relief, a* soupçon *or two of sheer gormless stupidity.*   (Guardian)

PRETENTIOUSNESS INDEX **!**

Soupçon doesn't do much that wouldn't be done by 'trace' or 'hint'. It implies a recipe – although now replaced in cooking by terms such as 'pinch' or 'dash' – and so is quite a handy term when a final, tiny item is to be added to a list. There's a faintly humorous overtone to the word.

SPIEL   *shpeel*   (German)

literally 'game'; 'glib talk', 'sales routine':

> *With a mixture of ignorance and reluctance, I accepted this whole spiel as a looming reality – until last weekend, when I bowed to corporate pressure and bought an iPod.*   (Daily Telegraph)

PRETENTIOUSNESS INDEX **Nil**

This word, long established in English, is always used disparagingly. The individual who's on the receiving end of another person's *spiel* will always feel that he's being sold something – and probably sold short.

STATUS QUO   *pronounced as spelled*   (Latin)

literally the 'state in which'; 'existing state of affairs':

Some will console themselves by saying that we always have low turnouts for EU elections, and that last month many people were content with the status quo and confident of a Labour win.   (Observer)

Pretentiousness Index **Nil**

Very widely used, *status quo* says in two words what would require a more cumbersome English phrase. Although the expression does not pass judgement, since the *status quo* may good or bad or somewhere in-between, I suspect that the term is weighted slightly more in favour of the positive. If people didn't, on the whole, like what is the *status quo* it would not be the *status quo* for very long.

STATUS QUO ANTE   *status quo anti*   (Latin)

literally the 'state in which before'; the 'situation which existed before some change occurred':

Poole and Macleod soon fell out, notably on who should be the successor to Macmillan – and within six months the status quo ante *of having a single chairman had been restored.*   (The Times)

Pretentiousness Index **Nil**

The *status quo ante* shouldn't be confused with the *status quo*. The first one was the state of affairs then, the second is how things are now. However, *status quo ante* doesn't necessarily imply that something is finished with, since it can be used to describe a restoration or return to some former practice (as in the *Times* quote above).

STURM UND DRANG   *shterm unt drang*   (German)

literally 'storm and stress'; traditional phrase describing a 'period of turmoil':

Only when all the Sturm und Drang *had been left far behind would he tip his flak helmet back wearily on his sweating head …*   (Joseph Heller, *Catch-22*)

Pretentiousness Index **Nil**

Something of a specialist term, *Sturm und Drang* originally described an artistic and literary movement in Germany towards the end of the eighteenth century characterised by the display of strong emotions and action. The phrase is occasionally used to describe any general period of 'turbulence' (and in the example describes a bombing raid on German positions during World War Two).

SUB JUDICE   *sub yewdissay*   (Latin)

literally 'under a judge'; 'under consideration by a judge or a court':

American jurisprudence dispenses with such niceties as sub judice and permits in-court cameras.   (Guardian)

PRETENTIOUSNESS INDEX **Nil**

If a matter is *sub judice,* it is barred from being discussed or commented on in a public forum (for example, in Parliament or the media) so as to prevent the conduct of the case being prejudiced. Although a 'technical' term, *sub judice* is widely used.

SUBPOENA   *suh-peena*   (Latin)

literally 'under penalty'; 'legal writ requiring someone's attendance in court'; 'to issue such a writ':

The company also issued subpoenas to several news websites [...] demanding that they disclose the sources of leaked information about new Apple products.   (The Times)

PRETENTIOUSNESS INDEX **Nil**

The meaning of *subpoena* comes from the first two words appearing on a medieval writ, indicating that failure to appear as a witness in court would incur a penalty. In British legal terminology *subpoena* has been replaced by 'witness summons', but the original Latin term is still current in the USA.

SUB ROSA   *pronounced as spelled*   (Latin)

literally 'under the rose'; 'in confidence', 'secret':

It may have brought him only the sum of $15,000 – just over a modest £9,000 – but how did he honestly imagine he could keep the revelation sub rosa?   (Daily Telegraph)

PRETENTIOUSNESS INDEX *!*

The rose was once a symbol of secrecy and this supposedly accounts for the slightly odd expression. Until recently *sub rosa* – the phrase sometimes carrying suggestions not just of privacy but of something a bit dodgy or illicit – wasn't much used or understood, but the world-wide success of *The Da Vinci Code* has given it a higher profile. In that book, the rose (*'la fleur des secrets'*) is associated with the Holy Grail, secrecy, womanhood...

SUB SPECIE AETERNITATIS   *sub speky-ay-tern-itah-tis*   (Latin)

'from the perspective of eternity':

Sub specie aeternitatis *the most powerful intellects among us might be no different from jackdaws, which, ethologists tell us, cannot keep track of quantities past four.*   (Prospect)

PRETENTIOUSNESS INDEX *!*

This fairly uncommon phrase is used to put things in the ultimate perspective, that of an eternity where all distinctions, differences and troubles may not matter at all. Coined by the 17th-century philosopher Spinoza, *sub specie aeternitatis* is the counterpart of a perhaps yet more unusual expression, *sub specie temporis* ('from the perspective of time').

SUCCÈS D'ESTIME   *souksay d'esteem*   (French)

a 'critical success' (rather than one that attracts a big audience or makes a lot of money):

He founded CNN and built it into a succès d'estime *in global broadcasting, as well as a multi-million dollar business.*   (Observer)

PRETENTIOUSNESS INDEX *!*

There are several kinds of success in French (see below). A *succès d'estime* is the most refined. Depending on your point of view, it may even be the most valuable – but it will not draw the biggest crowds or earn the largest cheques. The term is occasionally employed as a kind of consolation prize for low turn-out or bad box-office.

SUCCÈS DE SCANDALE   *souksay de scondall*   (French)

'success (of a book, film, etc) because of some scandalous subject-matter or other notoriety connected to it':

On its original publication in 1907, the book [Elinor Glyn's Three Weeks] had a succès de scandale, *largely because it depicted the woman as the seducer, making the running in the relationship from a recumbent position on her cushions and famous tiger-skin rug.*   (Andrew Lycett, *Ian Fleming*)

Of the three types of *succès* given here, this is the expression most frequently used. Even so, a *succès de scandale* is more likely to occur when people are easily scandalised. It's hard to imagine any current *succès* being built on sexual shenanigans, which is what the term almost invariably referred to. So the expression tends to be found in a historical context.

SUCCÈS FOU   *souksay foo*   (French)

literally 'mad success'; 'wild success':

Whichever of these titles – or, indeed, one that we've completely overlooked – does become the succès fou *of Christmas 2004, the book you get three copies of and never open, we learn something about ourselves from the phenomenon.*   (Observer)

PRETENTIOUSNESS INDEX **!**

Of the three 'success' phrases (see above) *succès fou* is the least often found. By definition it offers no explanation for the success, and indeed it suggests that the enthusiasm behind it is irrational.

SUGGESTIO FALSI   *suggest-ee-o fall-si*   (Latin)

'suggestion of falsehood'
See *suppressio veri* below.

SUI GENERIS   *sue-ee generiss*   (Latin)

'of its own kind', 'unique':

Next day I was in California, and the presidential election was seething all around me. Here it was, though, an election sui generis, *because California is so big, so rich and so different that national issues here are inextricably entangled with issues peculiar to the Golden State.*   (The Times)

PRETENTIOUSNESS INDEX **Nil**

Sui generis is handy as a way of expressing the idea of uniqueness without the sometimes problematic quality of that word. Anything described as *sui generis* makes comparison difficult because it is the only one of its precise type.

SUMMUM BONUM   *pronounced as spelled*   (Latin)

'highest good':

Consumer choice is regarded as the summum bonum of human life,

which results in an assertive but often not very intelligent individualism.
(Daily Telegraph)

<small>PRETENTIOUSNESS INDEX</small> **Nil**

Summum bonum is an expression from ethical or philosophical discussion, describing a supreme (moral) objective which should guide choices, actions, etc.

SUPPRESSIO VERI *seppress-ee-o very* (Latin)

literally 'suppression of the truth' and so describing a kind of lying in which facts which ought to be made known are kept hidden so that the true state of affairs is misrepresented:

Worse still, perhaps, [they] were found to have misled the judge who dealt with the case last month 'by a mixture of suppressio veri and suggestio falsi' – suppressing truth and suggesting falsehoods. (Daily Telegraph)

<small>PRETENTIOUSNESS INDEX</small> *!*

Suppressio veri is almost always accompanied by its twin Latin phrase, *suggestio falsi* (as above). Both are ways of lying without explicitly saying something which is untrue. Rather, the truth is deliberately not brought to light (*suppressio veri*), while what is untrue is implied (*suggestio falsi*) but never openly stated. The expressions are fairly obscure and legalistic, perhaps, but they apply to quite a lot of everyday conversation.

SYMPATHIQUE *sam-pah-teek* (French)

'pleasant', 'likable':

Ruddy, smiling, as sympathique a businessman as one could hope to meet, Forgeard waxed lyrical over a fine 1994 St Emilion while hosting lunch at Airbus HQ last week. (Observer)

<small>PRETENTIOUSNESS INDEX</small> *!*

Sympathique can be used of places and people, indicating that they are an agreeable fit to the mood of the person so describing them. The word is different from the English 'sympathetic', which generally occupies an area somewhere between understanding and pity.
See also *simpatico*.

T

TABLEAU VIVANT   *tab-lo vee-von*   (French)

literally 'living picture'; describing 'motionless figures arranged in some scene':

> *Up the stairs [of IKEA] they went along the only route available – the one that forces them through dozens of tableaux vivants (little theatre sets representing the nation's living rooms, very similar to the ones in the catalogue – except for the dirt).*   (Daily Telegraph)

PRETENTIOUSNESS INDEX **Nil**

A slightly technical term, *tableau vivant* applies to Madame Tussaud-style depictions of scenes and events against a realistic background. In the *Telegraph* example above, the rooms were presumably displayed without figures but the intention was to give the impression of 'real' places.

TABULA RASA   *tabula ra-za*   (Latin)

literally a 'scraped tablet' and so a 'clean slate'; something or somebody 'untouched by external impressions':

> *Our tendency [is] to paint political fantasies on to countries such as Ukraine which are tabula rasa for us.*   (Guardian)

PRETENTIOUSNESS INDEX **Nil**

Tabula rasa is not used literally, although the phrase originates with the writing-tablet which could be scraped clean to take more impressions. The expression can have the liberating meaning of the 'clean slate' by which someone is offered a fresh start. But more usually there is an ominous ring to *tabula rasa* since it suggests that whatever has been cleared of previous impressions – the mind of a child, an entire country (as in the quote above) – is ready to be written over by *somebody else.*

TAEDIUM VITAE   *tedium vee-tie*   (Latin)

'weariness of life':

Indeed, there are several aspects of human existence in a modern techno-logical world, it seems to me, that add to taedium vitae.   (The Times)

PRETENTIOUSNESS INDEX *!*

Taedium vitae is more than simple world-weariness or *ennui* (see entry) since the phrase hints at a disgust with life. It may be as much a philosophical or spiritual state as an emotional one.

TANT PIS   *ton pee*   (French)

'so much the worse', 'too bad':

Some critics [...] used to argue that, though admirable, these qualities so inhibited Enright that he lacked the amoral ferocity which great poetry requires. Tant pis, he would surely have replied.   (Guardian)

PRETENTIOUSNESS INDEX *!*

Tant pis pretty well has to be accompanied by a shrug of the shoulders and a little pout of the lips. Perhaps that is why it has never really caught on in English where anyway we have the perfectly serviceable 'too bad'. There is an opposite to *tant pis* in *tant mieux* – 'so much the better' – but I have been unable to find any examples of it in newspapers or elsewhere.

TENDRESSE   *ton-dress*   (French)

'tenderness', 'partiality', 'fondness':

Let me state, first of all, that this tendresse *for a key Blair ally has noth-ing to do with rumoured ambitions of of Rebekah's husband Ross Wade (Ross Kemp as was) to become a Labour MP.*   (Independent)

PRETENTIOUSNESS INDEX *!*

There are several English equivalents for *tendresse,* and it tends to be used when the writer wants to distance himself from a display of 'affection', either by the mild mockery of employing this arch French word in English or by questioning the motivation behind it (as in the example).

TERMINUS AD QUEM   *terminus ad kwem*   (Latin)

literally 'the end to which'; 'destination', 'the finishing-point of some project, argument, etc.':

In producing the original DNB [Dictionary of National Biography], the editors chose the end of the 19th century as their *terminus ad quem*, extending it to the date when the Queen died in January 1901. (Spectator)

Not often found, *terminus ad quem* may seem no more than an elaborate way of saying end-point, but the phrase does suggest that the destination is the one which was intended all along (rather than being arbitrarily chosen) and the word *terminus* gives a finality to the plan.

TERRA FIRMA *pronounced as spelled* (Latin)

'solid ground', 'dry land':

Lines were thrown ashore and for the first time since Nov 28 last year the trimaran made contact with terra firma. (Daily Telegraph)

One of those Latin phrases thoroughly established in general English, *terra firma* originally applied to large land masses rather than islands. Now used as a simple contrast to anything which isn't the sea.

TERRA INCOGNITA *terra incogneeta* (Latin)

'unknown territory':

This is New York's meatpacking district, a place long associated with tough blue-collar labour and which used to be terra incognita to most city-dwellers. (Daily Telegraph)

The phrase appeared on the earliest maps to signify those areas of the world which had never been explored. There isn't much *terra* left now which is truly *incognita*. However, the expression can still describe a place which is unknown to many, as in the quote above. It can also describe a metaphorical area of experience or learning ('Quantum physics is *terra incognita* for me').

TÊTE A TÊTE *tett-ah-tett* (French)

literally 'head to head' and so 'in private conversation':

The 72-year-old French leader […] also said that he believed he could influence Mr Bush if the pair could dine en tête-a-tête *when they meet on February 21.* (The Times)

As well as suggesting a confidential conversation, *tête-a-tête* is a valuable alternative to both 'face to face' and 'put heads together', since it lacks the slightly aggressive overtones of the former and the touch of intimacy in the second.

TOUR DE FORCE   *pronounced as spelled*   (French)

'feat of skill', 'very impressive performance':

James Wilby's reading is a tour de force of varied pace and tone, energetic, menacing and tender by turn.   (The Times)

PRETENTIOUSNESS INDEX **Nil**

Despite the implication of strength in the original French, *tour de force* is more to do with accomplishment and perhaps stamina. It almost always relates to some public performance, a single 'turn' sustained at the highest level of skill.

TOUR D'HORIZON   *tour d'orryzon*   (French)

literally a 'tour of the horizon' and so a 'wide-ranging survey':

This usually stretches to the first couple of pages of each chapter, the rest being filled in with an anthropological tour d'horizon of the many weird and wonderful ways by which people seek to improve on the appearance of their nose, lips, eyes or whatever.   (Daily Telegraph)

PRETENTIOUSNESS INDEX **!**

Tour d'horizon conjures up the image of an explorer leading the less well-travelled to some distant or obscure points in the landscape. It's more exotic than 'survey', which is essentially what it means.

TOUT COURT   *too core*   (French)

'simply, 'without anything extra':

Offal is off today, thankfully, but the meal he dishes up is nevertheless distinctly Meadesian, comprising a plate of brown meat tout court, with no vegetables, bread, pasta, or rice.   (Daily Telegraph)

PRETENTIOUSNESS INDEX **!**

There are several English phrases which would do the same job as *tout court* – 'that's it', 'in short' – but they don't have the elegant finality of the French expression.

TOUT LE MONDE *too le mond* (French)

'all the world', 'everyone':

We agree that while winter, spring and autumn are owned by tout le monde, summer is a fascist season, belonging almost exclusively to the young and the beautiful. (Observer)

PRETENTIOUSNESS INDEX *!*

Tout le monde appears in slightly humorous or camp contexts, and hasn't got the muscle to be used a serious synonym for 'everybody'.

TRAHISON DES CLERCS *trayzon day clerr* (French)

literally 'treachery of the clerks'; 'intellectual betrayal'. The phrase comes from the title of a book, *La Trahison des Clercs* (1927) by French writer and philosopher Julien Benda (1867–1956), and applies to the way in which some intellectuals betray their integrity by supporting causes which contradict the standards of honesty or morality they are supposed to uphold:

There's a phrase for what is happening – 'Trahison des clercs', or treason of the intellectuals, who glamorise drugs because they are too vain and stupid to understand what is really happening out on the unfashionable, hidden-away ghettos and estates of this country. (Guardian)

PRETENTIOUSNESS INDEX **Nil**

Although this is a fairly rarefied phrase, it has some force as an accusation or a piece of mud-slinging (depending on which side of the fence you are standing). Underlying it is the idea of an absolute standard to which intellectuals (the 'clercs' in French) should adhere, and from which they deviate when they distort the truth for racial or political reasons – or simply out of a desire to be fashionable (as in the *Guardian* passage above).

TRIAGE *tree-ahj* (French)

'sorting out'; in medicine the 'sorting of patients (particularly in war) according to those who most urgently need treatment and are most likely to survive':

As the wounded arrived on ships shuttling from Le Havre to Southampton, they were graded in a massive triage system and those who could travel were moved to one of 18 field hospitals built on Salisbury Plain, or to other facilities around the country. (Daily Telegraph)

Triage is a specialist term although one in quite widespread use, especially in the context of war or large-scale disaster. Originating in an old French word for 'sift', *triage* entails giving priority medical attention to those most likely to benefit from it and to survive afterwards.

TRICOTEUSE   *tree-cotterz*   (French)

'woman who knits'. The word was used to describe those women who, during the French Revolution, were present at public meetings or executions by guillotine and who sat and knitted throughout:

> *This new aristocracy may not have inherited its wealth and power, but it throws its weight about in a conspicuous fashion, filling us with the contempt the tricoteuses displayed for the aristos stepping up to the guillotine.*
>
> (Observer)

PRETENTIOUSNESS INDEX **Nil**

This is a word with a fairly precise historical application although it could be used to describe the attitude – one of gloating or anger – of those who watch the downfall of their enemies.

TRISTESSE   *treess-tess*   (French)

'sorrow', 'melancholy':

> *It all contributes to the hangover: a complex psychological result of consuming your bodyweight in dodgy rosé for 10 nights straight, combined with the sobering tristesse involved in realising that the party's almost over.*
>
> (Guardian)

PRETENTIOUSNESS INDEX *!!*

Tristesse is sadness with attitude. The French may use the term straight – *Bonjour Tristesse* was the title of Françoise Sagan's classic novel of the 1950s – but when found in English the term is almost always going to have an ironic tinge (as in the example above) or will describe a slightly cultivated and artificial mood.

TROIKA   *troy-ka*   (Russian)

'[Russian] horse-drawn vehicle' or 'team of three horses'; any 'group of three':

> *Diplomats and officials in Vienna following the Iranian nuclear saga at*

the International Atomic Energy Agency [predict] a breakdown of the diplomatic track the EU troika of Britain, Germany and France are pursuing with Tehran. (Guardian)

Pretentiousness Index **Nil**

Troika is most frequently found in a diplomatic/political context, to describe any grouping of three countries in which the participants have a roughly equal weight. It can also describe a trio of leaders.

TROMPE L'OEIL *tromp l'oy* (French)

literally 'deceives the eye'; applied to painted surfaces, etc. which, through positioning and detail, are so 'real' that they may trick the viewer:

Apparently the philosopher G.E. Moore, who believed that reality is what we perceive with our senses, once gestured towards the far end of his lecture room with the words: 'We know that to be a window.' It was actually a trompe l'oeil. (Daily Telegraph)

Pretentiousness Index **Nil**

There is no English term which concisely conveys what's meant by *trompe l'oeil*. As with a conjuring trick, part of the pleasure lies in being deceived.

TSAR *zar* (Russian; also **czar**)

historically the 'supreme ruler of Russia'; 'person given wide powers to do a particular task':

The new position of intelligence tsar was a central recommendation of the commission set up to investigate September 2001. (The Times)

Pretentiousness Index *tsar* is not so much pretentious as silly in most of its applications.

The *tsar* didn't quite disappear with the Russian Revolution of 1917. Indeed, in recent years tsars have multiplied so that a country may have a drugs tsar (in charge of suppressing rather than selling them), a crime tsar, a fitness tsar, and so on. I'm not sure why this word from imperial Russia should be used as a description of what are often deliberately created government posts, of dubious value. Maybe people consider that someone with a little despotic authority is the only one likely to solve an apparently insuperable problem.

TSUNAMI *tsoonah'mee* (Japanese)

literally 'harbour wave' but applying to any 'giant wave produced by earthquake or volcanic activity'. Until the disaster of December 2004 the word was rarely used in its absolutely correct meaning but rather had the general sense of 'tidal wave':

> *Regional heats have whittled 100,000 children down to 50 who managed to beat the onomatopoeia trap and ride the tsunami of the first televised national spelling competition.*   (The Times)

PRETENTIOUSNESS INDEX *!!* UNLESS USED IN ITS PROPER SENSE TO DESCRIBE WAVES PRODUCED BY UNDERSEA EARTHQUAKES, ETC.

Even before the end of 2004 *tsunami* was an oddly popular word – one newspaper site alone registered more than 250 occurrences up to that point. Yet, if used figuratively (as in the *Times* quote above) what job does *tsunami* do that 'tidal wave' won't perform equally well? The answer is none at all.

U

ÜBER- *oober* (German)

literally 'over'; widely used as a prefix in front of a noun and meaning 'ultimate', 'super-':

The Obvious Diet – the diet book that does exactly what it says, by the uber-agent Ed Victor – is still fattening its author's pockets. (Independent)

Much embarrassment at the BBC's children's department after a dressing-down from Ofcom, the Uber-watchdog with responsibility for broadcasting standards. (Private Eye)

PRETENTIOUSNESS INDEX *!*

The English 'super-' could do the job almost as well, but not quite. *Uber* carries overtones not just of superiority but has a touch of ruthlessness too. This may be because of its slightly tainted association with the Nazis and their racist 'theories' of the *übermenschen* (literally, the Third Reich 'supermen' who were destined to inherit the earth). Whatever its background, *über-* is being thrown around a bit casually at the moment.

UKASE *yew'kaze* (Russian)

a 'government order' (particularly in tsarist Russia); 'decree':

Peter the Great issued an ukase ordering that all previous ukases be obeyed. The government must often feel similar frustration. (Guardian)

PRETENTIOUSNESS INDEX *!* IF USED OUTSIDE ITS RUSSIAN CONTEXT.

As well as the *ukase* from Russia, other languages give us terms for arbitrary government decrees, words such as the German *diktat* (see entry) and the Persian *firman*. When they are applied to the British situation, the implication may be such things are alien to our democracy. They must be, since we don't have a word of our own for it.

ULTIMA THULE   *ultima thool*   (Latin)

literally 'farthest Thule'. The reference is to an island or land-mass somewhere north of Britain discovered by a Greek navigator in the 4th century BC. Thule's identity isn't known; it may be the Shetland Islands or Iceland or part of Norway, or somewhere else altogether. For the Greeks and Romans it represented the northermost region in the world. Hence the phrase *ultima Thule* comes to mean the 'extreme limit', the place beyond which no one can go:

> *Syd Barrett, the ultima thule of pop hermits whose departure from the Pink Floyd in 1968 was on a par with, say, Mick Jagger, unable to cope with being a Rolling Stone after Not Fade Away, scurrying back to Dartford to live quietly with his parents.*   (Guardian)

PRETENTIOUSNESS INDEX **!**

Ultima Thule is an oddity, not very widely used and probably not always understood when it does appear. That a term first coined nearly two and a half millennia ago to describe an unidentified island should be used to describe the legendary drop-out from Pink Floyd demonstrates the inexplicable staying power of some expressions.

ULTRA VIRES   *ultra vie-reez*   (Latin)

'beyond the powers [of]' and almost always in the sense of 'outside the legal power or authority of a person or a group':

> *Another was overruling the appeals panel that reinstated pupils in a school after they had issued death threats to their teacher. [...] From the safety of my armchair, I suspect I would have erred on the side of caution and taken precisely the same action, even if it was ultra vires.*   (Guardian)

PRETENTIOUSNESS INDEX **Nil**

Ultra vires has inescapable legal overtones, since it indicates that whatever action is being undertaken is outside the authority or the remit of the person doing it.

UTOPIA   *yew-towpee-a*   (Greek)

literally 'no-place' and originally the title of a book by Sir Thomas More (1478–1535) about an '(imaginary) state which is ideal in its social/political arrangements'; a 'perfect world':

Few ideologues can resist the allure of a blank slate – that was colonialism's seductive promise: discovering wide-open new lands where utopia seemed possible. (Guardian)

<small>PRETENTIOUSNESS INDEX</small> **Nil**

A *utopia* is more earth-bound than *paradise*. The words are often used interchangeably but while *paradise* tends to be found in a natural setting (a paradise island, etc.) and occasionally has spiritual overtones, *utopia* is more often used to refer to a social set-up which might just be humanly achievable. *Utopian* is sometimes applied to people or schemes considered impractical or too idealistic.

V

VADE MECUM   *vah-dee may-cum*   (Latin)

literally 'go with me'; 'handbook', 'guidebook':

Bradley did the City volume six years ago, and made of it a revelatory narrative as well as an eye-opening vade mecum.   (Guardian)

PRETENTIOUSNESS INDEX **Nil**

Vade mecum is a weightier term than guidebook, which might do no more than list the top ten sites and the cheapest bars in a city. As the meaning of the Latin suggests, a *vade mecum* is a companion, one who directs the traveller or the serious sight-seer.

VENDETTA   *pronounced as spelled*   (Italian)

literally '(blood-thirsty) revenge'; 'feud', 'drawn-out quarrel':

My children have horror stories to tell about boys who duff people up or girls who wage bitchy vendettas.   (Daily Telegraph)

PRETENTIOUSNESS INDEX **Nil**

The origins of *vendetta*, connected with honour and murder, have been diluted in current usage, so that it may apply to nothing more than a protracted spat. Strictly speaking, a *vendetta* is two-sided although it is sometimes used to describe a unilateral campaign against some (usually innocent/helpless) individual.

VERBATIM   *ver-bay-tim*   (Latin)

'word for word':

Those managers who chose to read the accompanying briefing notes verbatim rather than use them as guidelines often had a hard time doing so with a straight face.   (Spectator)

PRETENTIOUSNESS INDEX **Nil**

Verbatim implies an exact copying of something said or written elsewhere.

VERBOTEN ver'bowten (German)

'forbidden':

But I'm much more punctual now and I enjoy dancing, eating out and so many things that for years were verboten. (Daily Telegraph)

PRETENTIOUSNESS INDEX **!**

There's no reason for employing *verboten* in place of 'forbidden' or 'not allowed' other than to conjure up half-hidden associations with German discipline and belief in authority and, inevitably, Nazism. Oddly, this is never done for serious purposes and almost any use of the word in English is going to have slightly comic overtones.

VERISMO veriz'mo (Italian)

'truth to life', 'realism in the arts':

Verismo is not Belle's strong suit either. Her clients are all smart, clean and able to perform without too much coaxing. (Independent on Sunday)

PRETENTIOUSNESS INDEX **!**

Verismo has a particular association with Italian literature and opera from the late nineteenth century onwards. When used outside the context of artistic theory, it doesn't mean much more than 'plausibility' or 'credibility', as in the example above.

VERNISSAGE verni-sahj (French)

literally 'varnishing'; 'private view of an art exhibition before the public are admitted':

So, on the morning after all the critics and curators have gone home, vernissage over and only people proper in the gardens, I take it in and guess what? (Guardian)

PRETENTIOUSNESS INDEX **!**

Originally *vernissage* described the day when painters came in and varnished their painting just before an exhibition opened. Now the only varnishing likely to be going on is alcoholic. The term has a slightly specialist quality – one for those in the know.

VIA CRUCIS vee-ah crew-sis (Latin)

literally the 'way of the cross', the route taken by Christ to crucifixion on Calvary; by extension, a 'very painful experience':

...when I started out, their first talk when [doctors] met in the corridor or the coffee room was of patients and their illnesses, but now it is of the evils of management, government directives, bureaucratic tasks imposed upon them, and so forth. A longing for the end of this via crucis is all-pervasive ...

(Spectator)

PRETENTIOUSNESS INDEX !

The religious associations of *via crucis* are still strong (the phrase describes the 'stations of the cross' which appear as shrines in some church interiors). Not a widely used phrase, *via crucis* should be reserved for something which is a genuine ordeal.

VICE ANGLAIS *veece anglay* (French)

the 'English vice', generally used to describe the supposed English taste for getting sexual satisfaction out of beating or other forms of corporal punishment:

Old generals, barristers, lords, bishops and admirals were peculiarly in thrall to whipping. Flagellation has long been recognised as le vice anglais, but the Victorians were especially enthusiastic about birching.

(Spectator)

PRETENTIOUSNESS INDEX !

There's not much to say about this. *Le vice anglais* has a Victorian ring, and an alleged fondness for it among the upper classes (see above) is sometimes said to have been encouraged by the epidemic of beating and whipping in nineteenth-century public schools. Equivalent contemporary expressions such as S&M may be more democratic but not so elegant.

VICE VERSA *pronounced as spelled* (Latin)

'the other way round':

...our TV listings abound with soap operas, game shows and bone-headed fly-on-the-wall documentaries. It was Britain that exported The Weakest Link and Anne Robinson to America, and not vice versa. (Spectator)

PRETENTIOUSNESS INDEX **Nil**

Vice versa is so well established in English that it appears all over the place. It doesn't achieve anything that 'the other way round' would not except for being two words rather than four, and that's enough to justify it.

VIS-À-VIS *veez-ah-vee* (French)

literally 'face to face'; 'opposite to', 'in relation to':

> *If Labour wins by a narrow majority, it would undoubtedly be interpreted as bad for Mr Blair, and weaken his position vis-a-vis the chancellor.*

> (Guardian)

PRETENTIOUSNESS INDEX **Nil**

The slightly conflicting meanings of this useful and familiar expression are explained by its 'face to face' source. Although generally used to mean no more than 'in connection with' or 'about', *vis-à-vis* carries a suggestion of opposing forces, of two individuals or things being set in a position which is, however faintly, adversarial.

VIVE LA DIFFÉRENCE *veev la differ-onse* (French)

'long live the difference':

> *Her French sensibilities were clearly offended by the thought of champagne being poured into a plastic cup. She bit her lip thoughtfully, disappeared round the corner and reappeared with a proper glass. [...] Vive la différence.* (Daily Telegraph)

PRETENTIOUSNESS INDEX **!**

This exclamation originally celebrated the distinctions between the sexes. But it more commonly seems to be used now about the differences between the French and the English, differences which help to preserve a sense of national identity but which also give pleasure when encountered on the 'other' side.

VIZ *pronounced as spelled* (Latin)

a shortened form of *videlicet*, meaning 'namely', and used in front of an explanation:

> *Whatever truths there might be in her complaints ... they didn't amount to grounds for leaving me. There had to be another reason, viz., another man.* (David Lodge, *Therapy*)

PRETENTIOUSNESS INDEX **Nil**

Highly useful, this word has been around in English for at least five centuries.

VOLTE-FACE *volt-fass* (French)

'turn around', 'complete change in point of view':

The most likely explanation for the astonishing volte face was a realisation that the implications of this tour collapsing could be catastrophic for the game in Zimbabwe. (Guardian)

PRETENTIOUSNESS INDEX **Nil**

Volte-face is widely used, even though there are several ways of expressing the same idea in English. One reason for the popularity of *volte-face* may be that the English equivalents like 'about-face' or 'turn around' are too literal-sounding or reminiscent of military commands.

VOULU *voo-loo* (French)

'deliberate', 'contrived':

Harry's amazement is Rowling's anticipation of her ideal reader's, and so as such, seems a little too voulu, a self-conscious attempt to work up our awe. (Guardian)

PRETENTIOUSNESS INDEX *!*

Voulu literally means 'wished', and describes anything which does not seem to arise spontaneously from a situation but has been imposed on it or introduced from outside. *Voulu* is arguably a more delicate term than any of its English equivalents, hinting at a criticism rather than directly stating it.

VOX POPULI *vox pop-ewe-lie* (Latin; usually shortened to **vox pop**)

literally 'voice of the people'; 'popular opinion', 'common talk':

Piece by piece, and hour by hour, Bowen follows the events and the players … as well as drawing on a vox populi *of soldiers and civilians caught up in the bloodbath [of the Arab/Israeli 1967 War].* (Guardian)

PRETENTIOUSNESS INDEX **Nil**

The longer version of this old expression is *vox populi, vox Dei* ('the voice of the people is the voice of God') but the original idea – whether meant cynically or not – of the people's voice being all-powerful has been lost in modern applications. Now the phrase tends to be used, sometimes disparagingly, to describe the canvassing of public opinion in snippets, usually through brief telly interviews in the street, phone polling, etc.

VOYEUR *voy-err* (French)

'person who gets sexual pleasure from watching others having sex'; any 'illicit spectator':

> *In contrast to the posturings of pornography, the sex here seems to stem from a recognisable physical attraction. Yet as there is little emotional involvement for the audience, the viewer is placed in the position of voyeur.*
>
> (Observer)

PRETENTIOUSNESS INDEX **Nil**

Voyeur is such a frequently used term that a definition is hardly necessary. We haven't really got a word of our own for it although we have a homely English equivalent in Peeping Tom (from the legend of Tom the Tailor who peeped at the naked Lady Godiva as she rode past). But a *voyeur* may be interested in more than people's sexual activity, and the word implies a stealthy – and unhealthy – desire to spy on others.

W, Y, Z

WALLAH   *pronounced as spelled*   (Hindi)

'someone with a (usually administrative) job in an organisation':

I take it from his use of 'bolshie' that the quoted UN wallah is British.

                                                   (Daily Telegraph)

PRETENTIOUSNESS INDEX **Nil**

The use of *wallah* is a legacy from British rule in India, and will presumably fade over time. Generally taken to mean 'fellow', the term *wallah* was and still is joined to types of work or institutions – office *wallah*, UN *wallah* – in a slightly dismissive way.

WANDERLUST   *pronounced as spelled*   (German)

literally 'wander-longing'; 'urge to travel constantly':

As The New Yorker pointed out this week, even Ernest Hemingway's wanderlust might have been given a cold shower by today's exchange rates.

                                                            (The Times)

PRETENTIOUSNESS INDEX **Nil**

In the days of budget airlines and week-end breaks, any romance and rarity associated with *wanderlust* has disappeared. Everybody's doing it.

WELTANSCHAUUNG   *veltan-shau'ung*   (German)

'view of the world, 'philosophy of life':

Janet [Street-Porter] recently declared to a nation on the edge of its seat that her policy on men is that of a hungry diner approaching a buffet […] this is only one of a number of culinary metaphors offered in the continuously evolving and slightly mad Street-Porter Weltanschauung.   (Independent)

PRETENTIOUSNESS INDEX GENERALLY **!**

Weltanschauung embodies an idea that would take several words to convey in English but the term is, arguably, more cumbersome – to non-German ears – than those alternative expressions. *Weltanschauung* can be used seriously, of course, but most English references (and there aren't many of them) are going to be tinged with a self-regarding humour.

WELTSCHMERZ *velt-shmertz* (German)

literally 'world-pain'; 'sadness at the state of the world', 'weary pessimism':

> *There he was, poised to write a light comedy of manners, when someone served him the pickled mushrooms. And then, bam! Doom, gloom and Weltschmerz all the way.* (Sunday Telegraph)

PRETENTIOUSNESS INDEX *!*

Although *Weltschmerz* can be used relatively lightly (as above), it is a term which gives weight, even dignity to what may be quite run-of-the-mill feelings of melancholy. It can also be used to describe a prevailing mood in some artistic production such as a cycle of songs.

WUNDERKIND *vun'derkint* (German)

literally 'wonder-child'; a 'very talented child' but more usually applied to 'anyone who is very successful or who shows great skill at some activity early in life':

> *As a former* wunderkind *of the museum world, lauded for his restoration of the state apartments at Hampton Court Palace after the fire, Thurley is regarded as knowledgeable, energetic and outspoken.* (The Times)

PRETENTIOUSNESS INDEX *!*

Despite the derivation of the word, *wunderkind* rarely describes a child. Instead it operates as a benign version of the *enfant terrible* (see entry), someone who's made his or her mark on the world at an early stage and in a style that provokes a slightly patronising admiration. The *wunderkind* tends to be found in the arts and occasionally on the football field.

YANG *pronounced as spelled* (Chinese)

in Chinese philosophy *yang* is the 'active male principle', light and warm, while *yin* is the colder and more passive 'feminine principle', each being necessary to the other, held in a state of balance and tension, etc. The two terms are almost always found together:

How clever of [hotel] owner Anouska Hempel to reflect 'the bi-polarity of the world between yin and yang, black and white, hot and cold' (Daily Telegraph)

PRETENTIOUSNESS INDEX **!!**

As with various imports from Chinese culture, such as *feng shui*, originally serious ideas have been largely reduced to advertising props or lifestyle adornments for the west.

YIN (see **yang** above)

YURT *pronounced as spelled* (Russian)

'circular tent in eastern Asia, made of skins over a wooden frame':

In the Film and Video Yurt, a tent near the monkey houses, I watched a video of a Japanese man with bunny ears and lipstick. (Guardian)

PRETENTIOUSNESS INDEX AS WITH OTHER TERMS IN THIS BOOK, THERE'S NOTHING WRONG WITH THE *YURT* IN ITSELF. ANY PRETENSION INVOLVED IS IN BUILDING YOURSELF ONE AND THEN SITTING INSIDE IT – FOR THAT AT LEAST **!!!** ARE NEEDED.

Yurts have enjoyed a vogue recently – originally used by Mongolian nomads, they have acquired an exotic, hippy-ish tinge in the west. Yak milk doesn't seem to have caught on, though.

ZAFTIG *zoftick* (Yiddish)

'plump', 'well rounded':

Multitudinous aunts of northern extraction, zaftig dimensions (it wasn't until I hit puberty that I realised that brassieres didn't have to be made by Govan steelworkers) and indomitable will have swept, stately as galleons, through my life. (Guardian)

PRETENTIOUSNESS INDEX ARGUABLY **!** BUT THE WORD HAS A CERTAIN CHARM.

Zaftig isn't very often found in British English, more's the pity. Deriving ultimately from the German word for 'juicy', it is the Yiddish/ US colloquial equivalent of 'buxom', another term with somewhat hazy outlines.

ZEITGEIST *zite-guy'st* (German)

'spirit of the age', 'prevailing mood of the times':

Perhaps the quickest way to tap into the travel zeitgeist is to take a look at a DJ's booking diary. (Observer)

Like a number of other German expressions seeking to grapple with culture and philosophy, *zeitgeist*, when used in English (which it often is), has undergone a kind of dumbing-down. There is even an pseudo-adjectival form, *zeitgeisty*, not found in German and meaning 'hip', 'trendy'. In a serious context *zeitgeist* describes the moral and cultural 'feel' of a particular period.

INDEX OF WORDS IN *FAUX PAS?* BY LANGUAGE

fin de siècle
flâneur
folie à deux
folie de grandeur
force majeure
forte
(la) France
    profonde
franglais
frisson
froideur
frottage
galère
gamine
gauche
gaucherie
gigolo
gourmand
gourmet
grande dame
grande
    horizontale
Grand Guignol
habitué
haute couture
haute cuisine
hauteur
hommage
homme moyen
    sensuel
homme sérieux
honi soit (qui
    mal y pense)
hors concours
hors de combat
hors d'oeuvre
idée fixe
idiot savant
ingénue
j'accuse
je ne sais quoi

jeu d'esprit
jeunesse dorée
joie de vivre
joie de vivre
jolie laide
laissez-faire
largesse
legerdemain
lèse-majesté
longueur
louche
maîtresse en titre
malaise
malapropos
manqué
mariage blanc
marque
matériel
mauvais quart
    d'heure
mélange
mêlée
ménage
ménage à trois
métier
mise-en-scène
moi
monstre sacré
montage
motif
mot juste
mystique
naif
née
noblesse oblige
nom de guerre
nom de plume
nonpareil
nostalgie de la
    boue
nouveau pauvre
nouveau riche

objet d'art
objet trouvé
odalisque
oeuvre
on dit
oubliette
outré
panache
par excellence
parti pris
parvenu
pas de deux
pas devant les
    enfants
passé
persiflage
petit-bourgeois
petite
picayune
pièce de
    resistance
pied-à-terre
piquant
pique
pis aller
plus ça change
point d'appui
policier
portmanteau
poule de luxe
pourboire
pour encourager
    les autres
prêt-à-porter
proletariat
protegé
pudeur
quartier
qui vive
raconteur
raison d'être

rapport
rapporteur
rapprochement
recherché
réclame
reculer pour
    mieux sauter
rentier
revenant
risqué
rodomontade
roman fleuve
roman à clef
rosbif
roué
ruse de guerre
salon
salon des refusés
sang froid
sans-culotte
sauve qui peut
savant
savoir faire
sobriquet
soi-disant
soigné
soixante-neuf
soupçon
succès d'estime
succès de
    scandale
succès fou
sympathique
tableau vivant
tant pis
tendresse
tête-à-tête
tour de force
tour d'horizon
tout court
tout le monde

trahison des
    clercs
triage
tricoteuse
tristesse
trompe l'oeil
vernissage
vice anglais
vis-à-vis
vive la différence
volte-face
voulu
voyeur

German
angst
bildungsroman
blitzkrieg
diktat
doppelgänger
echt
ersatz
fest
Gemeinschaft
gemütlich
Gesellschaft
gestalt
Götterdäm-
    merung
kaput
kitsch
Lebensraum
leitmotiv
putsch
realpolitik
Schadenfreude
spiel
Sturm und
    Drang
über-
verboten

wanderlust
Weltanschauung
Weltschmerz
wunderkind
Zeitgeist

Greek
bathos
Diaspora
eureka
hoi polloi
hubris
kudos
nous
utopia

Hebrew
kosher
shibboleth

Hindi
pukka
wallah

Italian
a capella
al dente
al fresco
bella figura
bimbo
bordello
braggadocio
bravura
brio
capo
chiaroscuro
cognoscente
consiglieri
Cosa Nostra
crescendo
dilettante

diva
dolce far niente
(la) dolce vita
fiasco
furore
generalissimo
gonzo
imbroglio
inamorata/o
incognito
lingua franca
maestro
mafia
magnifico
numero uno
omertà
papabile
paparazzo
passeggiata
politico
prima donna
punctilio
risorgimento
sotto voce
vendetta
verismo

Japanese
bonsai
haiku
hara kiri
honcho
kaizen
kamikaze
seppuku
tsunami

Latin
ab initio
ad absurdum
a fortiori

ad hoc
ad hominem
ad infinitum
ad lib
ad litem
ad nauseam
alibi
alma mater
alter ego
alumnus
amanuensis
amicus curiae
annus horribilis
annus mirabilis
antebellum
apologia
a priori
arcanum
bona fides
camera obscura
carpe diem
casus belli
caveat emptor
cf (confer)
cognomen
compos mentis
cui bono
cum
curriculum vitae
decree nisi
de facto
de jure
delirium
    tremens
deo volente
deus ex machina
dictum
dramatis
    personae
e.g.
encomium

ergo
erratum
et al
ex cathedra
ex gratia
ex officio
ex parte
factotum
farrago
fiat
fons et origo
genius loci
gravitas
habeas corpus
horribile dictu
ibidem
id est
ignis fatuus
illuminati
impedimenta
imperium
imprimatur
in absentia
in camera
incubus
in flagrante
  delicto
infra dig
in loco parentis
in medias res
in propria
  persona
in situ
inter alia
interregnum
in utero
in vino veritas
in vitro
ipso facto
lacrimae rerum
lacuna

libido
literati
locum (tenens)
locus classicus
magnum opus
marginalia
mea culpa
membrum virile
memento mori
memorabilia
mirabile dictu
modus operandi
modus vivendi
moratorium
mores
mutatis mutandis
nem con
ne plus ultra
nil desperandum
noli me tangere
non sequitur
nostrum
nota bene
obiter dictum
omnium
  gatherum
pace
pari passu
passim
paterfamilias
pax Americana
per capita
perpetuum
  mobile
per se
persona
persona grata
persona non
  grata
placebo
post hoc

prima facie
primus inter
  pares
pro bono
pro forma
pro rata
pro tem(pore)
quasi
quid pro quo
quod erat
  demonstran-
  dum
quod vide
quondam
rara avis
reductio ad
  absurdum
redux
rus in urbe
sanctum
  sanctorum
Saturnalia
sic
sic transit (gloria
  mundi)
sine die
sine qua non
status quo
status quo ante
sub judice
subpoena
sub rosa
sub specie
  aeternitatis
suggestio falsi
sui generis
summum
  bonum
suppressio
  veri
tabula rasa

taedium vitae
terminus ad
  quem
terra firma
terra incognita
ultima Thule
ultra vires
vade mecum
verbatim
via crucis
vice versa
viz
vox populi

Persian
ayatollah
backsheesh
caravanserai
purdah

Portuguese
auto-da-fé
nabob

Russian
apparatchik
agitprop
dacha
glasnost
gulag
nomenklatura
perestroika
samizdat
shaman
troika
tsar
ukase
yurt

Sanskrit
ashram

guru
karma
mantra
nirvana
pundit

Spanish
aficionado
barrio
caballero
cojones
gringo
hasta la vista
hombre
incommunicado

junta
macho
mañana
mano a mano
nada
pecadillo
peon
simpatico

Swedish
ombudsman
smorgasbord

Tibetan
lama

Turkish
kismet

Welsh
hwyl

Yiddish
chutzpah
goy
klutz
kvetch
maven
mazeltov
mensch
nebbish

putz
schlemiel
schlepp
schlock
schmaltz
schmooze
schmuck
schnorrer
schtick
shikse
shtum
shtup
zaftig